United Nations Procurement Regime

# VÖLKERRECHT EUROPARECHT UND INTERNATIONALES WIRTSCHAFTSRECHT

Herausgegeben von Peter Hilpold und August Reinisch

Band 7

PETER LANG
Frankfurt am Main · Berlin · Bern · Bruxelles · New York · Oxford · Wien

Peter Neumann

# United Nations Procurement Regime

## Description and Evaluation of the Legal Framework in the Light of International Standards and of Findings of an Inquiry into Procurement for the Iraq Oil-for-Food Programme

PETER LANG
Internationaler Verlag der Wissenschaften

**Bibliographic Information published by the Deutsche Nationalbibliothek**
The Deutsche Nationalbibliothek lists this publication in the Deutsche Nationalbibliografie; detailed bibliographic data is available in the internet at <http://www.d-nb.de>.

ISSN 1862-457X
ISBN 978-3-631-58051-6



www.peterlang.de

*"The UN is not just a product of do-gooders. It is harshly real. The day will come when men will see the UN and what it means clearly. Everything will be all right – you know when? When people, just people, stop thinking of the United Nations as a weird Picasso abstraction, and see it as a drawing they made themselves"*

*(as quoted in 'The Times', London, 27th June 1955)*

*"It is not the Soviet Union or indeed any other big Powers who need the United Nations for their protection. It is all the others. In this sense, the Organization is first of all their Organization and I deeply believe in the wisdom with which they will be able to use it and guide it"*

*(Statement to the General Assembly of the United Nations, 3rd October 1960)*

*Dag Hammarskjöld.*
*United Nations Secretary-General 1953-1961*

# Prologue

The present publication was originally submitted as doctoral dissertation in international law to the University of Vienna. The dissertation resulted from an ambition to distil and capture insights and experience from a career as Legal Officer in the United Nations and Legal Adviser and Director of Procurement and Support Services in the United Nations Industrial Development Organization, which extended from 1968 until my retirement in 1998.

During my active years, I had the privilege of being charged with responsibilities that brought exposure to and involvement in manifold issues and decisions of considerable political, managerial as well as legal consequence. Many questions would have been interesting subjects to pursue for further analysis, but in view of the fast pace required to deal with the daily demands of rapidly changing requirements, I found little time to engage in research and was constrained to apply readily available knowledge.

The relatively early, mandatory retirement age practised by the United Nations System of Organizations finally presented me with the freedom and time to specialize in depth in procurement procedures and then to return to academia for an update of the numerous important developments in European and International Law that had occurred in the course of the last generation.

In searching for a legal subject on which to focus, I was hampered by the extensive, but also disjunctive nature of my practical working experience. At Vienna University, however, I had the good fortune that Professor Dr. August Reinisch, LL.M. kindly consented to supervise me as a doctoral candidate and guided me to choose a dissertation subject that was familiar. I wish to express my gratitude both to him and to the additional evaluator, Professor, Dr. Peter Hilpold, University of Innsbruck, for their constructive support during the writing of the dissertation. Their comments and views have been most helpful and any failure to take them fully into account remains my responsibility alone.

The presentation of the United Nations procurement regime, including the critical analysis and recommendations, does not necessarily in all respects correspond to the position or views of the United Nations or UNIDO. All responsibility for this publication rests with me.

It remains for me to thank my wife, Mag. iur. Ingrid Riener LL.M., whose understanding, encouragement and patience have been an indispensable source of strength.

Peter Neumann

# Abbreviations

| | |
|---|---|
| AALCO | Asian-African Legal Consultative Organization |
| AJIL | American Journal of International Law |
| BYB | British Yearbook of International Law |
| Charter | Charter of the United Nations |
| Cor. Int. L. J. | Cornell International Law Journal |
| CTBTO | Comprehensive Nuclear-Test-Ban Treaty Organization |
| CTBTO/PrepCom | Preparatory Commission for the CTBTO |
| ECLAC | Economic Commission for Latin America and the Caribbean |
| e.g. | *exempli gratia,* for example |
| ESCAP | Economic and Social Commission for Asia and the Pacific |
| ESCWA | Economic and Social Commission for Western Asia |
| FAO | Food and Agriculture Organization of the United Nations |
| fn./fns. | footnote/footnotes |
| IAEA | International Atomic Energy Agency |
| IAPSO | Inter-Agency Procurement Services Office |
| IAPWG | Inter-Agency Procurement Working Group |
| IBRD | International Bank for Reconstruction and Development (World Bank) |
| ICAO | International Civil Aviation Organization |

| | |
|---|---|
| ICLQ | International and Comparative Law Quarterly |
| ICPO | International Criminal Police Organisation |
| ICTR | International Criminal Tribunal for Rwanda |
| ICTY | International Criminal Tribunal for the former Yugoslavia |
| i.e. | *id est,* this is |
| IFAD | International Fund for Agricultural Development |
| IDA | International Development Association |
| IFC | International Finance Corporation |
| IIC | Independent Inquiry Committee into the United Nations Oil-for-Food Programme |
| ILO | International Labour Organization |
| ILM | International Legal Materials (published by the American Society of International Law) |
| IMF | International Monetary Fund |
| IMO | International Maritime Organization |
| Ind. Int'l & Comp. L. Rev. | Indiana International and Comparative Law Journal |
| Int'l L. | The International Lawyer |
| Interim Report | (first) Interim Report of the Independent Inquiry Committee into the United Nations Oil-for-Food Programme (3rd February, 2005) |
| ITC | International Trade Centre (UNCTAD/WTO) |
| ITU | International Telecommunication Union J. Energy |
| Nat. Resources L. | Journal of Energy and Natural Resources Law |
| J. World Trade | Journal of World Trade |

| | |
|---|---|
| MJIL | Melbourne Journal of International Law |
| OPCW | Organisation for the Prohibition of Chemical Weapons |
| Organization | United Nations Organization |
| p./pp. | page/pages |
| PAHO | Pan American Health Organization |
| para. | Paragraph |
| Pub. Cont. L. J. | Public Contract Law Journal |
| Pub. Proc. L. R. | Public Procurement Law Review |
| RFP | Request for Proposals |
| TIAS | Treaties and Other International Acts Series (published by United States Department of State) |
| UN | United Nations |
| UNIDO | United Nations Industrial Development Organisation |
| UNJYB | United Nations Juridical Yearbook |
| UN/PD | United Nations Procurement Division |
| UN/PS | United Nations Procurement Services |
| UNCTAD | United Nations Conference on Trade and Development |
| UNDP | United Nations Development Programme |
| UNDP/IAPSO | Inter-agency Procurement Services Office of the UNDP |
| UNECE | United Nations Economic Commission for Europe |
| UNESCO | United Nations Educational Social and Cultural Commission |

| | |
|---|---|
| UNFPA | United Nations Population Fund |
| UNHCR | Office of the United Nations High Commissioner for Human Rights |
| UNICEF | United Nations Children's Fund |
| UNIDO | United Nations Industrial Development Organization |
| UNOG | United Nations Office at Geneva |
| UNON | United Nations Office at Nairobi |
| UNOPS | United Nations Office for Project Services |
| UNOV | United Nations Office at Vienna |
| UPU | Universal Postal Union |
| UNRWA | United Nations Relief and Works Agency for Palestine Refugees in the Near East |
| UNU | United Nations University |
| UNV | United Nations Volunteers |
| UNTS | United Nations Treaty Series |
| UST | United States Treaties and Other International Agreements (by the United States Department of State) |
| WFP | World Food Programme |
| WHO | World Health Organization |
| WIPO | World Intellectual Property Organization |
| WMO | World Meteorological Organization |
| WTO | World Trade Organization |

# Contents

# I. SCOPE AND METHOD OF THE THESIS

## A. The United Nations, Specialized and Related Agencies

The United Nations system of organisations comprises, in addition to the United Nations itself, the specialized agencies of the United Nations and the other international organisations[1] which, although they are legally autonomous and have their own legal personalities and memberships, have concluded agreements with the United Nations that call for political, functional and administrative coordination among them. In the case of the specialized agencies, the agreements have been concluded pursuant to Chapters IX[2] and X[3] of the United Nations

---

1 These are sometimes referred to as "related agencies" to distinguish them from the specialized agencies proper and to indicate the lower degree of coordination formally required by their respective agreements with the United Nations. Among the related agencies are the International Atomic Energy Agency (IAEA), the Preparatory Commission for the Nuclear-Test-Ban-Treaty Organization (CTBTO), the Organization for the Prohibition of Chemical Weapons (OPCW) and the World Trade Organization (WTO). These organizations do not report to the Economic and Social Council of the United Nations (ECOSOC): the IAEA reports to the Security Council and the General Assembly, the CTBTO and the OPCW report to the General Assembly.

2 Art. 57: "1. The various specialized agencies, established by intergovernmental agreement and having wide international responsibilities, as defined in their basic instruments, in economic, social, cultural, educational, health, and related fields, shall be brought into relationship with the United Nations in accordance with the provisions of Article 63".
"2. Such agencies thus brought into relationship with the United Nations are hereinafter referred to as specialized agencies".
Art. 58: "The Organization shall make recommendations for the co-ordination of the policies and activities of the specialized agencies".

3 Art. 63: "1. The Economic and Social Council may enter into agreements with any of the agencies referred to in Article 57, defining the terms on which the agency concerned shall be brought into relationship with the United Nations. Such agreements shall be subject to approval by the General Assembly".
Art. 64: "1. The Economic and Social Council may take appropriate steps to obtain regular reports from the specialized agencies. It may make arrangements with the members of the United Nations and with the specialized agencies to obtain reports on the steps taken to give effect to its own recommendations and to recommendations on matters falling within its competence made by the General Assembly".
"2. It may communicate its observations on these reports to the General Assembly".

Charter[4] and, while the specialized agencies are autonomous, they coordinate their work with each other and the United Nations at the intergovernmental level through the coordinating machinery of the Economic and Social Council of the United Nations and at the inter-secretariat level through the Chief Executives Board.

## B. Scope of Procurement Activities

Notwithstanding that Articles 57, 58 and 63 of the Charter of the United Nations (hereinafter the "Charter")[5] as well as the network of relationship agreements, which grant the status of a specialized or of a related agency of the United Nations, provide a legal basis for coordination not only of activities and programmes but also of administrative matters, the allocation of responsibility for the performance of procurement services has remained highly decentralized. Indeed, not only does each specialized or related agency act through its own procurement service, but in the case of the United Nations Organization itself, a plethora of procurement services have been established so that the execution of the procurement function is decentralized to various organisational units of the United Nations Secretariat and programmes.

In 1984, in its resolution on "Financing operational activities for development",[6] the United Nations General Assembly requested to receive annually "data on procurement undertaken by organizations of the system engaged in operational activities". In response to this request, annual statistical data have been provided by the Inter-Agency Procurement Services Office (hereinafter "IAPSO") of the United Nations Development Programme (hereinafter "UNDP"). The most recently published Annual Statistical Report,[7] which covers

---

[4] Signed on 26 June 1945 in San Francisco at the conclusion of the United Nations Conference on International Organization and came into force on 24 October 1945. Depositary is the Government of the United States, USTS: 993. An amendment adopted on 17 December 1963 entered into force on 31 August 1965, another amendment adopted on 20 December 1965 came into force on 12 June 1968 and a further amendment adopted on 20 December 1971 entered into force on 24 September 1973. The membership of the United Nations is virtually global as it has grown from the 51 founding Member States in 1945 to 191 Member States at present. Switzerland and Timor-Leste who joined in 2002 are the most recent Members.

[5] Werner Meng, "Art. 57-60 and Art. 63", in B. Simma (ed.), *The Charter of the United Nations*, Vol. I, 944-966, 966-970 and 1002-1010 (2002).

[6] A/RES/39/220 of 18 December 1984, operative para. 9.

[7] Published in July 2005 by the UNDP/IAPSO. Available at http://www.iapso.org.

the year 2004, includes data submitted by 34 out of the ca. 41 procurement services[8] in the United Nations Organization and in the specialized and related agencies,[9] including data on the countries of the contractors and suppliers. As one of the procurement services, namely the UNDP, reported on the procurement undertaken by its 132 country offices, the total number of reporting procurement services amounted to 166. Ten of the procurement services belong to the legally independent specialized or related agencies while the remainder are part of the United Nations Organization.

According to IAPSO's Annual Statistical Reports, the total volume of procurement of goods and services[10] by the United Nations and its agencies is significant. It increased in value from 4.5 billion US dollars in 2002 to 5.08 billion US dollars in 2003, an increase of 9.3 %, again to 6.4 billion US dollars in 2004, a further increase of 25.4 %, and to 8.3 billion US dollars in 2005, which represented an increase of 21.6% over 2004 and comprised goods for 4.55 billion US dollars and services for 3.77 billion US dollars. The highest shares in terms of value were in 2005 accounted for by the World Food Programme (26.17%), the UN Procurement Services[11] (18.67%) and the UNICEF (13.63%). Although, strictly speaking, procurement for operational activities does not include the services and equipment required to establish and maintain the infrastructure at headquarters and other duty stations,[12] procurement for such requirements has been included in the report, and in the case of UNDP, procurement executed by Governments in implementation of UNDP assisted projects also has been included, thus to some extent inflating the figures. Moreover, the procurement undertaken by the non-reporting services, in particular by the CTBTO is significant, and is likely to exceed the value of procurement for insti-

---

8 The data for 2005 are based on reports from ECLAC, ESCAP, ESCWA, FAO, IAEA, IFAD, ILO, ITC, ITU, PAHO, UN/PS, UNCTAD, UNDP, UNDP/IAPSO, UNECE, UNFPA, UNHCR, UNICEF, UNIDO, UNOG, UNON, UNOPS, UNOV, UNRWA, UNU, UNV, WFP, WHO, WIPO, WMO and WTO. No data were reported by CTBTO, ICAO, ICTR, ICTY and UPU.

9 No information is provided on procurement undertaken by the so-called "Bretton Woods organizations", the World Bank Group (comprising the World Bank/International Bank for Reconstruction and Development (IBRD) the International Finance Corporation (IFC) and the International Development Association (IDA) as well as the International Monetary Fund (IMF). The reason may be that the procurement is undertaken either by the organizations themselves for their institutional needs or by Member Governments to execute projects financed by credits or loans extended by an organization in the World Bank Group.

10 This excludes the significant cost of the services of individual experts.

11 Formerly the UN Procurement Division.

12 Informally referred to as "headquarters procurement" or "institutional procurement".

tutional requirements. In this connexion, it should be noted that nearly all technical assistance and cooperation, as well as other forms of development aid provided by the United Nations system of organisations to the recipient countries are implemented through the method of subcontracting the delivery of services, equipment or of work to firms, institutions or individual experts. In addition, important institutional requirements arising at the headquarters and other duty stations of the organisations also are met through procurement of services, equipment or work, such as e.g. building construction and maintenance, office supplies, telecommunication, management or professional services.

## C. Coordination of Procurement

IAPSO also serves as the secretariat of the Interagency Procurement Working Group (hereinafter "IAPWG"), which is composed of the chiefs of the procurement services in the United Nations system. IAPWG meets annually to exchange information and views on common issues. Acting in a purely advisory capacity to the individual procurement services, IAPWG has drawn up and published certain documents that are descriptive of the principles, procedures and legal framework generally applied by the procurement services.[13] These descriptions are considered to constitute internal guidelines serving the purpose of coordination. The only legally binding provisions, however, are those found in the respective constitutive instruments, regulations and rules, as well as related administrative instructions of each organisation or agency.

The present, 20th edition[14] of the General Business Guide includes the following descriptive documents:[15]

a.) General Terms and Conditions for the Procurement of Goods[16]

b.) General Terms and Conditions for the Procurement of Services[17]

---

13 *See* UNDP/IAPSO, "United Nation's System General Business Guide for Potential Suppliers of Goods and Services with Common Guidelines for Procurement by Organizations in the UN System", published by UNDP/IAPSO. Available at http://www.iapso.org.

14 Version available at http://www.iapso.org.

15 *See* Ann. IV of the General Business Guide.

16 A more complete designation would be "General Terms and Conditions of Contract", since the same Terms and Conditions normally would be annexed as an integral part to the eventual procurement contract with the supplier and would supersede any deviating clause of the individual part of the procurement contract.

17 *Ibid.*

The General Business Guide further in its Annex I contains a document entitled "Common Guidelines for Procurement by Organizations in the UN System" (hereinafter "Common Guidelines").[18] The purpose of the Common Guidelines is stated to be to:

- Communicate basic principles for procurement by the organisations within the UN system;
- Guide procurement activities and facilitate harmonization of procurement procedure among the UN organisations.

While, according to the Business Guide, the Common Guidelines do not "state the details" of the procedures followed by the different procurement services, the relevant legal point to make is that, like the General Terms and Conditions, referred to above, the Common Guidelines are not legally binding. Their informative value for interested firms or institutions therefore is limited to that of a general description. As already mentioned, the legally binding provisions on the applicable procurement procedure are to be found in the respective rules of each organisation. While the constitutive instruments of the organisations, such as the Charter of the United Nations, are widely distributed and easily accessible, the full extent of the procurement rules is not made publicly available. Applicable rules on procurement set out in Financial Regulations and Rules[19] and in the related Administrative Instructions and Manuals are distributed internally, but as a practical matter often are unavailable to the general public and, of more crucial importance, also to the potential or actual suppliers to the organisations.

## D. Access to Internal Documentation

Lack of access to relevant documentation effectively constitutes an obstacle to an objective and systematic description of the rules and practices of procurement in the United Nations system. Although the organisations in the United Nations system in recent years have made use of internet homepages[20] to publish a significant portion of their respective official documents, and notwithstanding that

---

18 *See* Ann. I for Common Guidelines.

19 *See* Ann. II and III, respectively, for excerpts of the pertinent provisions of the Financial Regulations and Rules in United Nations documents ST/SGB/Financial Rules/1/Rev.3 (1985) and ST/SGB/2003/7 (2003).

20 For the United Nations, *see* http://www.un.org.

United Nations stated policy of transparency covers its six principal organs[21] and includes the resolutions and decisions, as well as the most important documents of the principal inter-governmental organs, i.e. the Security Council, the General Assembly and the Economic and Social Council, it generally excludes administrative instructions, guidelines and manuals that are issued by the Secretary-General acting as the chief administrative officer of the Organization.[22]

Thus, as far as procurement activities and procedures are concerned, the concept of transparency is not applied comprehensively, but merely selectively: while Financial Regulations and Rules, as well as Staff Regulations and Rules, are published, these sources contain only the basic rules. The more detailed administrative and procedural rules are set out in administrative instructions, guidelines and manuals that are not published and are available only to the staff concerned and to others with "internal" status. The recent posting on United Nations web site of its internal Procurement Manual does not amount to a genuine publication for the benefit of interested parties outside the Secretariat, nor does it purport to have any externally binding effect.[23]

In the context just described, it is fortunate for the inductive method, on which the present thesis largely relies, that the establishment of the Independent Inquiry Committee into the United Nations Oil-for-Food Programme (hereinafter

---

21 United Nations Charter, art. 7.1, "There are established as the principal organs of the United Nations: a General Assembly, a Security Council, an Economic and Social Council, a Trusteeship Council, an International Court of Justice, and a Secretariat.

22 *See* United Nations Charter arts. 97, 98 and 101.1.

23 The Procurement Manual of 320 pages was posted on 31 August 2006 and is preceded by the notice, "The United Nations Financial Regulations and Rules, as promulgated in Secretary-General's bulletin ST/SGB/2003/7 (2003), available at http://www.un.org/Depts/ptd/manual, govern the procurement functions of the United Nations. The United Nations Financial Regulations and Rules are accessible to the public through the United Nations website. The provisions of the Procurement Manual should be read as subordinate to the provisions of the United Nations Financial Regulations and Rules. The Procurement Manual is intended to serve as a guide to United Nations Personnel who undertake requisition and procurement function and is not intended to be exhaustive. The United Nations reserves the right to make exceptions to the provisions contained within the Procurement Manual, if and when necessary, and in the best interests of the Organization. The Procurement Manual is a living document and may be amended by the United Nations, as and when necessary, without prior notice." As additional emphasis the Procurement Manual above its copy-right symbol of January 2004 displays the notice that "No part of this publication may be reproduced, stored in a retrieval system, or retransmitted in any form or by any means, electronic, mechanical, photocopied, recorded, or otherwise, without the prior written permission of the United Nations.". The currently valid version of the Procurement Manual to be used by United Nations staff is available only to authorized officials on the internal web site http://intranet.un.org/PD.

the "IIC") and, in particular, the publication on 3 February 2005 of the (first) Interim Report of the IIC (hereinafter the "Interim Report"),[24] has provided unprecedented public access through its analysis and documentation of procurement processes in the United Nations.[25]

## E. Methodological Aspects

### *1. Findings of the Independent Inquiry Committee*

Given the unavailability of authentic source material on the procurement practices of the United Nations, comparable to the description and findings of facts in the IIC's Interim Report, the present thesis makes use of the Interim Report as its primary source in this respect. Although the Interim Report covers only three procurement actions, the treatment is both balanced and very detailed. The IIC has gone to such great lengths in collecting written data and interviewing the key actors in- and outside the United Nations Secretariat that it would be exceedingly difficult, if not practically impossible at a later date, to duplicate this exhaustive effort.

The first Interim Report examines the procurement from three companies of, respectively, banking and inspection services that together constituted the general framework for implementation of the Iraq Oil-for-Food Programme. It has been followed by two further interim reports addressing different aspects of the administration of the Oil-for-Food Programme and further reports have been published by IIC on the impact of the Programme on the Iraqi people, on the management and on the manipulation of the Programme, as well as on procedures for law enforcement requests for access to the IIC's documents and information. The final report was issued on 27 October 2005 and the procedures for law enforcement requests in November 2005. Although the IIC remained operational until the end of 2006 for the purpose of assisting national law enforcement authorities and regulatory agencies with cases they might be pursuing, the investigative work of the IIC itself has been concluded earlier and the Office of the IIC closed as of 31 December 2006. Accordingly, the factual description and findings in the IIC's reports can be regarded as definitive. To a considerable

---

[24] The Interim Report is available at http://www.iic-offp.org.

[25] Reportedly, the Interim Report "cited major failures to abide by UN procurement and contracting procedures in the oil-for-food program, and harshly criticized the program's former director." *See* the section on "Contemporary Practice of the United States" in 99 *AJIL* 496 (2005).

extent, however, the reports also state evaluations, conclusions and recommendations that constitute opinions of the IIC. The opinions rest on the authority of the IIC and have no further authoritative legal status. For this reason, the present thesis will rely only on the factual descriptions and findings regarding the actual execution of the three procurement actions, while mentioning and commenting on the opinions where appropriate. The importance of this distinction is particularly obvious with regard to any potentially incriminating evidence, considering that the IIC had neither mandate nor power to determine criminal culpability and relied on the criterion of "reasonable certainty" as its standard of proof, which is a significantly lower standard than the threshold commonly used in criminal proceedings of "beyond reasonable doubt".

It is not intended to posit that only three procurement actions are fully representative or typical for the thousands of different procurement actions undertaken and contracts entered into every year. The three procurement actions that are taken up were and remain, however, rightly perceived in the Secretariat and by Member States as having been of decisive importance for the possibility of successfully executing the Oil-for-Food Programme which is the largest in financial terms[26] and among the politically most sensitive undertaken by the United Nations. Taking these factors into account and realising the great attention paid to the execution of the three procurement actions concerned, it seems justified, with regard to the procedures in general and to the issue of accountability in particular, to consider drawing certain conclusions from the shortcomings, to which the IIC findings are pointing and which may be presumed to significantly affect all procurement undertaken by the United Nations.[27] Moreover, to the extent the procurement regime of the United Nations is generally similar to those of its specialized and related agencies, the same conclusions may be presumed to have validity for the agencies as well.

---

[26] The Programme was operated from December 1996 and terminated with the invasion of Iraq in March 2003. Proceeds for oil exports under the Programme amounted to 69.5 billion US$, of which 38.7 billion US$ were expended on requirements in Iraq, 18 billion US$ were allocated for compensation claims arising from Iraq's invasion of Kuwait in 1990 and 1.4 billion US$ were reserved for administrative expenses of the United Nations under the Programme.

[27] In making a general comment on all aspects investigated by the IIC, the Chairman of the IIC, Mr. Paul A. Volcker stated: "The results of the Committee's investigation into corrupt and illicit activity by many buyers of oil and sellers of humanitarian goods reinforce the Committee's central conclusion of failures in UN oversight and management. The need for stronger executive leadership, thoroughgoing administrative reform, and more reliable controls and auditing within the UN is underscored."

## 2. *Comparison with the Procurement Regime under the Government Procurement Agreement of the WTO*

The identification of apparent shortcomings or weaknesses in the United Nations procurement can serve to focus a search for appropriate remedies. A meaningful approach would be to compare the procurement procedures of the United Nations with those prescribed by well-established international regimes for public (Government) procurement, such as those set out in the Government Procurement Agreement of the World Trade Organization (hereinafter the "GPA" and the "WTO" )[28]. Such a comparison naturally must take into account any relevant legal or factual difference between the two procurement regimes, which may limit the validity of a comparison.

In this connexion, an apparent difference relates to the source of the applicable norms and rules, i.e. the legal authority from which they originate. In the case of the United Nations, the regulations, rules and administrative practices governing procurement have as their source of legal authority either the Member States acting as members of the competent United Nations organ, the General Assembly, or the Secretary-General acting to implement mandates received from the Member States acting through their representatives in the General Assembly. Turning to the GPA, it is an agreement adopted by an international conference of States in the context of undertaking international trade negotiations under the auspices of the General Agreement on Tariffs and Trade[29] (hereinafter the "GATT") and no authority or organ comparable to the Secretary-General of the United Nations has served as legal authority for the GPA. – This difference relates more to form than to substance, however, when it is considered that the authoritativeness and legitimacy of the Secretary-General's actions also derive from the sovereign Member States. It is the duty of the Secretary-General to execute mandates received from the General Assembly in line with the intent, policies and expectations of Member States. Ultimately, both the United Nations and the GPA procurement regimes result from multilateral cooperation between States exercising their sovereign authority and thus stem from the same source of legal authority.

The respective fields of applicability do constitute a difference between the procurement regimes. The United Nations procurement procedures apply to the

---

[28] *See* World Trade Organization, "WTO Analytical Index – Guide to WTO Law and Practice" (available at http://www.wto.org. WTO document LT/UR/A-4/PLURI/2.

[29] World Trade Organization, "WTO Analytical Index – Guide to WTO Law and Practice", 33 *ILM* 1154 (1994), available at http://www.wto.org.

Organization itself, i.e. to any procurement action undertaken by the United Nations in its own name. In contrast, the GPA is applicable to procurement actions by and for the account of governments, namely the governments of those Member States that have accepted, signed and ratified, or acceded to the GPA in accordance with the provisions in its Article XXIV.[30] Accordingly, the fields of applicability clearly differ, in as much as the actors subject to the regimes are in one case a global international organisation and in the other case sovereign governments accounting for a predominant share of the global government procurement market. Nevertheless, this difference is de-emphasized by the circumstance that the international organisation is a creation of and governed by governments of sovereign States.

Concerning their stated purposes, the procurement regimes expressly share the purposes of:

- Non-discrimination and transparency.[31]
- The purpose of maximising the economic benefit[32] of the procurer is represented for the United Nations by the principle of ensuring "best value for money", and in the GPA by the objective of liberalizing and expanding world trade.
- The United Nations Financial Regulations embrace the principles of fairness and integrity as such,[33] while the GPA takes these principles further by endorsing "a fair, prompt and effective enforcement of the international provisions on government procurement" and the maintenance of "the balance of rights and obligations" as purposes that will be furthered by the establishment of "international procedures on "notification, consultation, surveillance and dispute settlement".

---

30 The Parties to the GPA are the twenty-five Members of the European Communities: Austria, Belgium, Cyprus, Czech Republic, Denmark, Estonia, Finland, France, Germany, Greece, Hungary, Ireland, Italy, Latvia, Lithuania, Luxemburg, Malta, Netherlands, Poland, Portugal, Slovak Republic, Slovenia, Spain, Sweden, United Kingdom, as well as Canada, Hong Kong China, Iceland, Israel, Japan, Korea, Liechtenstein, Netherlands with respect to Aruba, Norway, Singapore, Switzerland, United States of America.
At present, the following are negotiating accession to the GPA: Albania, Bulgaria, Georgia, Jordan, Kyrgyz Republic, Moldova, Oman, Panama, and Chinese Taipei. Available at http://www.wto.org.

31 United Nations Financial Regulation 5.12 (b). GPA preamble, 2nd and 3rd recitals.

32 United Nations Financial Regulation 5.12 (a). GPA preamble, 1st recital.

33 United Nations Financial Regulation 5.12 (b). GPA preamble, 4th recital.

- Effectiveness[34] is listed as a criterion by the United Nations Financial Regulations in connection with the purpose of "effective international competition", while the GPA connects this criterion with the goal of an "effective multilateral framework of rights and obligations...regarding government procurement...". Although GPA does not refer expressly to international competition among the purposes listed in its preamble, the detailed procedures laid down in the GPA all serve to further that principle.
- Finally, certain purposes appear to be unique for either procurement regime. In this category falls for the United Nations the open-ended purpose of procuring in "the interests of the United Nations"[35] and, for the GPA, the objective of avoiding protection[36] of domestic products or services or domestic suppliers and the recognition of the needs of the developing and in particular the least developed countries.[37] Furthermore, while the issue of giving preference to domestic products, services or suppliers does not arise with respect to procurement by the United Nations, the absence from the United Nations Financial Regulations of a requirement of preferential consideration of the needs of the developing countries does contrast with the reference to their needs in the GPA.[38]

It follows that the purposes of the two procurement regimes to a considerable extent coincide. Certain purposes of the GPA are related to and justified by policy objectives peculiar to the WTO and the same applies to the invocation of "mutual reciprocity" as the basis for the amendment of the GPA that was undertaken in 1994.

The subject matters dealt with by the procurement procedures of United Nations and by those laid down by the GPA for procurement by governments are essentially the same. In both cases, the stated purposes are sought to be achieved through the requirement of detailed procedural steps and of clear substantive criteria for execution of procurement actions. While the GPA procedures are

---

34 United Nations Financial Regulation 5.12 (c). GPA preamble, 1st recital.

35 United Nations Financial Rule 5.12 (d).

36 GPA preamble, 2nd recital.

37 GPA preamble, 5th recital.

38 UNIDO's Financial Rule 109.21 (c), however, extends a price preference of up to 15% to suppliers from developing countries or countries undergoing economic transition.

more detailed and provide more alternatives than do the United Nations procedures, they are in substance very similar, though not identical.

In view of the foregoing analysis, it appears justified to undertake a comparison of the United Nations and the GPA procurement regimes on the basis of a detailed description of the context and contents of the applicable norms, as well as of the rules regarding accountability for, and remedies to enforce, compliance with the norms.

# II. REGULATORY FRAMEWORK OF THE UNITED NATIONS

## A. Procurement Rules

### *1. "Rules of the Organization"*

The internal legal norms of the United Nations, i.e. those adopted by its principal organs, form part of the "rules of the organization" as the latter term is defined in Article 2.1(j) of the Vienna Convention on the Law of Treaties between States and International Organizations or between International Organizations,[39] namely as comprising "in particular, the constituent instruments, decisions and resolutions adopted in accordance with them, and established practice of the organization".[40] According to that Convention,[41] the definition is applicable for the purposes of the Convention and without prejudice to the meaning or use of the term in the internal law of any State or in the rules of any organisation.

Formally, the United Nations internal rules and procedures on procurement fall under the above mentioned definition of "rules of the organization" since, as further detailed in the following, they have been adopted and issued by two of the principal organs,[42] the General Assembly and the Secretary-General.[43] They

---

[39] United Nations document A/CONF.129/14. The Convention was adopted on 21 March 1986 at an international conference of all States and major international organisations convened at Vienna by Res. 39/86 of the General Assembly of the United Nations. It was opened for signature on 21 March 1986 and will enter into force upon deposit of the 35$^{th}$ instrument of ratification or accession by States.

[40] Art. 1.1(34) of the Vienna Convention on the Representation of States in their Relations with International Organizations of a Universal Character, done on 14 March 1975, contains a nearly identical definition: "'rules of the organization' means, in particular, the constitutional instruments, relevant decisions and resolutions, and established practice of the Organization". The slight qualification "relevant" must be taken to refer to the subject matter of the Convention. Argueably, it therefore is unlikely that procurement rules will be seen to be relevant. As of November 2006 this Convention is not yet in force as it has been ratified only by 33 States out of the required number of 35 States.

[41] Art. 2 of the Convention.

[42] UN Charter art. 7.

[43] A general survey of the pertinent powers and functions of the General Assembly and of the Secretary-General is provided by E. Klein, "Art. 10 and Art. 17" as well as by W. Fiedler "Art. 97 and Art. 98", in B. Simma (ed.), *The Charter of the United Nations* Vol. I, 257-275, 332-352, 1191-1205 and 1205-1216 (2002).

deal with the procedure and criteria for selecting contractors and awarding contracts for supplies with or without competitive bidding. The procurement rules form part of public international law and with regard to the question of applicable law must be distinguished from the contracts for the procurement of supplies entered into by the United Nations. According to the United Nations, rather than having recourse to any particular municipal law, general principles of law should be relied on in the interpretation of such contracts with private parties.[44] Presumably, these general principles would encompass the principles of contract law common to the major legal systems and thus could be characterized as international private law. When concluding such procurement contracts, the United Nations exercises the legal capacity conferred on it by Article 104 of the Charter[45] and Article I of the Convention on the Privileges and Immunities of the United Nations (hereinafter the "CPIUN").[46] [47] The contracts are of a private law character and are mostly, but not exclusively, concluded with legal subjects that do not fall under international law.[48]

The Vienna Convention referred to above shall apply to (written) treaties between States and international organisations or between international organisations.[49] However, to treaties that are constitutive of an international organisation or adopted within an international organisation, the Convention merely shall be applicable without prejudice to the rules of the organisation concerned.[50] As an authoritatively established case of the rules of an interna-

---

44 Reply to a questionnaire from the Institut de droit international, section I, *UNJYB* 159-176 (1976).

45 UN Charter art. 104: "The Organization shall enjoy in the territory of each of its Members such legal capacity as may be necessary for the exercise of its functions and the fulfilment of its purposes."

46 1 UNTS 15 and 90 UNTS 327. Adopted by the General Assembly of the United Nations on 13 February 1946. Entered into force on 17 September 1946.

47 CPIUN art. I: "Section 1. The United Nation shall possess juridical personality. It shall have the capacity:

to contract;
to acquire and to dispose of immovable and immovable property;
to institute legal proceedings."

48 C. Schreuer, "Die Internationalen Organisationen", in H. Neuhold/W. Hummer/C. Schreuer (eds.), *Österreichisches Handbuch des Völkerrechts* Vol. I, 173, at 184 (2004).

49 Art. 1 of the Convention.

50 Art. 5 of the Convention. A similar provision is found in art. 3 of the Vienna Convention on the Representation of States in their Relations with International Organizations of a Universal Character, adopted on 14 March 1975.

tional organisation taking such precedence, reference may be made to the advisory opinion of the International Court of Justice in the *Namibia case*,[51] in which the Court found that the provision in Article 27.3 of the Charter of the United Nations requiring "an affirmative vote of nine members including the concurring votes of the permanent members" for the adoption of resolutions on all non-procedural matters had been modified by "the general practice of that Organization". The general practice as relied on by the Court had "been generally accepted by Members of the United Nations" and was evidenced by "presidential rulings and the positions taken by members of the Council" consistently and uniformly interpreting "the practice of voluntary abstention by a permanent member as not constituting a bar to the adoption of resolutions".[52] Accordingly, also internal, duly adopted procurement rules and legitimately established procurement practice may in principle, if generally accepted by the membership and those participating in the procurement, supersede even provisions of an international organisation's constitutive instrument. Normally, the intent to achieve such an effect would be lacking, however. Moreover, an international organisation that is party to a treaty may not invoke the rules of the organisation as justification of its failure to perform obligations under the treaty.[53] *A fortiori* it must be assumed that the rules of an international organisation similarly cannot serve as justification for not performing obligations arising under a contract governed by (international) private law.

## 2. *Codification or Progressive Development*

Regarding applicability at the level of international law of the Vienna Convention on the Law of Treaties between States and International Organizations or between International Organizations, Article 3 of the Convention provides that the fact that the Convention is not applicable as such to international agreements between one or more States or international organisations, on the one hand, and one or more subjects of international law that are not States or international organisations, on the other hand, shall not affect the legal force of such agree-

---

51 Legal Consequences for States of the Continued Presence of South Africa in Namibia (South West Africa) notwithstanding Security Council Res. 276 (1970). *ICJ Reports* (1971) paras. 21-22.

52 C. Schreuer explains the precedence of the general practice of the organisation as an effect of a customary law rule, C. Schreuer, "Die Internationalen Organisationen", in H. Neuhold/W. Hummer/C. Schreuer, *Österreichisches Handbuch des Völkerrechts* Vol. I, 173, at 202 (2004).

53 Art. 27 of the Convention.

ments and the application to them of those rules of the Convention, to which they would be subject under international law independently of the Convention.[54] This provision no doubt reflects the well-known difficulty of distinguishing between "progressive development" and "codification" of international law, which is inherent in the preparation of the text of international conventions.[55] [56] The Convention has been drawn up by the International Law Commission (hereinafter the "ILC"), which is a body of independent experts, established by the General Assembly of the United Nations[57] and given as "its object the promotion of the progressive development of international law and its codification".[58] In the experience of the ILC, a clear distinction between the terms, "codification", as referring to the more precise formulation and systematisation of rules of international law in fields where there already has been extensive State practice, precedent and doctrine, and "progressive development of international law", as referring to the preparation of conventions on subjects which have not yet been regulated by international law or in regard to which the law has not yet been

---

54 The relevant parts of art. 3 of the Convention read:

"The fact that this Convention does not apply:

to international agreements to which one or more States, one or more international organizations and one or more subjects of international law other than States or organizations are parties;

to international agreements to which one or more international organizations and one or more subjects of international law other than States or organizations are parties;

to international agreements not in written form between one or more States and one or more international organizations, or between international organizations; or

to international agreements between subjects of international law other than States or international organizations;

shall not affect:

the legal force of such agreements;

the application to them of any of the rules set forth in the present Convention to which they would be subject under international law independently of the Convention;"

55 S. Rosenne, "Codification of International Law", in R. Bernhardt (ed.), *Encyclopedia of Public International Law* Vol. I, 632 (1995).

United Nations, *The Work of the International Law Commission* 1-25 (1996).

56 C.-A. Fleischhauer, "Art. 13", in B. Simma (ed.), *The Charter of the United Nations* Vol. I, 298 (2002).

57 Pursuant to the mandate in art. 13.1(a) of the Charter.

58 Art. 1.1 of the Statutes of the International Law Commission, as adopted by the General Assembly of the United Nations.

sufficiently developed in the practice of States,[59] has in practice proved impracticable[60] to maintain, given that the systematisation and clarification of existing rules of necessity involve a certain degree of law development. Notwithstanding the difficulty of distinguishing in practice between the *lege lata* rules eligible for codification and the *lege ferenda* concepts found appropriate for progressive development of international law, the latter do acquire binding force when they are set out in an international convention and the convention is adopted and ratified.

Conversely, to the extent the Convention states *lege lata,* its rules can be considered to form part of already generally recognized general principles of international law and as such have legal force beyond the field of applicability strictly defined in Article 1 of the Convention. The *lege lata* rules will apply notwithstanding the Convention has not yet entered into force[61] and also for a State or an Organisation that has not signed, ratified or acceded to the Convention.[62] Taking into account the above mentioned advisory opinion of the ICJ, Article 5 of the Convention must be deemed to express *lege lata.*

---

59 Art. 15 of the Statutes of the International Law Commission provides that these meanings are used "for convenience" in the Statutes. While the convenience originally related to a compromise between opposing views, the comprehensiveness of the mandate has become widely accepted.

60 B. Simma, "Das Völkergewohnheitsrecht", in H. Neuhold/W. Hummer/C. Schreuer (eds.), *Österreichisches Handbuch des Völkerrechts* Vol. I, 42 (2004).

61 According to art. 85 of the Convention, ratifications by thirty-five States are required for entry into force. Only twenty-eight States had ratified and twelve international organisations, including the United Nations, had deposited an instrument of formal confirmation or accession, as of May 2007. Status of Multilateral Treaties deposited with the Secretary-General, available at http://www.untreaty.un.org.

62 In accordance with its Part VIII, Final Provisions, the Convention is open to signature by all States and those international organisations that participated in the drawing up and the adoption of the Convention. States become bound by the Convention upon ratification or accession and international organisations by deposit of an act of formal confirmation or an instrument of accession.
The Convention has been signed and formally confirmed by the United Nations and by the following specialized and related agencies: CTBTO, IAEA, ICAO, ICPO, ILO, IMO, OPCW, UNIDO, UPU, WHO, and WIPO.

## B. Hierarchy of Norms

An essential requirement for a concise description of the internal legal norms of the United Nations, as well as for a precise understanding of their legal nature and effect, is constituted by the necessity of always determining their source and thereby attribute the correct hierarchical rank to each applicable norm. This follows from the fact described below that the higher-ranking norm authorizes – and thus legitimises – the issuance of the lower ranking norm. Therefore, the higher ranking norm prevails over a norm of a lower rank, not only in case of a conflict between their plain textual meanings, but also in so far that the interpretation of a lower ranking norm must take into account and conform to the purposes of any applicable norm of a higher rank.[63]

A special application of the hierarchical order is represented by United Nations Staff Regulation 12. While authorizing the Secretary-General to make staff rules and amendments to implement the Regulations, it provides that such staff rules and amendments shall be reported to the General Assembly and remain provisional until on 1 January following the year during which they were reported. In particular, Regulation 12 provides that the General Assembly may direct that the rule or amendment be withdrawn or modified, if the Assembly finds it to be inconsistent with the intent or purposes of the Regulations.[64]

## C. Primary Source: Constitutive Treaty

### *1. United Nations Charter and Powers of its Principal Organs*

The primary source of internal norms of the United Nations is its Charter[65] (hereinafter the "Charter"), which has the status of a multilateral, international treaty, duly ratified by the 191 States Members of the United Nations.

---

[63] W. Münch, "Article 101", in B. Simma (ed.), *The Charter of the United Nations* Vol. II, 1256-1257 (2002).

[64] Staff Regulations 12.2 to 12.4. ST/SGB/2005/5 (2005).

[65] Signed on 26 June 1945 at San Francisco, entered into force on 24 October 1945. According to art. 111 of the Charter, the depositary is the Government of the United States. Full text available from *USTS* 993 and at http://www.un.org/aboutun/charter. Certain depository functions have been transferred to the Secretary-General of the United Nations, *see* http://untreaty.un.org.

The provisions of the Charter do not address procurement expressly, but are important in that they define the institutional framework, i.e. the decision-making organs and their respective powers and areas of responsibility. While all six principal organs[66] in principle are empowered to act with respect to the discharge of the procurement function, the most directly involved are the General Assembly and the Secretariat.

At the level of the provisions of the Charter, the functions and powers of the Secretariat are synonymous with those attributed to the Secretary-General, who is appointed by the General Assembly to head the Secretariat and to serve as "the chief administrative officer of the Organization".[67] In accordance with Article 98 of the Charter, the Secretary-General shall act "in that capacity" in all meetings of the deliberative principal organs: the General Assembly, the Security Council and the Economic and Social Council "and perform such other functions as are entrusted to him by these organs". The functions and responsibilities of the Secretary-General and of the Secretariat in the field of procurement can appropriately be classified as being based on Articles 97 and 98 and deriving from mandates given from time to time by the principal organ concerned, normally the General Assembly. This finding imposes itself by the broad formulation of Articles 97 and 98 and, in the absence of any other, more specific, provision in the Charter concerning this question,[68] also is compatible with the very broadly formulated Article 10.[69]

Chapter IV of the Charter sets out the powers as well as the decision-making procedure of the General Assembly. According to Article 10, the General Assembly has extensive power to deliberate, and by implication to adopt resolutions, on matters arising within the scope of the Charter or relating to the powers and functions of any organ of the United Nations referred to in the Charter. The power of the General Assembly to make recommendations addressed to

---

66 Charter, art. 7.1.

67 Charter, art. 97.

68 The Charter is formulated broadly in most respects and several provisions arguably may be deemed no longer to be fully adequate for the present complexity and size of the operations of the Organization.

69 Charter, art. 10: "The General Assembly may discuss any questions or any matters within the scope of the present Charter or relating to the powers and functions of any organs provided for in the present Charter, and, except as provided in Article 12, may make recommendations to the Members of the United Nations or to the Security Council or to both on any such question."

the Members or to the Security Council[70] relates to the external political sphere of international relations, including relations between States, whether Members of the United Nations or not, and relations between States and the Organization. Such recommendations are expressed in the form of resolutions and generally only have the force of recommendations, i.e. they are not considered to be legally binding. In this respect, the powers of the General Assembly thus differ from those of the Security Council.

According to Article 10, however, the General Assembly also is the deliberative principal organ that is responsible for discussing and, by implication, for adopting all general measures of a legislative or regulatory nature relating to the internal administration and management of the Organization, including the adoption of mandates to be executed by the Secretary-General and the Secretariat. Whether termed resolutions or decisions, in principle all such measures relating to the internal administration and management are binding on the Secretary-General, the Secretariat and the Member States.[71] The specific powers of the General Assembly that are expressly stated in Article 17,[72] namely the power to approve the budget of the Organization and to apportion the obligation to meet the expenses of the Organization among the Member States, also entail the power to make decisions that bind the Secretary-General, the Secretariat and the Member States.

## 2. *Power to Promulgate United Nations Financial Regulations*

While the Charter with respect to the administration and management of budgetary and financial matters does not contain a provision expressly referring to the

---

70 According to art. 14 of the Charter, in the specific area of "measures for the peaceful adjustment of any situation,....likely to impair the general welfare or friendly relations among nations", the General Assembly may address recommendations also to others than the Security Council and Member States, such as non-Members, other international organisations, non-governmental organisations or even private groups or individuals. O. Kimminich, "Art. 14" in B. Simma (ed.), *The Charter of the United Nations* Vol. I, 321 (2002).

71 *See further* B. Sloan, "The binding force of a "recommendation" of the General Assembly of the United Nations", *BYB* 397-424 (1948) and M. Sørensen, *Grundtræk af international organisation* 44-46 (1952).

72 Charter, art. 17: "1.The General Assembly shall consider and approve the budget of the Organization.
2. The expenses of the Organization shall be borne by the Members as apportioned by the General Assembly."

promulgation of Financial Regulations similar to Article 101.1[73] on the establishment of Staff Regulations, nevertheless, ever since the first session of the General Assembly adopted[74] the initial, Provisional Financial Regulations, the General Assembly has maintained a set of comprehensive Financial Regulations[75] in force and, as necessary from time to time, adjusted the Financial Regulations through revisions.[76] Implied authority may be derived from Article 17 concerning the General Assembly's mandate to consider and approve the budget and to apportion the expenses to be borne by the individual Member States.

For the discussion by the present thesis of the findings of the IIC, the Financial Regulations and Rules set out on ST/SGB/Financial Rules/1/Rev.3 of March 1985[77] are particularly relevant, since they were applicable during the relevant period.

---

[73] Charter, art. 101.1: "The staff shall be appointed by the Secretary-General under regulations established by the General Assembly."

[74] General Assembly Res. 14(I) (1946). According to para. A.1, the General Assembly resolved that "Arrangements be made on the basis of the general principles set out in section 2 of chapter IX of the Report of the Preparatory Commission and of the provisional financial regulations, for budgetary procedures, the collection and custody of funds, the control of disbursements and the auditing of accounts." Ann. I to the resolution contained the initial version of the Provisional Financial Regulations.

[75] The presently applicable, revised Financial Regulations, effective as of 1 January 2003, were approved by the General Assembly in its decision 57/573 (2002). *See* the Secretary-General's bulletin of 9 May 2003, ST/SGB/2003/7. Bulletin ST/SGB/2003/7 "supersedes bulletins ST/SGB/Financial Rules/1/Rev.3 (1985) entitled "Financial Regulations and Rules of the United Nations" and ST/SGB/Financial Rules/1/Rev.3/Amend.1 (1998) entitled "Amendment of Financial Rule 110.32: Property Survey Board" and any other communication concerning revisions to the Financial Rules."

[76] E. Klein informs that at the San Francisco Conference where the United Nations Charter was adopted, it was decided "not to specify budgetary procedures or assessment methods in the Charter", but only to clarify "the member States' obligation to bear the expenses of the Organization through the present formulation of art. 17(2). The subsequent discussions in the Preparatory Commission and its Executive Committee laid the groundwork for the future financial mechanisms of the Organization. An Advisory Group of Experts assisted in establishing a provisional budget, the Working Capital Fund, and the financial regulations. This Group later developed into the Advisory Committee on Administrative and Budgetary Questions (ACABQ). .... Likewise a Committee on Contributions (COC) was recommended, and the principle of apportioning the expenses broadly according to capacity to pay was agreed upon." E. Klein, "Art. 17", in B. Simma (ed.), *The Charter of the United Nations* Vol. I, 334-335 (2002).

[77] *See* App. A for an extract of pertinent provisions of the Financial Regulations and Rules (1985).

### *3. Power to Promulgate United Nations Staff Regulations*

With respect to the administration and management of staff, the fundamental principles and norms are stated in Articles 100 and 101 of the Charter. Article 100 is especially important in that it establishes the independence of the Secretariat, including independence from the Member States, as a fundamental requirement.[78]

Article 101.1 provides for the establishment of Regulations by the General Assembly to govern the appointment and service of staff.[79]

## D. Secondary Source: Regulations

### *1. United Nations Financial Regulations*

Apart from the Financial Rules and such *ad hoc* resolutions and decisions as the General Assembly has adopted from time to time to address specific situations and questions concerning budgetary or financial matters of the Organization, the Financial Regulations of the United Nations constitute the single most important legislative measure in this field due to their comprehensive and semi-permanent nature. They are a secondary source of applicable norms, ranking after the provisions of the Charter.

With respect to procedures for procurement, the Financial Regulations never have been detailed, however. In the version in force during 1996,[80] i.e. the period investigated by the IIC, and until 1 January 2003, under the heading "Contracts

---

[78] Charter art. 100: "1. In the performance of their duties the Secretary-General and the staff shall not seek or receive instructions from any government or from any authority external to the Organization. They shall refrain from any action which might reflect on their position as international officials responsible only to the Organization.
2. Each Member of the United Nations undertakes to respect the exclusively international character of the responsibilities of the Secretary-General and the staff and not to seek to influence them in the discharge of their responsibilities."

[79] Charter, art. 101.1: "The Staff shall be appointed by the Secretary-General under regulations established by the General Assembly.".

[80] Secretary-General's Bulletin of March 1985: Financial Regulations and Rules of the United Nations. (ST/SGB/Financial Rules/1/Rev.3 (1985)). *See* Ann. II for an extract of pertinent provisions.

and purchases", the only directly pertinent regulation was Regulation 10.5, which read:

> "Regulation 10.5: Tenders for equipment, supplies and other requirements shall be invited by advertisement, except where the Secretary-General deems that, in the interests of the Organization, a departure from the rule is desirable."

The foregoing provision formed part of Article X, entitled "Internal Control" and was the only provision in a subsection with the subtitle "Contracts and purchases".

With effect from 1 January 2003, the General Assembly has approved[81] certain amendments to the Financial Regulations,[82] including the renumbering of Regulation 10.5 to become Regulation 5.13,[83] as well as the addition of a new Regulation 5.12, which reads:

> "Regulation 5.12: Procurement functions include all actions necessary for the acquisition, by purchase or lease, of property, including products and real property, and of services, including works. The following general principles shall be given due consideration when exercising the procurement functions of the United Nations:
>
> - Best value for money;
> - Fairness, integrity and transparency;
> - Effective international competition;
> - The interest of the United Nations."

These Regulations form part of Article V, entitled "Utilization of funds" and are the only provisions in Section C, entitled "Procurement".

The additional Financial Regulation 5.12 had been proposed by the Secretary-General, together with certain changes to the Financial Rules, in response to requests by the General Assembly[84] and following extensive consultations within an inter-agency Task Force on Common Services.[85] According to the explanation

---

81 General Assembly Dec. 57/573 (2002), *see* the General Assembly's Summary Records (A/57/PV.78).

82 The amended version is set out in the Secretary-General's bulletin of 9 May 2003: Financial Regulations and Rules of the United Nations (ST/SGB/2003/7). *See* Ann. III for an extract of pertinent provisions.

83 The former Financial Regulation 10.5 was transposed unchanged, except for replacing "the rule" with "this regulation".

84 General Assembly Res. 52/226 A (1998), 54/14 (1999) and 52/247 (2001).

85 Report of the Secretary-General: Proposed revisions to the Financial Regulations of the United Nations (A/57/396) (2002).

given by the Secretary-General,[86] the proposed "harmonized and simplified" revisions would "place greater emphasis on the overall guiding principles for procurement while providing greater authority for the Chief Procurement Officer (the Under-Secretary-General for Management in the case of the Secretariat) to develop specific procurement procedures." The above mentioned amendment of the Financial Regulations aimed to ensure the first objective: emphasizing the guiding principles, while the second objective: to enhance the authority of the Chief Procurement Officer, was pursued through the changes to the Financial Rules that are discussed below.

## 2. *Power to Issue United Nations Financial Rules*

As of 1985,[87] Financial Regulation 10.1(a) provided that the Secretary-General shall

> "establish detailed financial rules and procedures in order to ensure effective financial administration and the exercise of economy."

Accordingly, the Financial Rules issued pursuant to this Financial Regulation constituted a tertiary source of norms, the validity of which was subject to, primarily, the Charter of the United Nations and, secondarily, the Financial Regulations. This point was indirectly confirmed by Financial Rule 114.5, which allowed for the Rules to

> "be amended by the Secretary-General in a manner consistent with the Financial Regulations."

As of 2003,[88] the authority and mandate to establish financial rules and procedures is contained in Financial Regulation 5.8(a) in identical terms. That no equivalent of the former Financial Rule 114.5 has been retained does not imply any substantive change such as authorizing the issuance of Financial rules at variance with the Financial Regulations. Unlike the Staff Regulations with reference to the Staff Rules, as discussed in Section D.4 below, the Financial Regulations do not call for Financial Rules to remain provisional until reviewed, and not modified or withdrawn, by the General Assembly before 1 January. No such special mechanism is therefore available to determine whether a new Finan-

---

86 *Ibid.*

87 ST/SGB/Financial Rules/1/Rev.3 (1985).

88 ST/SGB/2003/7.

cial Rule is inconsistent with the Financial Regulations or otherwise issued without the Secretary-General having had the requisite authority to do so.[89]

### 3. *United Nations Staff Regulations*

As mentioned, Article 101.1 of the Charter provides for Staff Regulations to be "established" by the General Assembly.[90] The Staff Regulations, like the Financial Regulations, constitute a secondary source of applicable norms subject in ranking to the provisions of the Charter. The presently applicable version went into force on 1 January 2005 and is set out in the Secretary-General's bulletin ST/SGB/2005/3 of 15 March 2005.[91]

Certain Staff Regulations define the principles and standards of performance required of the staff and therefore are relevant for an analysis of questions arising in the course of the execution of procurement. The Staff Regulations applicable during 1996, the year of the procurement actions investigated by the IIC, were promulgated by the Secretary-General in a bulletin,[92] that also reiterated those provisions of the Charter of the United Nations, which directly relate to the service of the staff,[93] including Article 100 quoted above. Staff Regulation I, entitled "Duties, obligations and privileges" stated the fundamental requirements for the performance by the staff of their duties. While the requirements were generally applicable, their direct relevance for the performance of functions in the field of procurement is obvious. Especially the provisions in Staff Regula-

---

89 In his comment "Executive (Ab)use of the Procurement Power: *Chamber of Commerce v. Reich*", G. M. Clay finds that the United States Procurement Act, which states as its goals "economy" and "efficiency" in government contracting, does not empower the United States President to use the procurement power to shape labour policy or to pursue broad economic or social goals by issuing executive orders conditioning awards on the contracts complying with such policies. 84 *Geo. L.J.* 2573-2596 (1995-1996).

90 Already at its first session the General Assembly, on 13 February 1946, by operative para. 10 of its Res. 13(I), adopted the Provisional Staff Regulations contained in Ann. II to the resolution. Subsequently, the General Assembly has amended the Staff Regulations at fairly frequent intervals, most frequently to adjust the salary scales and other benefits and conditions of service.

91 The presently applicable bulletin was preceded by the bulletins ST/SGB/2001/8 (2001), ST/SGB//2000/7 (2000), ST/SGB/1999/2 (1999), ST/SGB/1998/20 (1998), ST/SGB/1998/8 (1998), ST/SGB/Staff Regulations/Rev.23 (1995), as well as by previous issuances.

92 Secretary-General's Bulletin, Staff Regulations (ST/SGB/Staff Regulations/Rev. 23) (1995).

93 Charter arts. 8, 97, 100, 101 and 105.

tions 1.1, 1.3 and 1.5[94] must be noted as they elaborated and reinforced the requirement of independence already stated in Article 100 of the Charter of the United Nations. The same requirement was further emphasized by Staff Regulation 1.9, which obliged staff members to subscribe to an explicit oath of office or declaration, which is normally done by signature on the occasion of countersigning the letter of appointment.[95]

The presently applicable version of the Staff Regulations, issued under the document symbol ST/SGB/2005/5, essentially has retained the foregoing Staff Regulations, including the oath or declaration. In addition to some editorial changes, a slight strengthening is noticeable in that the second sentence of the oath or declaration – which now is found in Regulation 1.1.b[96] – obliges staff not to seek or accept instructions from "any Government or other source external to the Organization" rather than to "any Government or other authority external to the Organization". The same amendment has been made in the new Staff Regulation 1.2(d) which corresponds to the former Regulation 1.3. Thus, also instructions from private sector entities, such as firms or individuals, are now expressly prohibited.

---

94 These Staff Regulations read: "1.1: Members of the Secretariat are international civil servants. Their responsibilities are not national but exclusively international. By accepting appointment, they pledge themselves to discharge their functions and to regulate their conduct with the interests of the United Nations only in view."

....

"1.3: In the performance of their duties members of the Secretariat shall neither seek nor accept instructions from any Government or from any other authority external to the Organization."

....

"1.5: Staff members shall exercise the utmost discretion in regard to all matters of official business. They shall not communicate to any person any information known to them by reason of their official position that has not been made public, except in the course of their duties or by authorization of the Secretary-General. Nor shall they at any time use such information to private advantage. These obligations do not cease upon separation from the Secretariat."

95 The oath or declaration read: "I solemnly swear (undertake, affirm, promise) to exercise in all loyalty, discretion and conscience the functions entrusted to me as an international civil servant of the United Nations, to discharge these functions and regulate my conduct with the interests of the United Nations only in view, and not to seek or accept instructions in regard to the performance of my duties from any Government or other authority external to the Organization."

96 *See* ST/SGB/2005/5 (2005).

### 4. *Power to Issue United Nations Staff Rules*

Staff Regulation 12[97] allows the Secretary-General to issue Staff Rules and amendments thereto in order to implement the Staff Regulations. Moreover, issued Staff Rules shall remain provisional and shall be reported to the General Assembly on an annual basis. Unless the General Assembly finds a provisional Staff Rule to be inconsistent with the Staff Regulations and therefore directs that it shall be modified or withdrawn, the provisional Staff Rule enters into "full force and effect" on 1 January following the year in which it was reported to the General Assembly. It follows that Staff Rules constitute a tertiary level of norms subject in validity to the Charter of the United Nations and to the Staff Regulations. Although there is no enabling provision[98] in the United Nations Staff Rules authorizing the issuance of any additional rules with a lower rank, numerous Administrative Instructions, Directives and Circulars have been issued at the tertiary level to complement or implement the Staff Rules.[99]

## E. Tertiary Source: Rules

### 1. *United Nations Financial Rules*

As of 1985 and until the promulgation in 2003 of a revised edition, the subject of procurement was treated in United Nations Financial Rules 110.16 – 110.31.[100] The emphasis was placed on financial accountability and control within the Secretariat. Much less emphasis, if any, was placed on the goals of ensuring the efficiency, fairness and transparency of the procurement process and of acquiring goods, services and work of the required quality and at the lowest comparable cost. A result of the limited objectives of financial accountability and control has been that the Financial Rules, neither in the 1985 version nor in the presently applicable 2003 version, set out a comprehensive description of the administra-

---

97 Since ST/SGB/Staff Regulations/Rev.23 (1995), Staff Regulation 12 has remained unchanged.

98 United Nations Staff Rule 112.3 refers to the violation of any "regulation, rule or administrative instruction" as a legal basis for personal liability of a staff member but does not otherwise establish any norm on liability.

99 W. Münch, "Article 101", in B. Simma (ed.), *The Charter of the United Nations* 1259-1260, Vol. II (2002).

100 ST/SGB/Financial Rules/1/Rev.3 (1985). The 1985 bulletin has been superseded by ST/SGB/2003/7 (2003).

tive procurement procedure, which thus has been left to be addressed by a variety of manuals, guidelines and administrative issuances of a lower ranking order of authority.

Considering the following chapter will contain a comprehensive description of the procurement processes, including the administrative procedure typically followed, the present chapter will only deal with the fundamental aspects of the 1985 and 2003 versions of the United Nations Financial Rules as applicable to procurement actions.

## 2. *Institutional aspects*

In the 1985 version, UN Financial Rules 110.16 – 110.17 addressed the institutional questions of authorization of procurement officials or staff and the requirement of approval of certain procurement actions by an interdepartmental Committee on Contracts, while the remaining rules prescribed specific conditions that must be met in order to perform particular forms of procurement. Under Financial Rule 105.13 of the 2003 version, the Under-Secretary-General for Management[101] has overall responsibility for the United Nations procurement functions and for the establishment of "all United Nations procurement systems", including establishment of "review committees at Headquarters and other locations, to render written advice…on procurement actions….". The composition of the review committees and their terms of reference, including the types and monetary values of proposed procurement subject to their review, shall be established by the Under-Secretary-General.

### a.) authority

The authority to enter into a procurement contract was defined by Financial Rule 110.16 which provided that procurement contracts "shall be entered into" only by officials (i.e. staff members) duly authorized for this purpose. According to

---

[101] The Under-Secretary-General for Management serves at the highest rank below the Secretary-General and traditionally is a national of the United States.

the same Financial Rule, the entering into of procurement contracts[102] extended to include the bidding process and negotiations with suppliers.[103]

Under the presently applicable rules, set out in ST/SGB/2003/7, Financial Rule 105.13(a) requires that the Under-Secretary-General for Management "shall designate the officials responsible for performing procurement functions." It follows *a contrario,* that officials not so designated are not authorized to perform procurement functions and the rule therefore has effected no change in this respect. "Procurement functions" are not defined, however, and the former implied definition[104] regrettably has not been retained, thus loosening regulatory and, potentially, administrative control.

In practice, the authorized officials were and remain synonymous with all the staff members of the Secretariat's procurement service, who hold a professional grade, and selected staff members at the senior general service grade level. Collectively and individually, they are referred to as "procurement officers".[105]

### b.) control

Notwithstanding their being formally authorized[106] to conclude contracts, procurement officers are not empowered to act alone, however, but must obtain the prior approval of the "certifying officer" designated for the relevant internal account, from which the contract is to be financed. The certifying officer must sign off on all proposed expenditures "before the expenditure is actually incurred". Subsequently, after conclusion of the contract, another designated

---

102 Referred to as "contracts for the purchase, rental or sale of services, supplies, equipment or other requirements."

103 Referred to as "the invitation of proposals or tenders and the negotiation with potential suppliers or purchasers on the basis of detailed specifications."

104 *See supra* notes 101 and 102.

105 In the common system of conditions of service adhered to by United Nations and its specialized and related agencies, those appointed to the professional grades P-1 to P-5 and D-1 to D-2 normally hold university level degrees and serve internationally in posts that are filled in accordance with quotas based on nationality, while those appointed to the General Service are recruited locally, normally do not hold advanced degrees and are not subject to nationality quotas for appointment.

106 Previously pursuant to Financial Rule 110.16, presently pursuant to Financial Rule 105.13 (a).

official, the "approving officer" must approve the obligation before it is entered into the accounts or any payment is made.[107]

These internal controls have been retained in Bulletin ST/SGB/2003/7, in particular in Financial Rules 105.5 concerning certifying officers and 105.6 concerning approving officers. A new subparagraph (b) of Financial Rule 105.5, provides that certifying officers also are responsible for managing the efficient and effective utilization of the resources, in accordance with the purposes for which they have been approved and the Financial Regulations and Rules. A further strengthening of the control system is the now express prohibition of any certifying officer also exercising the functions of an approving officer, or vice versa.

### c.) "substantive" or "technical officers"

In addition to these financial controls, the procurement officer is dependent, during the acquisition process, on the cooperation of those officers in the various organizational units of the Secretariat, who for official purposes require goods, services or work that are to be met through procurement and who are commonly referred to as "substantive" or "technical officers". They not only request the initiation of procurement actions and provide a detailed description of their requirements, but also are involved in the evaluation of bids or offers and in the supervision of the performance of contractors or suppliers. As part of the financial management and control system, certain substantive/technical officers, designated as "allotment holders", were authorized by the Under-Secretary-General for Administration and Management, in accordance with Financial Rule 110.1, to commit funds.[108] Also the revised Financial Rules refer to allotment

---

[107] These important requirements were stated in ST/SGB/Financial Rules/1/Rev.3, Rule 110.3, entitled "Certification and approval of obligations and expenditures", which read: "Every obligation or proposal for the incurring of expenditure shall require:

Certification by a certifying officer designated for the purpose by the Controller before the expenditure is actually incurred, provided that the Controller shall have authority to certify obligations and expenditures under all accounts; and

Subsequent approval by an approving officer designated for that purpose by the Controller before the obligation is recorded or payment made."

[108] Financial Rule 110.1: "(a) The USG/AM is responsible to the Secretary-General for ensuring that the expenditures of the Organization remain within the appropriations as voted and are incurred only for the purposes approved by the General Assembly (*See also rule 106.1 with respect to authority for expenditure*)."

holders, namely in revised Financial Rule 105.3 which reiterates the substance of former Financial Rule 110.1.

### d.) Committee on Contracts

The mandate of the Committee on Contracts was determined in Financial Rule110.17[109] to be to render written advice to the Assistant Secretary-General for General Services or to the above mentioned authorized officials on contracts about to be entered into or to be amended. The main Contracts Committee was established at the United Nations Headquarters while local Contracts Committees were established at other major duty stations such as Geneva, Vienna, and Nairobi or at the regional economic commissions.[110] The Contracts Committee at the United Nations Headquarters as of 1985[111] was made responsible for reviewing all proposed contractual commitments to be entered into with a single contractor for a cost of US$ 40.000 or more as well as all proposed amendments or modifications to such contracts. On 1 November 1996[112] the monetary limit was raised to US$ 200.000. For proposed income producing contracts the limit was set at US$ 10.000 in 1985 and raised to US$ 40.000 in 1996, provided that where one or more amendments to an income producing contract would increase the amount by more than 20% or cause the aggregate amount to exceed US$ 40.000, the advice of the Committee on Contracts also would be required prior to any contractual commitment being made. The local Contracts Committees were given responsibility for reviewing and advising on transactions involving lower

---

Such authorization may take the form of:

An allotment of funds or other authorization to commit funds covering a specific period and/or a specific purpose; and/or

An authorization for the employment of staff or of consultants."

109 Replaced by Financial Rule 105.13, *see* ST/SGB/2003/7 (2003), which confers responsibility on the Under-Secretary-General for Management for the procurement functions of the United Nations and for the establishment of review committees to render advice before final action is taken to award or amend a procurement contract. The specific monetary limits are no longer stated in the Financial Rules.

110 ECA at Addis Ababa, Ethiopia, ECLA at Santiago, Chile, and ESCAP at Bangkok, Thailand.

111 ST/SGB/Financial Rules/1/Rev.3 (1985).

112 Policy Guidelines of the Procurement and Transportation Division, contained in the Annex to the Fourth Report on Procurement Reform of the Advisory Committee on Administrative and Budgetary Questions. United Nations document A/51/7/Add.3 (1996).

monetary amounts and concerning activities and requirements arising at the duty station concerned.

In its present version, Financial Rule 105.13(b) vests the responsibility to "establish review committees, at Headquarters and other locations, to render written advice to the Under-Secretary-General for Management on procurement actions leading to the award or amendment of procurement contracts..." in that senior official, the Under-Secretary-General for Management, rather than as previously in the Secretary-General. This change clearly has diminished the role – but not the ultimate responsibility – of the Secretary-General in providing control and oversight over procurement.

While there was no provision in the Financial Rules of 1985 for waiving the procedure of seeking the advice of the competent Committee on Contracts wherever required, the advice was not binding. However, paragraph (g) of Financial Rule 110.17 provided that in a case where the authorized official "decides not to accept the advice of the Committee, he or she shall record in writing the reasons for that decision". Similarly, in the revised version, Financial Rule 105.13(c) provides that where the advice of the competent Review Committee is required, no "final action leading to the award or amendment of a procurement contract" may be taken before the advice has been received. Should the Under-Secretary-General decide not to accept the Review Committee's advice, he or she shall record the reasons in writing.[113]

According to paragraph (b) of Financial Rule 110.17 of 1985, the Secretary-General determined the composition of the Headquarters Committee on Contracts while paragraph (c) provided that the composition of local Contracts Committees "shall be determined by the head of the office concerned in consultation with the Secretary-General." Under the presently applicable Financial Rule 105.13(b), the Under-Secretary-General for Management establishes the composition and the terms of reference of the review committees on procurement actions. Invariably, the central administrative services have been represented.[114]

113 Financial Rule 105.13 (c) in ST/SGB/2003/7.

114 As of 1 November 1996, the Headquarters Contracts Committee was composed of a chairman appointed by the Assistant Secretary-General for the Office of Conference and Support Services from among a staff member from each of the following units: Office of Conference and Support Services, Office of Programme Planning, Budget and Accounts, Office of Legal Affairs and Department for Development Support and Management Services. (A/51/7/Add.3, Ann. IV).
As of 19 May 2005, the local Contracts Committee at Vienna was composed of the Chief, Financial Resources Management Service, Division for Management, UNODC, the Chief, General Support Section, Division for Management, UNOV and the Senior Legal Liaison Officer, UNOV/UNODC. *See* UNOV/INF.210. UNODC/INF.211.

## *3. Substantive aspects*

### a.) competition

As a general rule, Financial Rule 110.18 of 1985 provided that procurement contracts "shall be let after competitive bidding or calling for proposals." The principle of awarding contracts on the basis of competition was and remains fundamental for procurement by the United Nations. The revised Financial Regulation 5.12 demands that "due consideration" must be given to a) best value for money, b) fairness, integrity and transparency, c) effective international competition and d) the interest of the United Nations. Although the weight of "effective international competition" is now tempered by its having been placed as one among several criteria of seemingly equal importance, it continues to rank as a fundamental principle supported by detailed procedural provisions ensuring its observance. Competition also is a condition according to the revised Financial Rule 105.14 which requires that "procurement contracts shall be awarded on the basis of effective competition" and that the competitive process, as necessary, shall include certain specific features such as formal or informal methods of solicitation and public bid openings.[115]

### b.) advertising

While the Financial Rules did not describe the competitive process comprehensibly, Financial Rule 110.18 required tenders to be invited by advertising, normally through either "publication or distribution of formal invitations to bid" and, exceptionally, "where the nature of the work involved precludes invitation of tenders", proposals could be called provided a "comparative analysis of such proposals" was kept on record.

For a global international organisation, the practical feasibility of publishing tenders through advertisement in the printed media is frustrated by the implicit expectation of Member States that potential bidders from in principle every Member State be afforded an equal opportunity to participate in the bidding process. Quite apart from linguistic barriers, until the arrival and general use of the Internet web, none of the available media could be considered to have uni-

---

[115] Other features that are required "as necessary" are i) acquisition planning for the development of an overall procurement strategy and procurement methodologies, ii) market research for identifying potential suppliers and iii) prudent commercial practices.

form global reach. Therefore, this modality has been used only in special cases, such as where only firms from the duty station concerned would be capable of implementing the contract, e.g. building construction.

### c.) formal invitation of tenders versus informal calling for proposals

The distinction between formal invitation of "tenders" and informal calling for "proposals" is clear in principle, and although recognized by long established United Nations practice,[116] it was not addressed by the internal Procurement Manual until 1998.[117] The procurement procedure can in either case be understood as being quasi- or pre-contractual in nature[118] and United Nations practice has recognized the following distinction:

A *tender* is a formal bid that must meet all specifications and requirements set out in the formal invitation and state the asking price which will vary between the competitive bids. Formal invitation of tenders constitutes a quasi-contractual offer and therefore there is no room for modifying a tendered bid through negotiations. It constitutes acceptance of the procurer's offer and must be approved or rejected as it is presented. Accordingly, the exchange consisting of the formal invitation of tenders and the tendering of a bid can be considered to have a quasi-contractual nature.

---

116 *See* Memorandum of 19 June 1991 from the Chief, Procurement Services, to a Senior Legal Officer, objecting to the public opening of proposals since "those present would have every expectation that the award will be made to the lowest bidder, all other things being equal. In the case of proposals, these do not lend themselves to public opening because of the judgemental considerations which have to be used in determining which proposer has, in the final analysis, submitted the best offer. The technical evaluation may well result in the contract being awarded to other than the lowest proposer." Third Interim Report, Independent Inquiry Committee into the United Nations Oil-for-Food Programme, 8 August 2005, available at http://www.iic-offp.org/documents/ThirdInterimReport.pdf, App. B, 12-13.

117 A revised version of the United Nations Procurement Manual, issued on 31 March 1998, addressed this point.

118 When reviewing a complaint lodged by a disappointed bidder, the United States Court of Claims recognized that an implied-in-fact contract to negotiate in good faith exists between offerors and the Government, which may constitute a cause of action. *See* J. R. Cantor, "Bid Protests and Procurement Reform: The Case for Leaving Well Enough Alone", 27 *Publ. Cont. L. J.* 161-162 (1997-1998), analysing *Heyer Products Co.* v. *United States* 140 Supp. 409 (Ct.Cl.1956), *modified*, 177 F. Supp. 251 (Ct.Cl.1959).

A *proposal*, on the other hand, is considered to be the response to an informal call by the procurer. The call naturally will indicate the specifications and other requirements as far necessary in order to enable the bidding suppliers to present comparable competitive proposals, but room will be left for the bidders to formulate the details and, in certain circumstances, even the choice of technology or other implementation modalities. Accordingly, negotiations with the best-placed bidder or bidders may take place in order to reach agreement on all the technical and contractual terms prior to the formal award of the contract. The informal call for proposals and the submission of proposals in response is not quasi-contractual, but rather pre-contractual in nature.

The above-mentioned distinction, as well as its disregard, was invoked by the Secretariat's Joint Disciplinary Committee[119] during its investigation of alleged misconduct by certain procurement officers during 1992. In its report,[120] the Joint Disciplinary Committee stated among its General Findings as follows:

> "….the Panel observed that the *Procurement Manual* was inadequate in that, while it covered the bidding process, it did not cover the Request for Proposal ("RFP") process although this had become a key instrument for meeting the needs of peace-keeping missions. It is important to distinguish between the two: while the bidding process asks for quotes for products with clear and unambiguous specifications, making the evaluation process relatively straightforward, the RFP process asks for quotes on services, leaving it to the vendors to specify *how* they intend to meet the RFP's requirements. This is a far more flexible process, and is more demanding in terms of the technical and financial analysis needed to evaluate proposals and select the most suitable vendor. Yet, official guidelines for the RFP process were still lacking in 1992. Moreover, the *Procurement Manual* did not cover emergency where immediate action was required, nor did it cover situations involving on-going changes in requisition and RFP requirements."

---

119 Established by the Secretary-General pursuant to Staff Regulation 10.1 to advise him in disciplinary cases. Staff Rule 110.6 provides that each case before the Joint Disciplinary Committees shall be considered by a Panel composed of a chairperson, a member appointed by the Secretary-General and a member elected by the staff. According to Staff Rule 110.4(b) "no staff member shall be subject to disciplinary measures until the matter has been referred to a Joint Disciplinary Committee for advice as to what measures, if any, are appropriate", except where the referral has been waived by mutual agreement of the staff member and the Secretary-General or in case of summary dismissal where immediate separation from the service is warranted by the seriousness of the misconduct (ST/SGB/Staff Regulations/Rev.23).

120 Cited after Judgment No. 744 of the United Nations Administrative Tribunal (United Nations document AT/DEC/744), published on 22 November 1995, which referred *in extenso* to the report of Joint Disciplinary Committee.

The present Financial Rules[121] have retained certain aspects of the distinction discussed above. They employ a revised terminology, but do not comprehensively regulate the matter. Financial Rule 105.15 distinguishes between cases where "a formal invitation to bid" and where "a formal request for proposals" has been issued and, as a new development, relies on this distinction to determine which selection criteria are applicable. In the former case, the award shall go to "the qualified bidder whose bid substantially conforms to the requirements set forth in the solicitation documents and is evaluated to be the one with the lowest cost" and in the latter case to "the qualified proposer whose proposal, all factors considered, is the most responsive to the requirements set forth in the solicitation documents". That the award criteria are formulated flexibly may be convenient for the procurement officer, but does not provide the desirable level of legal certainty and predictability regarding the award decision. In this regard, the criterion of being "most responsive to the requirements" cannot be understood objectively without further detailed criteria such as an enumeration of specific requirements and an indication of how and with which weight, i.e. quantification, each requirement will be evaluated.

Financial Rule 105.15 addresses only the "formal methods of solicitation" and not the "informal methods of solicitation such as requests for quotations" – the latter being referred to in Financial Rule 105.14(d). The informal methods are available only in the enumerated instances where a formal competitive procedure is not feasible. Under the informal procedure the award shall go to "a qualified vendor whose offer substantially conforms to the requirement at an acceptable price." Clearly, the criterion of "an acceptable price" is not unambiguous and therefore fails as a guarantee of legal certainty and predictability in the selection.

### d.) exceptions to competition

Financial Rule 110.19 listed several exceptions to the basic requirement in Financial Rule 110.18 of concluding procurement contracts only after competition between interested potential contractors.

One ground was a relatively low value of the intended contract, which in 1985 was set at 10.000 US$ for procurement actions at the United Nations Headquarters and only 5.000 US$ at the duty stations with locally established Contracts Committees. These thresholds have since been raised, *inter alia* to

---

[121] ST/SGB/2003/7.

reflect price inflation. The presently applicable provision in Financial Rule 105.16(a)(x) retains the principle of exempting low value procurement from competition, but leaves the monetary threshold to be established by separate administrative action by the Under-Secretary-General for Management.

Exemption also was permitted on the grounds that the prices were fixed by legislation or regulation or that the Contracts Committee had approved standardisation of the category of supplies or equipment intended to be acquired. The same grounds are retained in the revised Financial Rule 105.16(a)(i) and (ii) which have added a reference to monopoly situations.

According to Financial Rule 110.19(d), a further ground for exemption was if the delay that would be caused by following a competitive procedure could not be permitted in view of the exigency of effecting the procurement. This ground also is contained in the revised Financial Rule 105.16(a)(vii).

Also the nature of the goods or services to be acquired could be a ground for exemption. That was the case for proprietary articles[122] or perishable supplies, external professional services, medicines, medical supplies, hospital or surgical supplies or prosthetic appliances.[123] The revised Financial Rule 105.16(a) retains the category of professional services in subparagraph (viii) under "services that cannot be evaluated objectively". Proprietary articles are not mentioned but may be included under "monopoly" in subparagraph (i). Likewise, the omission of perishable supplies would seem to be neutralized by the retention of "exigency" under subparagraph (vii). A substantive change has been effected by no longer retaining the taxonomic listing of medicines, medical supplies, hospital or surgical supplies or prosthetic appliances as exempt categories.[124] A further substantive change is the addition of three broadly formulated grounds for exemption, i.e. where offers for identical products and services have been obtained competitively within a reasonable prior period (subparagraph (iv)), where a formal solicitation of competitive offers has not produced satisfactory results (subparagraph (v)) or where it is intended to purchase or lease real estate and market conditions do not allow for effective competition (subparagraph (vi). As

---

122 This term has been taken to refer to items where ownership rights prevent or severely restrict competition, such as where a unique item is available from only one supplier. This may be due to a market monopoly or to intellectual property rights.

123 Financial Rule 110.19(d) to (g). ST/SGB/Financial Rules/1/Rev.3 (1985).

124 Due to the involvement of the United Nations in post-conflict rehabilitation and reconstruction programmes, the volume of such medical and hospital procurement has significantly increased.

was also previously the case,[125] the Chief Procurement Officer, the Under-Secretary-General for Management, under the revised Financial Rule 105.16(a) (ix) can make an advance determination that a formal solicitation will not give satisfactory results, provided that the Officer records the reasons for the determination in writing. Under the revised Financial Rules, such recording of the respective reason also must be made in all other cases of exemption from the competitive procedure, i.e. all the instances where informal methods of solicitation may be used.

While the revised Financial Rules do not offer any substantial change in the grounds for exemption from competition, they are formulated more clearly and enhance the personal responsibility of the Chief Procurement Officer by requiring him or her to record any ground for exemption in writing. Previously, in most instances the written record of the ground relied on was found only in the minutes and recommendations of the Committee on Contracts.

### e.) public opening of bids

Financial Rule 110.20[126] required that all bids must be opened publicly at the time and place specified in the respective invitation to bid and that an immediate record be made of the bids. The formulation of the corresponding revised Financial Rule 105.14(e)[127] is less absolute; it merely requires that procurement contracts shall be awarded "on the basis of effective competition" and that "the competitive process shall, as necessary, include:....Public bid openings". In fact, in this respect the revision of the Financial Rules merely has codified the established practice, under which bid openings open to attendance by representatives of the bidders had become the exception so that, in the vast majority of cases, only designated members of the Secretariat attended the opening.

### f.) selection criteria

In spite of the overarching role played by the selection criteria for the execution of procurement actions, only the brief rule that "contracts shall be awarded to the

---

[125] Financial Rule 110.19(h). ST/SGB/Financial Rules/1/Rev.3 (1985).

[126] ST/SGB/Financial Rules/1/Rev.3 (1985).

[127] ST/SGB/2003/7.

lowest acceptable bidder" was contained in Financial Rule 110.21.[128] In particular, this rule did not determine the relative weights to be given to the criteria of cost (or of price), on the one hand, and to qualitative criteria, on the other hand, and thus left it to administrative practice to act *ad hoc* or, in the best case, to elaborate more detailed guidelines on the formulation, calculation and weighting of the various selection criteria.

One modality that was widely followed was to apply the selection criteria literally: first the technical aspects of the bids were screened for compatibility with the technical requirements stipulated in the invitation and those found to meet the technical requirements were then reviewed further to establish and compare their respective cost, whereupon the award went to the bidder having submitted the least costly bid among those that had been retained as technically acceptable and compatible given the requirements. In the course of the 1990ies, however, more differentiated guidelines were developed and included in the internal Procurement Manual of the United Nations and in training modules prepared by the UNDP and IAPSO. Basically, as mentioned above, a distinction was drawn on the basis of the type of solicitation document used. A Request for Quotation (RFQ) or an Invitation to Bid (ITB) was prescribed for the procurement of goods and services, for which simple but comprehensive specifications could be stated, so that the price would be the main variable in the offers. The evaluation of the quotations or bids and the selection of the awardee therefore would follow the method outlined immediately above. In contrast, a Request for Proposals (RFP) was to be used for the acquisition of goods, services or works where the requirements could be described only in a general manner, e.g. by specifying the desired result or performance, and where an independent and creative contribution was expected from the interested potential contractor in composing its proposal.

The revised United Nations Financial Rules[129] formally endorse the above distinction and differentiate between the selection criteria accordingly. Thus, pursuant to Financial Rule 105.15(a), when a *formal invitation to bid* has been issued, the award shall be given to

> "the qualified bidder whose bid substantially conforms to the requirements set forth in the solicitation documents and is evaluated to be the one with the lowest cost to the United Nations."

---

[128] ST/SGB/Financial Rules/1/Rev.3 (1985).

[129] ST/SGB/2003/7.

On the other hand, Financial Rule 105.15(b) provides that when a *formal request for proposals* has been issued, the award shall go to

> "the qualified proposer whose proposal, all factors considered, is the most responsive to the requirements set forth in the solicitation documents."

As can be seen, under paragraph (a) the selection criteria essentially remain the traditional ones of the least costly and technically acceptable bid, while the criteria under rule (b) are less transparent in as much as an objective application presumes the use of a list of the requirements that must be evaluated and a point system to define the respective weight to be given to each requirement, whether financial or technical.

### g.) currency availability

Reflecting the practice of certain Member States of liquidating their voluntary financial commitments to the Organization in non-convertible currencies, it was further provided that due consideration should be given to "the utilization of currencies available to the Organization and which require special management." In practice this meant that only suppliers, including state trading agents, from the country making a contribution in its own non-convertible currency could be considered for the award of contracts to be financed from that contribution. – That this rule has been not included among the revised Financial Rules reflects the decreased use of non-convertible currencies in the economies of Member States.

### h.) rejection of all bids

Finally, Financial Rule 110.21 allowed that all bids could be rejected "where the interests of the Organization so require" and that in such instances, the reasons should be recorded in writing by the responsible procurement officer.[130] An effect of invoking this rule was that none of the rules requiring procurement actions to follow a prescribed procedure, such as the references to "formal solicitation", constituted a ground that could be relied on by a bidder wishing to pursue a claim against the United Nations based on alleged procedural irregularity. Moreover, Financial Rule 110.21 did not require the United Nations to inform bidders of the reasons for rejecting all bids – the written record of the

---

130 The Assistant Secretary-General for General Services or a procurement officer.

reason had merely internal status. No change in this respect has been made in the revised Financial Rules,[131] nor do they entitle unsuccessful bidders to be advised of the reason for not retaining their bids. Rather, the Under-Secretary-General for Management is entitled to opt between undertaking a new solicitation, directly negotiating a contract with a qualified vendor, or terminating or suspending the procurement action. Accordingly, there was and still is no consistency with the notion that the formal bidding process forms part of a pre-award phase of a quasi-contractual nature, in the course of which a bidder whose bid meets all the conditions stipulated in the invitation and offers the lowest price may possess an enforceable claim either to be awarded the contract or, alternatively, to receive compensation.

## F. Quaternary Source: Administrative Instructions

### *1. Power to Issue United Nations Administrative Instructions*

In the 1985 version,[132] United Nations Financial Rule 114.5 stated what would have been applicable also without that rule, i.e.:

> "These Rules may be amended by the Secretary-General in a manner consistent with the Financial Regulations."

A fourth level of norms was foreseen by Financial Rule 114.4, entitled "Amplification of Rules", which provided that

> "These Rules may be amplified by administrative instructions issued by the USG/ADM".[133]

From a practical, administrative viewpoint, the delegation of authority to an Under-Secretary-General to issue administrative instructions *de facto* affects the normative function of the Secretary-General in a manner that tends to limit the Secretary-General's ability to effectively manage the financial affairs of the Organisation. This risk could well materialize even in face of the precautionary qualification that the purpose of the administrative instructions merely shall be to amplify the Financial Rules. The revised Financial Rules, issued in 2003,[134] have

---

131 ST/SGB/2003/7, Financial Rule 105.15 (c).

132 ST/SGB/Financial Rules/1/Rev.3(1985).

133 The acronym stands for 'Under-Secretary-General for Administration and Management.

134 ST/SGB/2003/7.

enhanced the risk by omitting any rule corresponding to the former Financial Rules 114.4 and 5 and by emphasizing and detailing the delegated authority in a manner that tends to further suppress the authority of the Secretary-General to issue and to implement norms and, thus, to directly manage all financial matters, including, especially, in the field of procurement. As a practical example may be mentioned that due to the hierarchical structure of the Secretariat, the Executive Office of the Secretary-General is likely to be more inclined than the immediate advisers of an Under-Secretary-General, to request and rely on advice and assistance from the Secretariat's Office of Legal Affairs in the preparation of administrative instructions and similar issuances.[135] In this respect the now applicable Financial Rule 101.1 provides the general rule that

> "The Secretary-General hereby delegates authority and responsibility for implementation of the Financial Regulations and Rules to the Under-Secretary-General for Management. The Under-Secretary-General may in turn delegate by administrative instruction authority for specified aspects of the Financial Regulations and Rules."

In the field of procurement, additional authority, responsibility and control has been delegated to the Under-Secretary-General for Management by several Financial Rules, among which Rule 105.13(a) is particularly comprehensive:

> "(a) The Under-Secretary-General for Management is responsible for the procurement functions of the United Nations, shall establish all United Nations procurement systems and shall designate the officials responsible for performing procurement functions."

Further Financial Rules now complement the general delegation by elaborating on important aspects. Thus, Financial Rule 105.13(b) charges the Under-Secretary-General for Management with the task to "establish review committees at Headquarters and other locations, to render written advice ...on procurement actions leading to the award or amendment of procurement contracts,..." including to "establish the composition and the terms of reference of such committees...". The review committees have replaced the former Contracts Committees, which performed similar functions but whose composition and terms of reference were determined by the Secretary-General[136] to the extent the terms of reference were not already fixed in the Financial Rules.

---

[135] This observation is not limited to the procurement field, but is equally valid *e.g.* for personnel administration, budgetary and financial management and legal aspects of technical assistance programmes for development.

[136] ST/SGB/Financial Rules/1/Rev.3 (1985), Rule 110.17.

The motivation for delegating authority so extensively, appears to be the realization that the Secretary-General is primarily dealing with a large number of complex and important political questions, with which he is charged by Member States, and that, consequently, little time is left for the equally time-consuming tasks connected with the administration of the Secretariat and implementation of the programmes of the Organisation. Although, unquestionably, this is a common view that realistically reflects the situation of several Secretaries-General, the device of delegating authority to an Under-Secretary-General cannot diminish the accountability of any Secretary-General for the full range of responsibilities, whether they are those of a Chief Administrative Officer under Article 97 of the Charter or follow from other pertinent Charter provisions. Moreover, the creation of a dichotomy between the indirect management of financial and other administrative matters and the "hands-on" management of political matters is an invitation to contradictions and inefficiencies.

## G. United Nations System

A similar, hierarchically structured order of norms prevails in the specialized and related agencies of the United Nations. As mentioned in Chapter I, their procurement rules also are similar to those of the United Nations. Due to the origin of the United Nations Industrial Development Organization[137] (hereinafter referred to as "UNIDO") as a department of the United Nations, the framework of its procurement regime exhibits the greatest affinity with that of the United Nations.

[137] The Constitution of the United Nations Industrial Development Organization was adopted at Vienna on 8 April 1979. It entered into force on 21 June 1985, pursuant to its art. 25, when at least eighty States that had deposited instruments of ratification, acceptance or approval also had agreed, after consultations among themselves, that the Constitution should enter into force. United Nations document: ST/LEG/SER.E/10.

## 1. *Constitution of UNIDO and Powers of its Principal Organs*

The Constitution of UNIDO is a multilateral, international treaty,[138] duly ratified by the 171 Member States of UNIDO. UNIDO was established through the conversion[139] of a former subsidiary organ[140] of the United Nations to become a legally independent international organization with the status of a specialized agency of the United Nations.[141] The legal origin of UNIDO is reflected in the preamble to its Constitution and in Article 26.2[142] thereof, which provided for the continued applicability to the new UNIDO of the "rules and regulations" of the former UNIDO, such as the Financial Regulations and Rules, until new provisions had been adopted by the new organization. UNIDO has three principal organs:[143] the Secretariat, the Industrial Development Board and the General Conference. All Member States[144] are represented in the General Conference, which is the deliberative and legislative organ with general competence.

---

[138] Signed 8 April 1979, entered into force 21 June 1985, 1401 *UNTS* 3.

[139] The present UNIDO is the legal successor to the former organisation of the same name, which had been formally established by General Assembly resolution 2089 (XX) of 20 December 1965 while General Assembly resolution 2152(XXI) of 17 November 1966 provided it with the institutional framework of an autonomous organisation within the United Nations.
By section IV, paragraph 9, of its resolution 3362 (S-VII) (1979), the United Nations General Assembly endorsed the recommendation of the Second General Conference of UNIDO to convert that organisation into a specialized agency of the United Nations. The endorsement of the recommendation to convert UNIDO further was recalled by the General Assembly's resolution 34/96 (1979), entitled "Transitional arrangements relating to the establishment of the United Nations Industrial Development Organization as a specialized agency." The latter resolution, *inter alia*, laid down rules for the transfer of assets from the former to the new organisation and decided to terminate the existing UNIDO at the end of the calendar year in which the General Conference of the new UNIDO would first be convened. The General Conference held its first session in 1985 and the former UNIDO thus was terminated at the end of the date of 31 December 1985.

[140] J. Klabbers, *An Introduction to International Institutional Law* 11 (2002).

[141] For a succinct account of the legal measures taken to implement the conversion of UNIDO, *see* *UNJYB* 184-192 (1986).

[142] UNIDO Constitution, art. 26.2: "The rules and regulations governing the organization established by the United Nations General Assembly resolution 2152 (XXI) shall govern the Organization and its organs until such time as the latter may adopt new provisions."

[143] Constitution art. 7.1.

[144] UNIDO presently has 172 Member States. UNIDO document IDB.33/2-PBC.23/2 (2006).

Whether the new UNIDO is the legal successor[145] to the former UNIDO and to this extent to the United Nations became a matter of contention between the United Nations and the new UNIDO related to the assets of the former UNIDO, in which respect the United Nations Office of Legal Affairs held that the disappearance of the former UNIDO implied the lack of legal succession of the new the new UNIDO, while legal succession was favoured by UNIDO.[146]

## *2. Power to Approve UNIDO Financial Regulations*

Article 8.3 of the Constitution provides that the General Conference, *inter alia*, shall "approve the financial regulations of the Organization".

The General Conference first exercised this power by taking note[147] of a decision[148] of the Industrial Development Board to approve the application by the Director-General of the Financial Regulations of the United Nations as of 31 December 1985 *mutatis mutandis* pending adoption of financial regulations of UNIDO by its General Conference. The interim lasted two years: On 12 November 1987, the General Conference decided,[149] in accordance with Article 8.3 of the Constitution, to approve the Financial Regulations for the UNIDO, which

---

[145] J. Klabbers analyses practice involving dissolution and succession of international organisations, *supra* note 140, 320-332.

[146] Karin Rudolph holds that "as the legal personality of the old UNIDO was not considered as continuing in the new UNIDO" it was necessary, on 10 December 1985, to conclude a series of tri-partite and bilateral exchanges of letters between the United Nations, UNIDO and Austria, which continued in force the existing agreements relating to the headquarters in the Vienna International Centre of the two organizations, pending the conclusion of permanent headquarters agreements. *See* K. Rudolph, "Article 104", in B. Simma (ed.), *The Charter of the United Nations* Vol. II, 1307 (2002). This alone is not conclusive, however. Indeed, the old UNIDO had been part of the legal personality of the United Nations and, in the diction of the General Assembly's resolutions, *converted* into the new UNIDO, to which, under its Constitution, the United Nations rules and regulations continued to apply until replaced by UNIDO. In accordance with this notion, most of the existing staff chose to exercise their right to transfer to the new organisation with retention of their rights acquired as staff of the United Nations. Moreover, none of the international agreements of the former UNIDO, other than the headquarters agreements, and none of the several thousand commercial contracts with private parties were formally novated but *de facto* treated as continuing commitments applicable to and binding on the new UNIDO. The case for legal succession therefore appears more convincing.

[147] UNIDO General Conference decision (GC.1/Dec.31) (1985).

[148] UNIDO Industrial Development Board decision (IDB.1/Dec.12) (1985).

[149] General Conference decision (GC.2/Dec.25) (1987).

were annexed to the decision and scheduled to come into force on 1 January 1988.[150]

### 3. *Power to Establish UNIDO Staff Regulations*

Article 11.5 of the Constitution of UNIDO provides, *inter alia*, as follows:

> "The staff shall be appointed by the Director-General under regulations to be established by the Conference upon recommendations of the Board…."

Accordingly, also with respect to the adoption of Staff Regulations, the General Conference is the competent principal organ. Initially, in accordance with Article 26.2 of the Constitution, the Staff Regulations of the United Nations continued to be applied *mutatis mutandis*. Thereafter, the General Conference on 12 November 1985 adopted a decision[151] establishing the Staff Regulations of UNIDO, which were annexed to the decision and entered into effect on 1 July 1988.[152]

### 4. *UNIDO Financial Regulations*

Regarding procurement matters, the Financial Regulations of UNIDO are even more sparse than those of the United Nations.[153] The only rule is Regulation 9.5, which reads:

> "Regulation 9.5: The Director-General shall as part of the financial rules establish rules for the procurement of equipment, supplies and other requirements including rules governing the invitation of tenders and the calling of proposals."

---

150 With respect to the subject of a Tax Equalization Fund, no agreement was reached on the proposed Financial Regulations 5.2(e) and 5.3 due to objections by the United States. Instead, it was decided to continue to apply the corresponding United Nations Financial Regulations: the chapeau and sub-paragraph (e) of regulation 5.2.

151 General Conference decision (GC.2/Dec.29) (1987).

152 As in case of the Financial Regulations (*see supra* note 147) the lack of agreement on a Tax Equalization Fund caused the General Conference to opt for the continued applicability of the corresponding United Nations Staff Regulations 3.3(e) and 3.3(f) instead of the proposed regulations 6.8(c), 6.8(d) and 13.4.

153 Approved by the General Conference's Dec. GC.2/Dec.25 (1987) and amended by Dec. GC.3/Dec.21 (1989). Promulgated in the Director-General's bulletin UNIDO/DG/B.74/Rev.1 (1990). Financial Regulation 9.5 came into effect on 1 January 1988 and has not been amended.

## *5. UNIDO Staff Regulations*

The relevant substantive Staff Regulations of UNIDO[154] correspond *mutatis mutandis* to those of the United Nations, except for minor variations that do not alter the fundamental principles or the essential meaning of the provisions.[155]

## *6. Power to Issue UNIDO Financial Rules*

UNIDO Financial Regulation 12.1 provides that the Director-General shall

> "issue financial rules which shall govern the administration of all financial activities and transactions of the Organisation. In the financial rules, the Director-General may delegate authority to officials of the Organization."

This provision should not be read as providing an exclusive mode of delegating authority in financial matters, however, since individual procurement officials have been delegated authority in the form of an internal memorandum from the Director-General.

## *7. Power to Issue UNIDO Staff Rules*

As described for the United Nations, also in the case of UNIDO, the Staff Regulations empower the Director-General, to issue Staff Rules and amendments thereto for the purpose of implementing the Staff Regulations.[156] The Director-General must report such rules and amendments to the Industrial Development Board, which may direct amendment or withdrawal in case it finds the rule, or amendment to be inconsistent with the intent or purpose of the Staff Regulations. Contrasting with the United Nations, however, newly issued rules or amendments are immediately applicable, but shall not give rise to acquired rights if withdrawn or amended at the direction of the Board. This slight deviation from

---

154 Adopted by the General Conference of UNIDO on 12 November 1987 by its Dec. GC.2/Dec.29. Issued, together with the Staff Rules, as UNIDO DG/B/Staff Rules/1/.

155 UNIDO Staff Regulation 1.2 corresponds to United Nations Staff Regulation 1.2(d), except for the addition of the following sentence: "Staff Members should note that Member States have on their part undertaken to respect the exclusively international character of the responsibilities of the Director-General and the staff and not to seek to influence them in the discharge of their responsibilities." The addition enhances the independence requirement by referring to a potential source of infringement.

156 UNIDO Staff Regulations 13.4. UNIDO/DGB/Staff Rules/1/.

the United Nation's rule making newly issued staff rules applicable only at the conclusion of the year during which they have been reported to the General Assembly, is compatible with the requirement in Article 11.5 of the Constitution of UNIDO that "the conditions of service of staff shall conform as far as possible to those of the United Nations common system." The margin for deviations is narrow, however. Mostly, new Staff Rules or amendments are issued to implement rules already adopted in other *fora* of the common system of organizations.

## 8. *UNIDO Financial Rules*

In accordance with UNIDO Financial Regulation 12.1, the Director-General has issued Financial Rules which took effect on 1 January 1988.[157] They did not differ in substance from the then applicable Financial Rules of the United Nations in any important respect, except that with respect to procurement the criteria for selecting the winning bid were set out in more detail. UNIDO Financial Rule 109.21.(b) did not distinguish between formal bids and informal proposals but provided that

> "contracts shall be awarded to those firms or institutions that have tendered the lowest, technically acceptable bid or submitted the lowest, technically acceptable proposal....".

Another special feature of UNIDO's Financial Rules[158] is the price preference allowed for bids from developing countries. Provided the condition is clearly stated in the invitation to bid or to submit competitive proposals, a price preference of up to 15% may be allowed for bids or proposals from firms or institutions in the so-called recipient countries, i.e. the Member State(s) that are the beneficiaries of the development assistance, for which the procurement is undertaken. As is the case under the United Nations rules, all bids or proposals may be rejected "where the interests of the Organization so require."

## 9. *Power to Issue UNIDO Administrative Instructions*

UNIDO Financial Rule 112.4 provides that they "may be amplified by administrative instructions issued by" the Deputy Director-General for Administration in consultation with the Director-General.

---

157 UNIDO/DG/B.74 and UNIDO/DG/B.74/Rev.1.

158 *Ibid.*, Financial Rule 109.21(c).

Similarly, also UNIDO Staff Rule 113.02(c) provides for the issuance of a fourth level of norms, namely Administrative Instructions, by the Director of the Personnel Services Division, who must act in consultation with either the Director-General or the Deputy Director-General for Administration.[159]

## H. Purposes of the Formal Norms

Although the earlier versions of the United Nations Financial Regulations did not explicitly state the overriding purposes of the formal norms on procurement actions as such, Financial Regulation 10.1(a)[160] implicitly provided guidance as it required the Secretary-General to "establish detailed financial rules and procedures in order to ensure effective financial administration and the exercise of economy". Applicable at present is the revised United Nations Financial Regulation 5.12[161] which states four general principles and requires that they "be given due consideration when exercising the procurement functions." It would seem appropriate to consider these additional principles to express purposes that had been implicitly recognized also prior to their being incorporated in an express norm. They are:

a.) Best value for money;

b.) Fairness, integrity and transparency;

c.) Effective international competition;

d.) The interest of the United Nations.

No priority has been established in the revised Financial Regulations between these principles, nor would there seem to be any logical need to do so, since they are intertwined and overlapping. The principles under (a) to (c) clearly are not mutually exclusive. Depending on the circumstances at hand, the fourth criterion: the interest of the United Nations, can be understood either as a general reference that encompasses the other three principles or as a distinct ground for

159 UNIDO Staff Rule 113.02(c) "The present rules may be amplified by administrative instructions issued by the Director, Personnel Services Division, in consultation with the Deputy Director-General, Department of Administration, or the Director-General, as appropriate." UNIDO/DG/B/Staff Rules/1.

160 ST/SGB/Financial Rules/1/Rev.3 (1985).

161 ST/SGB/2003/7.

making exceptions thereto. – The former view was implied by the Secretariat's Office of Legal Affairs when advising that so-called "tied contributions", i.e. voluntary contributions encumbered by the condition that purchases funded from the contribution be made in the donor country, were incompatible with the Financial Regulations and Rules of the United Nations, in particular with "the usual practice of international competitive bidding for procurement, the scope of which is supposed to be established solely in the Organization's interest and in accordance with its policies".[162]

Presumably, the single most important purpose or principle is to ensure the economical use of the Organizations financial resources. The systemic placement of the procurement norms as part of the Financial Regulations and Rules speaks for this view, as does the emphasis placed in the selection criteria on the lowest cost and the effectiveness of the international competition.

UNIDO's Financial Regulations and Rules are silent on the purposes of the procurement regime. Nevertheless, taking into account UNIDO's legal origin, its status as a specialized agency of the United Nations and the great similarity between the prescribed procedures, it can be assumed that the purposes are analogous to those of the United Nations procurement regime.

## I. Promoting Observance of the Procurement Norms and Procedures

### 1. *Variety and Effectiveness of Measures*

In principle, recourse can be had to various measures in order to promote observance of, or to discourage infringements of, the prescribed procurement norms and procedures of the United Nations. Given the existence of different modalities, the question self-evidently can be raised, to which extent a possible measure is effective in ensuring compliance in general and, in particular, in preventing a recurrence of infringements such as those indicated by the factual findings of the IIC.

---

162 Letter of 18 October 1982 to the Legal Liaison Officer of UNIDO. *UNJYB* 183 (1982). – In 1982 UNIDO still formed a part of the United Nations.

## 2. *Reform of the Formal Procedural Norms*

A revision of the present Financial Regulations and Rules, and of the associated administrative instructions, guidelines and manuals, is a possible remedial measure. The present regulatory framework applicable to procurement by the United Nations is complex due to its multi-layered, hierarchical structure. The complexity poses a difficult challenge to procurement officers and other staff without specialized legal training and diminishes their ability to understand and apply the prescribed norms correctly, in particular when account is taken of the operational need to respond swiftly to procurement requests. The existing structure also determines the actors that would have to participate in a revision, which implies that action would be required by both the Secretary-General and by Member States acting through the General Assembly.

Preferably, in order to enhance clarity and facilitate comprehension and compliance, a revision should be comprehensive and aim at reducing the number of hierarchically layered levels and instruments. A single comprehensive instrument to be promulgated by the Secretary-General and possibly constituting a section of the Financial Rules could replace the provisions found in the current Financial Rules, administrative instructions and manuals. Thus, the General Assembly only would be have to adopt any consequentially required amendments to the Financial Regulations.

Questions not adequately covered at present should be addressed. That includes the important issue of defining the selection criteria clearly, including the use of alternative selection criteria, and, in all events, requiring the criteria to be disclosed to the potential bidders by being stated expressly in the Solicitation Documents. It is particularly important to disclose the relative weights that will be given during evaluation to the factors related to cost versus those related to quality. A further issue is to clarify the differences, if any, between the "formal" procedure of inviting bids and the "informal" procedure of calling for proposals. In this connexion, the procedures must, comprehensively and progressively, set out the respective roles, duties and responsibilities of programme managers, financial certifying officers, procurement officers and substantive officers. The duty of confidentiality owed to the suppliers participating in a competitive bidding process must be clarified and described in relation to members of the Secretariat as well as to all other persons, including, especially, representatives of Member States.

## 3. *Internal Reorganisation, Selection and Training of Staff*

In the light of the duties and responsibilities to be discharged, consideration should be given to upgrading the status of the Procurement Services in relation to other units of the Secretariat. An enhanced status would assist members of the Procurement Services in efforts to more effectively resist pressures from other units and from external actors not to observe the letter or the spirit of the prescribed procedure. Practical measures to this end could include the consolidation of the multitude of procurement services found throughout the Organization into a few but larger units. Such a step would strengthen the capacity and professionalism, especially if combined with training of the staff. In this connexion, it also would be beneficial to establish the precise educational and professional requirements that must be met by procurement officers and, last but not least, to apply the requirements rigorously.

## 4. *Criminal Law Enforcement and Disciplinary Measures against Staff Members*

### a.) criminal jurisdiction

Despite the helpful effect of the foregoing remedial measures, they are not likely to fully prevent future infringements. Experience bears out this lesson which ought not to be ignored by the United Nations but lead to consideration of more incisive measures.

It is common ground that the United Nations does not have jurisdiction of a criminal law nature over members of its staff. This was confirmed already in the case of *the People of the State of New York v. Nicholas Coumatos.*[163] The defendant, a United States citizen employed by the United Nations, had been arrested by the New York police outside the United Nations Headquarters and indicted for grand larceny. He claimed the court lacked jurisdiction as he was a United Nations employee and the alleged crime had taken place within the Headquarters. Having first examined the provisions of Section 7(b) of the United States International Organizations Immunities Act of 1945,[164] which provide immunity

---

[163] Judgement of 19 January 1962 of the Court of General Sessions, New York County, 224 N.Y.S. 2d 507. *See also* Gen. Sess., 224 N.Y.S. 2d 504. *UNJYB* 294-295 (1962).

[164] United Nations Legislative Series, Legislative Texts and Treaty Provisions concerning the Legal Status, Privileges and Immunities of International Organizations, Vol.1 (ST/SGB/SER.B/10), 128.

from suit and legal process only for acts performed in an official capacity, the judge noted that in the case at hand defendant's claim rested on, Article III, Sections 8 and 9, of the Headquarters Agreement of 26 June 1947,[165] and after reviewing its pertinent provisions found that

> "... it would appear from this agreement that the local law shall have jurisdiction over any acts done or transactions taking place within the Headquarters District which are in violation of such laws and the courts of the appropriate American authorities shall have jurisdiction to try and determine issues between the parties. However, such Federal, State and local laws shall, of course, not be inconsistent with any regulation that has been authorized by the United Nations...."
>
> "For the Court to recognize the existence of a general and unrestricted immunity over suits or transactions, as proposed by the defendant, would be to establish a large preferred class of people within our borders who would be immune to punishment inasmuch as the United Nations has no tribunal for the control and punishment of defendants among its personnel. It can at best expel or eject them from the Headquarters District and such persons would escape trial and punishment completely. Such a blanket immunity is contrary to our sense of justice and cannot be supported by any reference to the United Nations Charter, Acts of Congress or executive orders of the President."

The United Nations Secretariat has concurred with the above-mentioned construction of the Headquarters Agreement[166] in the *Coumatos* case. Equivalent to the functional immunity enacted by the United States International Organisations

---

165 Agreement between the United Nations and the United States of America regarding the Headquarters of the United Nations. TIAS 1676; 11 *UNTS* 11.

166 United Nations Headquarters Agreement, art. III, reads in its pertinent parts:
Section 7: "(a) The headquarters district shall be under the control and authority of the United Nations as provided in this agreement.
(b) Except as otherwise provided in this agreement or in the General Convention, the federal, state and local law of the United States shall apply within the headquarters district.
(c) Except as otherwise provided in this agreement or in the General Convention, the federal, state and local courts of the United States shall have jurisdiction over acts done and transactions taking place in the headquarters district as provided in applicable federal, state and local laws.
(d) The federal, state and local courts of the United States, when dealing with cases arising out of or relating to acts taking place in the headquarters district, shall take into account the regulations enacted by the United Nations under Section 8".
Section 8: "The United Nations shall have the power to make regulations, operative within the headquarters district, for the purpose of establishing therein conditions in all respects necessary for the full execution of its functions. No federal, state or local law or regulation of the United States which is inconsistent with a regulation of the United Nations authorized by this section shall, to the extent of such inconsistency, be applicable within the headquarters district...".
Section 9: "The headquarters district shall be inviolable...".

Immunity Act, the CPIUN[167] extends immunity to officials of the United Nations "from legal process in respect of words spoken or written and all acts performed by them in their official capacity".[168] After the *Coumatos* case, on 29 April 1970 the United States acceded to the CPIUN and in a legal opinion of 1 April 1974[169] the United Nations Office of Legal Affairs stated that a staff member (except someone of a high rank enjoying diplomatic status)

> "would have no special immunity from local prosecution for a criminal offence by virtue of his United Nations employment. Whether or not he was prosecuted would not be a matter of direct concern to the United Nations although the United Nations would intervene to ascertain whether in fact his official functions were involved..."

More recently, at the request of a United States attorney, the Secretary-General has waived the immunity of a procurement officer who had been suspended from service and charged with misconduct following an internal investigation.[170] The official thereafter was arrested under indictment of corruption in the award of procurement contracts.[171]

Apparently, there is a presumption that a criminal act falls outside the official functions of a staff member so that the Secretariat merely needs to establish to its own satisfaction the *bona fide* nature of the criminal charge and to confirm to law enforcement authorities that the Official enjoys no immunity with respect to the alleged criminal act.

### b.) disciplinary measures

In the absence of conferring criminal jurisdiction over the staff, the General Assembly has by Staff Regulation 10.1 empowered the Secretary-General to establish an "administrative machinery with staff participation" to advise him in disciplinary cases. The Secretary-General has implemented this power through the issuance of Staff Rules 110.4 to 110.7 which provide for (i) a standing "Joint Disciplinary Committee" (hereinafter the "JDC") to advise the Secretary-General

---

167 1 *UNTS* 15, and 90 *UNTS* 327.

168 CPIUN Section 18(a). Section 19 grants full diplomatic privileges and immunities to the Secretary-General and senior officials at (or above) the rank of Assistant Secretary-General.

169 Advice by the Office of Legal Affairs in a letter to the Assistant Secretary-General of an international organization, *UNJYB* 188 (1974).

170 United Nations news release of 2 November 2006. Available at http://www.un.org/apps/news.

171 "U.N. Corruption Probe 'At Full Throttle'", *New York Times*, 3 November 2006.

in disciplinary matters, (ii) the composition of the JDC and (iii) the procedure and principles of due process in disciplinary proceedings. Under Staff Regulation 10.2 the Secretary-General is authorized to "impose disciplinary measures on staff members whose conduct is unsatisfactory" and to "summarily dismiss a member of the staff for serious misconduct." Staff Rule 110.3 lists the possible disciplinary measures as follows:

i.) Written censure by the Secretary-General;

ii.) Loss of one or more steps in grade;

iii.) Deferment, for a specified period, of eligibility for within-grade increment;

iv.) Suspension without pay;

v.) Fine;

vi.) Demotion;

vii.) Separation from service, with or without notice, or without compensation in lieu thereof notwithstanding rule 109.3 (a rule requiring a notice period in case of termination of staff or compensation in lieu of notice);

viii.) Summary dismissal.

Certain other measures – not classified as disciplinary measures – also may be taken, namely:

i.) Reprimand, written or oral, by a supervisory official;

ii.) Recovery of moneys owed to the Organization;

iii.) Suspension pursuant to rule 110.2 (i.e. suspension during investigation and disciplinary proceedings).

Considering the range and nature of disciplinary and related measures available, the Secretary-General appears to have comprehensive and normally effective means at his disposal to prevent recurrences of infringements committed by staff that have engaged in misconduct. Imposition of disciplinary measures as well as prosecution before a criminal court require the existence of adequate proof of the misconduct or criminal act and, therefore, are essentially reactive measures, although they can be presumed to possess a certain generally preventive effect as well.

## J. Accountability for Compliance with the Procurement Norms

The concept of "accountability of international organizations" is, as recognized by the International Law Association[172] (hereinafter the "ILA"), a multifaceted phenomenon linked to the international organisation's authority and power and entailing the organisation's duty to account for its exercise thereof.[173] Accountability may arise in legal, political, administrative or financial forms and a combination of these forms may best ensure the necessary degree of accountability. In this connexion, it may well be asked whether the political accountability of organs of international organisations, especially of those that are highly dependent on their Member States, can effectively preclude the possibility of harm to third parties.[174] In any event, the effectiveness of accountability measures, including political measures, is a function of the procedures and remedies available to assert responsibility and ensure compliance, eventually through the imposition of sanctions. Where effective procedures and appropriate remedies do not exist, accountability rules arguably are mere moral as opposed to legal norms. The question of effectiveness will be further explored in the following.

Although the ILA's concept of accountability of international organizations, will be taken into account, the structure of the present study will differ from that

---

172 International Law Association, *Final Report of Berlin Conference on Accountability of International Organisations* 5 (2004).

173 The ILA Committee defined the following three interrelated and mutually supportive levels of accountability:
First level: "the extent to which international organizations, in the fulfilment of their functions as established in their constituent instruments, are and should be subject to, or should exercise, forms of internal and external scrutiny and monitoring, irrespective of potential and subsequent liability and/or responsibility;"
Second level: "tortious liability for injurious consequences arising out of acts or omissions not involving a breach of any rule of international and/or institutional law (*e.g.* environmental damage as a result of lawful nuclear or space activities);"
Third level: "responsibility arising out of acts or omissions which do constitute a breach of a rule of international and/or institutional law (*e.g.* violations of human rights or humanitarian law, breach of contract, gross negligence, or as far as institutional law is concerned acts of organs which are ultra vires or violate the law of employment relations."

174 It has been asserted that "In particular, in the case of international organizations that are highly dependent upon their member states, the political accountability of their organs toward their member constituency serves as an effective restraint and internal control mechanism that precludes even the mere possibility of harm to third parties." A. Reinisch, "Securing the Accountability of International Organizations", 7 *Global Governance* 132 (2001).

of ILA's report, the scope of which extends to "all component entities of the international community at large provided their interests or rights have been or may have been affected by acts, actions or activities of IO-s",[175] since the focus of this study more narrowly is on procurement actions and rules.

## *1. Accountability of the Secretary-General to Member States*

In his capacity of chief administrative officer of the Organization,[176] the Secretary-General of the United Nations is accountable to Member States for the activities of the Secretariat, including the observance by procurement officers of the applicable rules and guidelines on procurement. Remedies available to Member States wishing to react to perceived infringements of the applicable norms normally are circumscribed, however, by the need for Member States to act either collectively within a competent organ of the organization or alone, whether or not within the rules of the Organization, and by the *post-facto* nature of the available remedies.[177] These remedies, referred to in sections (a) – (b) below, correspond to the first level of accountability in the ILA's definition.

### a.) management and oversight

Member States can exercise direct influence on the management of the Secretariat, in particular by their powers to appoint and to withhold re-appointment of the Secretary-General,[178] or to adopt the budget[179] and by their regulatory powers over the staff.[180] As members of the General Assembly they also have ample opportunities through their votes in the competent organs to insist on specific measures being taken by the Secretary-General and on particular procedures being followed by the Secretariat. These opportunities are clearly inherent in, but by no means limited to the budgetary process in the General Assembly and its competent subsidiary organs such as the Fifth Committee and the Advisory Committee on Administrative and Budgetary Questions (hereinafter the

---

175 *Supra* note 172.

176 Charter art. 97. *See also* arts. 98, 100 and 101.

177 K. Wellens, *Remedies against International Organizations* 29-32 (2002).

178 Charter art. 97.

179 Charter art. 17.

180 Charter art. 101.1.

"ACABQ"). The Secretariat, indeed, is faced with a constant need for receiving mandates and approvals from Member States in order to be able to continue to carry out its work in a legitimate manner.

Member States have acted to institute general reviews of the activities of the Secretariat, either by instituting standing bodies such as the Board of Auditors appointed by the General Assembly pursuant to Financial Regulation 12,[181] the Office of Internal Oversight Services[182] or the endorsement of ad hoc investigations, such as the inquiry into the Oil-for-Food programme by the IIC, which is discussed in chapter V.[183] While such review or investigation measures necessarily are *post-facto* in nature, they do serve to prospectively regulate the manner of exercise by the Secretary-General of his constitutional powers, without affecting their essence however, and to limit any risk of abuse.

### b.) appointment of staff

Accountability of the Secretary-General to Member States for the activities of the Secretariat presupposes the Secretary-General has the necessary authority over the staff, including the power of appointment. For this reason and in view of the formulation of Article 101.1 of the Charter,[184] which qualifies the appointment power only by a reference to the Staff Regulations, it is questionable from a strictly legal viewpoint that the General Assembly by certain resolutions has eliminated, or to various degrees imposed restrictions on, the Secretary-General's power to appoint the staff. Especially serious instances are those where appointments of executive heads of certain subsidiary organs have been

---

181 The United Nations Board of Auditors was established by GA Res. 74 (I) (1946) and is mandated to exercise oversight, monitoring and control by the General Assembly of the administrative and financial functioning of the United Nations. Additionally, a Panel of External Auditors of the United Nations, Specialized Agencies and the International Atomic Energy Agency was established by General Assembly Res. 1438 (XIV) (1959). It is composed of the members of the United Nations Board of Auditors and the appointed external auditors of the specialized agencies and of the IAEA.

182 The Office of Internal Oversight Services was established by General Assembly Res. 48/218 B (1994) to assist the Secretary-General in the oversight of the resources and staff of the Organization through monitoring, internal auditing, inspection and evaluation.

183 The Committee was launched by the Secretary-General and endorsed by the Security Council in its Res. 1538 (2004), which also called on Member States to cooperate fully with the inquiry.

184 Charter art. 101.1, "The staff shall be appointed by the Secretary-General under regulations established by the General Assembly."

made subject to special conditions, such as the election of the Executive Director of the United Nations Environment Program (hereinafter "UNEP") by the General Assembly merely on nomination by the Secretary-General, or the subjection of the Secretary-General's appointment of the Secretary-General of the United Nations Conference for Trade and Development (hereinafter "UNCTAD") to confirmation by the General Assembly.[185] – It is arguable that such restrictions on the appointment power are incompatible with the prerogatives of the Secretary-General under the Charter and, when taking into account that the Secretary-General's powers extend to promotions and other decisions in the administration of personnel, that the unified character of the Secretariat is thereby undermined.[186]

The Constitution of the United Nations Industrial Development Organization,[187] adopted on 8 April 1979, provides in its Article 11.5 that "Appointments at the level of Deputy Director-General shall be subject to approval by the Board." With respect to other staff, however, Article 11.5 provides that they "shall be appointed by the Director-General under regulations to be established by the Conference on the recommendation of the Board" and Article 11.3 states that "Under the authority and subject to the control of the Board, the Director-General shall be responsible for the appointment, organization and functioning of the staff". The influence given to the Board by these provisions does not appear significantly to detract from the Director-General's ability to control and manage the staff. Moreover, when taking into account the preparatory works leading to the adoption of Article 11 of the Constitution of UNIDO as well as the principle of legal continuity[188] between the former UNIDO as an autonomous organisation within the United Nations and the present UNIDO established pursuant to the Constitution of UNIDO, it follows that, apart from the requirement of approval by the Board of appointments of Deputy Directors-General, the appointment

---

[185] Additional instances are critically reviewed by the Secretariat's Office of Legal Affairs in a study of 26 February 1982 prepared for the Secretary-General. *UNJYB* 189-200 (1982).

[186] A corresponding decentralization in the field of procurement is provided by Financial Rule 110.16(b) of ST/SGB/Financial Rules/1/Rev.3 (1985) with regard to certain departments and programmes located in Africa, Asia, Europe and Latin America.

[187] United Nations document A/Conf.90/19.

[188] UNIDO's Constitution art. 25.2 provides: "The rules and regulations governing the organization established by the United Nations General Assembly Res. 2152 (XXI) shall govern the Organization and its organs until such time as the latter may adopt new provisions."

authority of the Director-General of UNIDO is as exclusive as that of the Secretary-General of the United Nations and must be exercised as independently.[189]

## 2. *Other Remedies of Member States*

In describing what he refers to as the "first level of accountability" and defines as the "daily functioning of the international organisation that does not give rise to non-contractual liability or organisational responsibility", Karel Wellens[190] posits that Member States may, *inter alia*, avail themselves of certain remedies of a more political/administrative nature.

While accountability no doubt may manifest itself in political or administrative forms, it is essential to clearly distinguish between remedies foreseen or legitimated by applicable rules of law and "other remedies", including some that consist in disregard for or infringement of established procedural or substantive obligations. While it may well be legitimate for a Member State to withhold approval of proposed measures, including reappointment of an executive head, or to vote for revocation of delegated authority, a refusal to pay assessed contributions under the regular budget would in the case of the United Nations infringe the obligation arising under Article 17.2 of the Charter to bear the expenses of the Organization as apportioned by the General Assembly.[191] Voluntary contributions are *per definitionem* not obligatory, but an irrevocable pledge to make such a contribution does constitute an obligation that would become meaningless if the donor State were free to dishonour the pledge.

Karel Wellens further contemplates temporary withdrawal from membership as a potential remedy suitable for enhancing the bargaining power of a Member State beyond that afforded by permanent withdrawal. Regarding the United Nations, the fact that withdrawal is not addressed in the Charter presumably does not preclude a Member State from discontinuing its membership by denouncing the Charter, although the intent of the drafters may have been that such with

---

189 Memorandum to the Director-General from the Legal Adviser of UNIDO, dated 28 April 1986. *UNJYB* 334-337 (1986).

190 K. Wellens, *supra* note 177, 28-35. The levels of accountability discussed by professor Wellens correspond to those defined by the ILA's Committee on the Accountability of International Organizations, on which he served as Co-Rapporteur together with professor Malcolm Shaw. Sir Franklin Berman served as Chair.

191 P. Sands/P. Klein, *Bowett's Law of International Institutions*" 578-580 (2001).

drawal should be permissible only under exceptional circumstances, e.g. in connexion with Charter amendments.[192]

No denunciation of the Charter has been recorded by the depositary, the United States Government.[193] The dissolutions of Czechoslovakia, the Socialist Federal Republic of Yugoslavia and the USSR in 1991 and 1992 did give rise to lapse of membership,[194] or to legal succession as the case may be, but did not involve denunciation of the Charter.[195] – In the case of UNIDO, withdrawal is regulated by Article 6 of its Constitution and has occurred four times,[196] while "temporary withdrawal" is unknown.

When the Government of Indonesia in a letter of 20 January 1965 informed the Secretary-General it had "decided at this stage and under the present circumstances to withdraw from the United Nations", its participation in certain organs of the United Nations and its financial contributions did lapse. Eventually, however, on 19 September 1966, the Ambassador of Indonesia to the United States in a cable to the Secretary-General referred to the letter of 20 January 1965 and conveyed the decision of his Government "...to resume full participation in the United Nations and to resume participation in its activities...". In a statement to

---

192 United Nations, Repertory of Practice of the United Nations Organs, Supplement No 3, Vol. I, art. 4, at 189-191 (1959-1966).

193 *See* United States Treaties and Other International Agreements of the United States in Force on 1 January 2005, 519.

194 J. Klabbers, *supra* note 140, 127.

195 The memberships of Czechoslovakia, the Socialist Federal Republic of Yugoslavia (SFRY) and the USSR were discontinued by the dissolution of these States: Czechoslovakia dissolved on 31 December 1992 at midnight and the USSR on 25 December 1991, while the exact date of dissolution of the SFRY – and the consequential lapse of its membership – seems less certain, *see* United States Treaties and Other International Agreements of the United States in Force on 1 January 2005, 75, 320 and 346 respectively. While the Legal Counsel of the United Nations took the view that General Assembly Res. 47/1 (1992) neither terminated nor suspended the membership of the SFRY of the United Nations, the Security Council previously in the preamble to its Res. 777/1992 (1992) had considered that "the state formerly known as the Socialist Federal Republic of Yugoslavia has ceased to exist." *UNJYB* 460 (1991) and United Nations: Repertory of Practice of United Nations Organs, Supplement No.8, Vol. I, art. 4, at 6 (1989-1994). *See also* United Nations, Summary of the Practice of the Secretary-General as Depositary of Multilateral Treaties, ST/LEG/7/Rev. 1, para. 89, and para. 297.

196 Denunciations were made twice by Australia: on 24 December 1987 with effect from 31 December 1988 and on 23 December 1996 with effect from 31 December 1997 (Australia acceded a second time on 1 January 1992). United States denounced on 4 December 1995 with effect from 31 December 1996 and Canada on 3 December 1992 with effect from 31 December 1993. United Nations: Status of Multilateral Treaties deposited with the Secretary-General.

the General Assembly, its President indicated the general view of the membership to be that Indonesia's "recent absence from the Organization was based not upon a withdrawal from the United Nations but upon a cessation of cooperation" and that "Indonesia should resume full participation in the activities of the United Nations". The General Assembly concurred with the statement of the President in as much as it attracted no objection.[197] Whether this temporary situation is termed cessation of cooperation or of full cooperation, it must be distinguished from (temporary) withdrawal.[198]

In the event a Member State were to avail itself of "temporary withdrawal" for the purpose, as suggested, of enhancing its bargaining power compared to that afforded by a permanent withdrawal, it appears such action in the case of the United Nations or of UNIDO would be without a legal foundation in the constituent instrument concerned.

The suggestion that a Member State may set up a parliamentary Commission of Inquiry to investigate particular aspects of a peace-keeping or humanitarian mission implies a unilateral measure that might infringe the obligation of Member States to respect the exclusively international character of the responsibilities of the executive head and the staff and not to seek to influence them in the discharge of their responsibilities.[199]

In the description of remedies of Member States at the second and third levels of accountability, the author briefly refers to the possibility of instituting judicial proceedings against an international organisation and also discusses the possibility of a State rendering the continued stay on its territory of officials of an international organisation "difficult or even impossible", as a "remedial action that may be taken all the way through to the actual expulsion of the officials of the organisation from a state's territory, eventually resulting, in a finally deteriorating scenario, in the termination of the Headquarters Agreement. Such a decision is clearly political in the essence and by nature, and at the same time constitutes a legal act entailing legal consequences".[200] The very brief description regrettably does not refer to the dispute settlement provisions commonly found in headquarters agreements and in conventions on the legal status, privileges and immunities of international organisations, which would be applicable in the event any of the above mentioned "remedies" were to be invoked. It also

---

197 United Nations, Repertory of Practice of United Nations Organs, Supplement No 3, Vol. I, art. 4, paras. 29-36 (1959-1966). General Assembly, XXI Plenary Session, 1420th meeting, paras. 1-9.

198 *See also* J. Klabbers, *supra* note 140, 124-125.

199 Charter, art. 100.2, UNIDO Constitution, art. 11.4.

200 K. Wellens, *supra* note 177, 33.

seems that such measures may amount to lack of good faith in observing obligations undertaken by the host Government.

It follows that certain of the above mentioned "remedies" constitute dysfunctional actions, rather than legally available measures. A similar view has been implied in the report of the ILA's Committee on Accountability of International Organizations, which stated that "Remedial actions belonging to the political/administrative sphere may also give rise to legal problems of a constitutional nature, such as in cases of refusal to pay the assessed contribution under the regular budget of an IO, or temporary or permanent withdrawal from the IO".[201]

## 3. *Third-Party Settlement of Procurement Disputes*

### a.) immunity from jurisdiction

A claim, whether by a state or a non-state actor, against the United Nations arising out of a dispute involving the Organization's procurement activities, generally cannot be adjudicated by any court of a Member State due to the Organization's immunity from jurisdiction.[202] The immunity rests on Article 105.1 and 2 of the Charter, which lays down the principle of functionality[203] as a criterion for the privileges and immunities to be enjoyed by the Organization itself and by officials of the Organization as well as by representatives of the Member States.[204] Article 105.3 of the Charter empowers the General Assembly to determine more closely the extent of privileges and immunities possessed by the

---

201 *Supra* note 172, at 32.

202 In this respect, the Final Report of the ILA's Committee on the Accountability of International Organizations found (p. 41) that "In the framework of the implementation of accountability of IO-s, jurisdictional immunity remains a decisive barrier to remedial action for non-state claimants."

203 Charter, art. 105:
"1.The Organization shall enjoy in the territory of each of its Members such privileges and immunities as are necessary for the fulfilment of its purposes."
"2. Representatives of the Members of the United Nations and officials of the Organization shall similarly enjoy such privileges and immunities as are necessary for the independent exercise of their functions in connexion with the Organization."
"3. The General Assembly may make recommendations with a view to determining the details of the application of Paragraphs 1 and 2 of this Article or may propose conventions to the Members of the United Nations for this purpose."

204 *See also* the statement made on 6 December 1967 by the UN Legal Counsel to the Sixth Committee of the General Assembly. *UNJYB* 311-314 (1967).

Organization, its officials and representatives of its Member States. The General Assembly did so by adopting, on 13 February 1946, the CPIUN which is open to accession by and enters into force as regards each Member State on deposit of its instrument of accession.[205] The detailed definition of the jurisdictional immunity of the Organization is stated in Section 2 of the CPIUN as follows:

> "Section 2. The United Nations, its property and assets wherever located and by whomsoever held, shall enjoy immunity from every form of legal process except insofar as in each particular case it has expressly waived its immunity. It is, however, understood, that no waiver of immunity shall extend to any measure of execution".

The Charter's functionality principle thus has resulted in absolute immunity for the Organization itself, while with respect to the Organization's officials,[206] Section 18(b) of the CPIUN stipulates a limitation based on their functions by specifying that they shall

> "be immune from legal process in respect of words spoken or written and all acts performed by them in their official capacity."

Section 18(b) applies to most members of the staff, except for the relatively small number who due to their high rank are accorded diplomatic immunities under section 19 of the CPIUN or under certain headquarters agreements concluded *inter alia* with Austria and Switzerland. In connexion with claims arising out of procurement activities, however, the immunity of officials is not of primary relevance in view of the official nature of the acts of any official involved. In this connexion reference is made to a report of the Secretary-General submitted to the General Assembly,[207] which explains it to be the policy of the Organization that

> "if a claim is against an official for acts performed in his or her official capacity, the Organization will inform the claimant that the action is against the Organisation itself and then the normal procedures for dispute resolution" [followed for claims

---

205 CPIUN art. 31. Practically all Member States have acceded.

206 The officials coming within the purview of arts. V and VII of the CPIUN are, in accordance with General Assembly Res. 76 (I) (1946), "all members of the staff of the United Nations, with the exception of those who are recruited locally and assigned to hourly rates." *See* letter of 3 July 1964 from Office of Legal Affairs to the Permanent Representative of a Member State. *UNJYB* 264-265 (1964).

207 United Nations document A/AC.5/49/65 (1995). Report of the Secretary-General, submitted in response to the General Assembly's decision 48/493 B (1994), on the procedures in place for implementation of art. VIII, Section 29, of the CPIUN.

> against the Organization] "should apply. It is only if an act relates to private activities of the official that the issue of waiver is examined."

## b.) determination of official acts and waiver of immunity

Moreover, it is a well established position of the United Nations[208] [209] that the Secretary-General has exclusive competence[210] to determine whether an act is carried out in an official capacity and that this question is not subject to review by authorities of a Member State.[211] This point was made by the Office of Legal Affairs in a letter of 12 December 1977[212] addressed to the Legal Liaison Officer, UNIDO, and stating as follows:

> "The Secretary-General's position with respect to suggestions of immunity has always been that he and he alone may decide what constitutes an official act, when to invoke immunity and when to waive immunity.
>
> There is no precise definition of the expressions "official capacity", or "official business". These are functional expressions and must be related to a particular context. Indeed it is doubtful whether a definition would be desirable since it would not be in the interest of the Organization to be bound by a definition which may fail to take into account the many and varied activities of United Nations officials."

While the immunity of staff is subject to the duty of the Secretary-General to waive the immunity in any case where, in his opinion, it would impede the course of justice and can be waived without prejudice to the interests of the United Nations, as provided in section 20 of the CPIUN, these express conditions for a waiver are unlikely to be met in the event the act involves the carrying out of procurement. In case it should be established *prima facie* that an official has committed a criminal act in the course of carrying out procurement, it

---

208 "...not without reason, the UN claims exclusive competence to decide – in general and on a case by case basis – what constitutes an 'official act'. Immunity of the UN would be jeopardized if precedence of scrutiny and decision had to be left to national courts". D. Rotenberg, "Article 105", in B. Simma (ed.), *The Charter of the United Nations* Vol. II, 1320 (2002).

209 J. Klabbers recalls the finding in the Advisory Opinion of the ICJ on *Applicability of Article VI, Section 22, of the Convention on the Privileges and Immunities of the United Nations (Mazilu)* that the Secretary-General's opinion "creates a presumption which can only be set aside for the most compelling reasons". J. Klabbers, *supra* note 140, 161.

210 *UNJYB* 237-238 (1976).

211 Office of Legal Affairs' memorandum of 5 April 1983 to the Assistant Secretary-General for General Services. *UNJYB* 214-215 (1983).

212 *UNJYB* 247-248 (1977).

would seem incumbent on the Secretary-General to waive the official's immunity, however.[213] Alternatively, the Secretary-General might take the position that the alleged criminal activity consists in private acts and for this reason choose not to make any suggestion of immunity for the official.[214]

### c.) CPIUN, CPISA and UNIDO

The CPIUN is not applicable to the specialized and related agencies. However, with a view to unify as far as possible the privileges and immunities enjoyed by the United Nations and by the specialized agencies, the United Nations General Assembly on 21 November 1947 adopted the Convention on the Privileges and Immunities of the Specialized Agencies (hereinafter the "CPISA"), and thereby established a legal regime approximating the legal personality, capacity, privileges and immunities of the specialized agencies, their officials and representatives of their Member States to those provided under the CPIUN.[215]

Regarding the UNIDO, a provision corresponding to Article 105.1 and 2 of the Charter is included as Article 21.1 of the Constitution of UNIDO. Moreover, the great similarity in structure and substance between the CPIUN and the CPISA has made it possible in the Constitution of UNIDO to allow its Member States to opt for the applicability of either the CPIUN or the CPISA to UNIDO.[216]

---

213 "It depends on careful scrutiny of every individual case whether a sufficiently close connection between the event in question (*e.g.*, a traffic accident) and the official act proper justifies the acknowledgment of functional immunity". D. Rotenberg, "Article 105", in B. Simma (ed.), *The Charter of the United Nations* Vol. II, 1320 (2002).

214 Office of Legal Affairs' memorandum of 11 July 1963 to the Deputy Chef de Cabinet of the Secretary-General. *UNJYB* 188 (1963).

215 Section 4 of the CPISA defines the immunity from legal process of the specialized agencies, their property and assets, in terms identical to those of section 2 of the CPIUN and section 19 (a) of the CPISA sets forth the immunity from legal process of the officials of the specialized agencies in the same terms as used in section 18 (a) of the CPIUN regarding the officials of the United Nations.

216 Art. 21.2 of the Constitution of UNIDO provides for the applicability to UNIDO of the CPISA in the Member States having acceded to that Convention in respect of UNIDO and of the CPIUN in those Member States having acceded to that Convention, but not to the CPISA in respect of UNIDO. In fact, the CPIUN is applied to UNIDO by almost all its Member States.

### d.) the nature of immunity

The immunity of the United Nations and of its officials must be distinguished from, respectively, the sovereign immunity of States and the diplomatic immunity enjoyed by representatives of States under the multilateral Vienna Convention on Diplomatic Relations of 18 April 1961.

The source of state immunity is the sovereignty and equality of States recognized under general international law. The immunity of a State as well as of its representatives is based on generally accepted principles and doctrines forming part of general international law. The extent of the immunity of the State itself is determined especially by invoking the distinction between acts *jure imperii* and acts *jure gestionis,* while the extent of the immunity of representatives of States, who have diplomatic status, is set out in the Vienna Convention on Diplomatic Relations. – In contrast, the source of immunity of an international organization is the constitutive treaty concluded between sovereign States to establish the organization concerned or other applicable treaties, In the case of the United Nations, Article 105 of the Charter establishes functionality as the basic principle underlying the extent of both the Organization's immunities (and privileges) and those of the officials of the Organization while leaving the detailed determination of the extent of the immunities to further multilateral treaties, or conventions, to be elaborated by the General Assembly. Accordingly, the immunities of the United Nations, of its specialized agencies and of their officials are attributable to and delimited by the pertinent multilateral treaties, wherefore neither the nature nor the extent of these immunities are determined by general principles of international law.[217]

As far as procurement by the United Nations or its specialized agencies is concerned, it follows from the foregoing that all procurement activities undertaken for the purposes of the functioning of the Organization including the execution of its mandates and programmes, constitute official acts of the Organization, for which it enjoys immunity pursuant to article 105 of the Charter and the pertinent provisions of the CPIUN, in the case of the United Nations, or pursuant to equivalent provisions in the constitutive treaty of the specialized agency concerned, f. i. in the case of UNIDO Article 21 of its Constitution, and of the CPISA or CPIUN.

---

[217] *See* the Decision of 8 January 1980 by the United States Court of Appeal for the District of Columbia in the case of *Marvin R. Broadbent et al.* v. *The Organization of American States. See* also the *Amicus Curiae* Brief submitted by the United Nations Legal Counsel in that case. *UNJYB* 224-242 (1980).

### e.) waiver of the Organization's immunity

Where a claim against the United Nations or a specialized agency involves official acts of the Organization, for which it enjoys immunity, judicial settlement is only possible in the event the immunity is waived by the Organization. Apart from the easily understandable requirement that a waiver must be express, such waivers also are subject to two conditions that materially diminish their practical utility from the viewpoint of the claimant.

According to section 2 of the CPIUN and section 4 of the CPISA, the Organization enjoys immunity "except insofar as in any particular case it has expressly waived its immunity." In reliance on the formulation "in any particular case", this phrase has in the practice of the United Nations been understood normally[218] to exclude the possibility of a general waiver, i.e. an advance waiver, for cases or categories of cases where the nature of any claim or dispute is not yet known. In line with this interpretation, the practice of the United Nations is to refrain from waiving its immunity for claims or disputes arising out of procurement contracts by means of inserting a waiver clause in the contract concerned. While the obligations under the contract would be known in general terms at the time the contract is concluded, the particular circumstances that subsequently might give rise to a claim or dispute under the contract could not be known in advance. Insertion of a waiver clause in the contract therefore would not satisfy the condition of "in any particular case".

Furthermore, with respect to claims arising out of procurement activities leading to the conclusion of a contract, including the competitive bidding procedure, the fact that no instance of any waiver is known may be attributable to, on the one hand, the policy preference of the United Nations for arbitration as the means for the settlement of disputes and, on the other hand, the length of time involved in a judicial proceeding, which typically would preclude any possibility of effective and prompt redress for the claimant.

Section 2 of the CPIUN and section 4 of the CPISA further provide that "no waiver of immunity shall extend to any measure of execution". Therefore, even in the event of a waiver opening the way for a judgment against the Organisation, no enforcement action could be taken. Notwithstanding the procedural

---

218 One exception where the United Nations would be prepared to waive its immunity in advance would be where it has contracted for third party liability insurance as it normally would not be feasible to obtain such insurance, *e.g.* for automobiles, without giving the insurance carrier the right to defend the Organization against suits. Reply by the Office of Legal Affairs to a questionnaire from the *Institut de droit international* 176. *UNJYB* 159-176 (1976).

barring of measures to execute or enforce, the Organisation would be under a clear substantive legal obligation to comply with the judgment, however.

### f.) non-judicial dispute settlement: arbitration

#### *(1) standard clauses*

As a counterbalance to the extensive grant to the United Nations of immunity from legal process, including especially immunity from the jurisdiction of the courts of Member States, Section 29 of the CPIUN[219] imposes on the Organization the obligation to

> "make provisions for appropriate modes of settlement of
>
> (a) disputes arising out of contracts or other disputes of a private law character to which the United Nations is a party;
>
> (b) disputes involving any official of the United Nations who by reason of his official position enjoys immunity, if immunity has not been waived by the Secretary-General."

The obligation to "make provisions for appropriate modes of settlement of disputes" has not resulted in the establishment of generally applicable procedures for the settlement of disputes of a private law character involving the Organization or against officials whose immunity has not been waived.[220]

In this regard, the Secretary-General, in a report[221] submitted in response to a request by the General Assembly,[222] has provided a comprehensive account of the procedures in place for implementation of section 29 of the CPIUN. The

---

219 Section 31 of the CPISA contains the corresponding provision for the specialized agencies, *mutatis mutandis*.

220 In a legal opinion, dated 16 July 1986, the United Nations Office of Legal Affairs expressly confirmed that "Neither the United Nations, nor, to the best of our knowledge, any of the specialized agencies has agreed with a State, in general terms, on procedures for the settlement of disputes of a private character." This opinion merely described the practice of agreeing *ad hoc* to arbitration of disputes arising under individual contracts. *UNJYB* 324 (1986).

221 UN document A/C.5/49/65 (1995).

222 General Assembly Dec. 48/493 B (1994).

report (prepared by the Office of Legal Affairs) concludes with the statement that the procedures and mechanisms set out in the report

> "in the view of the Secretary-General, implement the obligation to provide an appropriate means of dispute resolution in respect of disputes arising out of contracts or other disputes of a private law character or involving any official of the United Nations who by reason of his official position enjoys immunity that has not been waived by the Secretary-General."

Notwithstanding the contention in the report that the obligation imposed by section 29 of the CPIUN has been adequately implemented, a closer analysis shows that fully adequate procedures for the resolution of disputes arising out of procurement activities have yet to be established.[223]

The report refers to the two studies prepared by the Secretariat to assist the International Law Commission of the United Nations with respect to its work on the status, privileges and immunities of the United Nations, which were published in 1967[224] and 1985,[225] and recalls that in order to implement section 29 of the CPIUN:

> "it has been the practice of the United Nations to make provision in its commercial agreements (contracts and lease agreements) for recourse to arbitration in the event of disputes that cannot be settled by direct negotiations."

Accordingly, standard arbitration clauses have been developed by the Office of Legal Affairs for the purpose of inclusion in commercial contracts and lease agreements – which ensue from completion of the applicable procurement procedure.

According to its established practice, the Secretariat further incorporates a standard clause regarding privileges and immunities, which follows upon the arbitration clause and reads

> "Nothing in or relating to this Contract shall be deemed a waiver of any of the privileges and immunities of the United Nations, including, but not limited to, immunity from any form of legal process."

---

223 R. H. Harpignies, "Settlement of disputes of a private law character to which the United Nations is a party – A Case in Point – The Arbitral Award of 24 September 1969. In Re Starways Ltd. v. the United Nations" 7 *Revue belge de droit international* 451-68 (1971).

224 United Nations document A/CN.4/L.118 and Add. 1 and Add. 2, 2 *Yearbook of the International Law Commission* 154-324 (1967).

225 United Nations document A/CN.4/L.383 and Add. 1-3, 2 *Yearbook of the International Law Commission* 145-210 (1985) addendum.

Among the intended effects of this clause is, of course, that the arbitration clause should not afford a basis for any judicial or administrative authority of a Member State to acquire jurisdiction over the Organization, a result that arguably otherwise might be justified by interpreting the Organization's consent to arbitration to imply a waiver of immunity. This argumentation is weak, however, since the CPIUN requires all waivers to be express. Nor would there seem to be any necessity of enforcement measures as the United Nations can be expected to comply with legal obligations arising out of an arbitration award and in its standard arbitration clause expressly undertakes to do so. Moreover, since a waiver in any event could not cover execution measures, the practical importance of the privileges and immunities clause is limited to excluding any possibility of a judicial review of the arbitration award and the proceedings leading to the award.

### *(2) scope of arbitration*

The standard arbitration clause defines the scope of arbitration as follows:

> "Any dispute, controversy or claim arising out of or relating to this Contract, or the breach, termination or invalidity thereof, shall, unless it is settled amicably by direct negotiation, be settled by arbitration in accordance with the UNCITRAL Arbitration Rules then obtaining. ....The Parties agree to be bound by the arbitration award rendered in accordance with such arbitration, as the final adjudication of any such dispute, controversy or claim."

The formulation of the purview of the arbitration clause, i.e. the phrase "arising out of or relating to this Contract", has resulted in a practice of including arbitration clauses in commercial contracts of the United Nations that do not provide any remedy to bidders in matters relating to the conduct of the procurement process by the United Nations. Moreover, the circumstance that the contracts containing the clause, are those concluded with successful bidders, serves to underline the weight of the absence of any remedy for disappointed bidders – who might well have grievances concerning the award of the contract to another bidder or otherwise relating to the conduct of the procurement process.

The lack of standing of participants in the competitive procurement procedures conducted by the United Nations to avail themselves of either the standard arbitration clause or of language in the bidding documents, is clearly illustrated by the letters of 4 and 30 September 1981, addressed by the United Nations Office of Legal Affairs to the Administrator of a commercial arbitration tribunal.[226] The letters were occasioned by a Demand for Arbitration and a Notice of Filing for the appointment of three arbitrators, which the Administrator had addressed to a subsidiary organ of the United Nations and which related to a claim of a disappointed bidder, whose offers had not been accepted. The principal argument of the United Nations, in its letter of 4 September 1981, was that the claimant's Demand for Arbitration suffered from the "fundamental defect" of being based on the Organization's Invitation to Bid form, which clearly had characterized the bid as an offer from the bidder that was subject to acceptance by the Organization. As the claimant's offer had not been accepted, no contract had been concluded, on which an entitlement to arbitration might have been based, according to the Office of Legal Affairs. In the letter of 30 September 1981, the same position was maintained although a condition stated in the Invitation to Bid form provided as follows "Any claim or controversy arising out of or relating to *this* or to any *contract* resulting here from, or the breach thereof, shall be settled by arbitration....". (emphasis added). In this connexion the United Nations letter relied on a quite formalistic reasoning by rejecting the claimant's contention that the demonstrative adjective "this" should mean the bid itself and claiming instead that "the demonstrative adjective 'this' modified the word 'contract' and a 'contract' does not result until the bid (i.e., the offer) is accepted." While conceding that the bid contained the arbitration provision as it was one of the conditions printed on the reverse of the Invitation to Bid form, the letter maintained that the arbitration provision remained a part of the offer until the offer was accepted. For these reasons, the United Nations held that there was "no basis, in the absence of a submission agreement, for the [commercial arbitral tribunal] to find even a colourable contractual basis for the claimant's present Demand for Arbitration."

The energetic rejection of arbitration and the strenuous argumentation to show that there had been no agreement to arbitrate, serve to illustrate the reluctance of the Secretariat to commit itself to the scrutiny involved in third party settlement procedures, i.e. arbitration, of disputes involving its conduct of competitive procurement procedures. Rather than offering to enter into an *ad hoc compromis* to arbitrate the claims of the disappointed bidder, the Secretariat construed grounds, on which to avoid arbitration.

In addition to referring, as discussed above, to commercial agreements, namely contracts and lease agreements, the above-mentioned report of the Secretary-General on the implementation of section 29 of the CPIUN, under the heading "other disputes of a private law character", also refers to such matters as

---

226 *UNJYB* 156-158 (1981).

third-party claims for personal injury, claims arising from vehicle accidents or third-party claims for compensation for personal injury or death, or property loss or damage, related to peace-keeping operations, all of which, upon examination, appear to involve contractual or statutory obligations. Under the heading "other claims", the report finally sets forth the Secretariat's reasons for not being agreeable to "engage in litigation or arbitration" with either "disappointed job applicants, i.e. individuals who are aggrieved that they were not selected for a United Nations position" or with the "numerous third parties that submit claims (often seeking substantial monetary compensation) based on political or policy-related grievances against the United Nations, usually related to actions or decisions taken by the Security Council or the General Assembly in respect of certain matters." – Also these further categories are devoid of any reference to claims concerning the conduct and observance of procurement procedures, and the report therefore does not refer to procedures for the settlement of disputes arising out of such claims.

# III. THE PROCUREMENT PROCESS AND ITS ACTORS

## A. Introduction

The formal legal norms – described in the preceding chapter – pursue limited specific objectives. An analysis merely of the formal legal framework therefore does not provide a comprehensive description of the respective roles of the actors in the Secretariat nor of the processes followed by the staff when executing procurement actions. To facilitate a better understanding of the context, in which the legal norms are being applied, this chapter offers a description of the organisational structure and the administrative procurement processes as seen from the vantage point of the authorized procurement officers and other staff members involved in procurement actions.

## B. Organisational Structure

The following organizational units typically interact in performing key roles during the execution of procurement actions:

*Financial Services*: formulates the biennial budget, receives and safeguards the funds, keeps the accounts, controls the allocation of funds and undertakes the disbursement of funds, including the payment of contractors and suppliers. In the course of implementing the biennial budget, available funds are allotted to individual officers with substantive responsibilities for specific programmes or projects. An allotment constitutes the authorization of allotment holders[227] to initiate the commitment of the allotted funds for the purposes authorized in the budget, including by requesting the initiation of a procurement action.[228]

*Legal Services*: drafts procedures and model contracts and advises on their implementation. When situations arise that are not foreseen in the established procedures or model contracts, the Legal Service analyses the issues and advises on the legal position and administrative steps to be taken. The legal advice may take the form of clearing a particular formulation or text for use in a specific situation.

---

[227] *See* Section II.E.2 (c), p. 30.

[228] ST//SGB/Financial Rules/1/Rev.3 (1985): Financial Regulation 10.2; Financial Rule 110.1(b). ST/SGB/2003/7: Financial Regulation 5.9; Financial Rule 105.3(a).

*Substantive Units and Officers*: are responsible for the preparation and implementation of mandated activities defined and described in short and medium term programmes and in portfolios of specific project documents. The Units are organised according to the substantive and technical contents of the activities and are staffed with specialists possessing the relevant professional or technical expertise. Each Unit prepares for its area of responsibility an initial draft of the biennial budget and these draft texts then are coordinated and consolidated into a single budget proposal prior to the adoption of the final budget by the organisation's Member States. Some substantive officers are allotment holders and, as such, authorized to raise requisitions for procurement actions for the acquisition of goods, services or work for the implementation of activities mandated in the budget.[229]

*Procurement Services*: are responsible for implementing the procurement actions in compliance with the prescribed procedures and in accordance with the requisitions raised by the substantive units and/or officers within their respective areas of responsibility. Under the Financial Rules, the Procurement Officers have the exclusive authority to commit the organisation externally to procurement contracts, i.e. to the purchase, rental or sale of services, supplies, equipment or other requirements of the organisation.[230]

While the staffing levels of the Financial, Legal and Procurement Services tend to be kept at a constant but modest level consistent with a policy of ensuring low cost of administrative and statutory functions, a higher degree of volatility often characterizes the composition and level of the personnel resources made available to the substantive units, which are called upon to pursue frequently changing programmatic priorities. Consequently, centralized planning of procurement requirements is circumscribed accordingly and the capacity of the Procurement Services to undertake such planning is reduced.[231]

## C. Procurement Planning

Notwithstanding the aforementioned obstacles to comprehensive procurement planning, important advance preparations are made by the extensive registration

---

229 Raising a requisition is synonymous with proposing an expenditure in the sense of Financial Rules 110.2(a) and 110.3 of ST/SGB/Financial Rule/1/Rev.3 (1985).

230 ST/SGB/Financial Rules/1/Rev.3 (1985), Financial Rule 110.16(a). ST/SGB/2003/7, Financial Rule 105.13(a).

231 ST/SGB/2003/7, Financial Rules 105.14(a) and (b).

of potential suppliers who are deemed to be capable of and interested in participating in competitive bidding for procurement opportunities.[232] Electronic databanks of potential suppliers of equipment and of firms or institutions that potentially could enter into contracts for the delivery of services or work are kept and updated both by the individual organisations in the United Nations system and by the IAPSO on behalf of the participating procurement services. Questionnaires are used to collect information directly from the firms and institutions on their respective capacities and data are also derived from evaluation of the performance of contractors under previous contracts. Due to the development of a comprehensive system of coding of the categories of equipment, services and work that might be required, the searchable databanks are effective tools for rapid identification of potential suppliers and future contractors. The databanks are maintained and used by the Procurement Services on a case by case basis to establish lists of firms or institutions that are invited to submit bids or proposals[233] for specifically described procurement requirements. Exceptionally, the databanks also may be used either to identify a single firm or institution for the purpose of initiating negotiation of a procurement contract[234] or, in the so-called pre-qualification procedure, to draw up an extensive list of firms or institutions to be invited to explain their capacity to meet procurement requirements that are described only in a general outline, the purpose being on the basis of the responses to select a smaller number of the best qualified and invite them to participate in a competitive bidding procedure, for which the full and detailed requirements are disclosed.

Considering the global membership of the organisations in the United Nations system, a *de facto* preference has developed for using limited competitive bidding, i.e. to invite only pre-selected firms or institutions to participate in the bidding. The classical device of advertising[235] procurement opportunities in the print media, which is often a prescribed procedure at the level of individual Member States, clearly is not a practically feasible method for a global international organisation to employ in most cases. It may exceptionally be used, e.g. where only firms located in a single Member State can be considered or where

---

232 *See* Section 2 of the Common Guidelines.

233 ST/SGB/Financial Rules/1/Rev.3 (1985), Financial Regulation 10.5, Financial Rule 110.18. ST/SGB/2003/7, Financial Rules 105.14(d); 105.15(a) and (b).

234 ST/SGB/2003/7, Financial Rules 105.14(d); 105.16.

235 ST/SGB/Financial Rules/1/Rev.3 (1985), Financial Regulation 10.5. ST/SGB/2003/7, Financial Regulation 5.13.

only a few firms with the required capacity exist globally. In such cases, it may be feasible to identify print media with adequate circulation.

More recently, Procurement Services are making use of the Internet to contact interested suppliers by posting invitations on the home page of the organisation concerned. This electronic modality is used for the registration of potential suppliers or contractors and also for the publication of detailed requirements and invitations of competitive bids and proposals for the published requirements.

The process of planning for those future requirements of the organisation that shall be met through procurement, forms part of the preparation and approval of the organisation's bi-annual budget and program of work. The Chief, Procurement Services, when preparing the request for the future budget and work programme for the Procurement Services, must take the nature and volume of such future requirements for procurement into account. The Chief, Financial Services, must take into account the procurement requirements that have been included in the approved bi-annual programme of work when allotting funds and other resources to the substantive Allotment Holders and to the Procurement Services.

## D. Coordination of Legal Aspects

In consultation, as necessary, with the Chief, Legal Services, the Chief, Procurement Services, is responsible for preparing and authorizing the texts of such Model or Sample Contracts as are required in view of the varying categories and nature of the goods, construction or services to be procured.[236] The texts shall be prepared before actual procurement proceedings are commenced and may include *inter alia*: (i) Contracts for Studies or Consultancy Services, (ii) Contracts for the Design, Supply, Integration, Installation, Testing, Inspection and Commissioning of Machinery or of a Plant, (iii) License Agreements for Computer Equipment and/or Software and (iv) Purchase Order Contracts for Goods – as well as the corresponding General Terms and Conditions of Contract.

The Procurement Services normally are required to include such texts in the solicitation documents and in general are guided in their work by these already established texts.

Whenever it is desirable or necessary to deviate from the established texts, the Procurement Officer concerned will consult the Legal Services to seek guid-

---

236 *See* Section 6 of the Common Guidelines.

ance, except in case of minor modifications that have no legal implications. Such consultations should be held before a commitment is given to any external party.

## E. Requisitions, Terms of Reference and Technical Specifications

### *1. The Raising of Requisitions*

Allotment Holders must ensure that requests to incur obligations against allotments under their responsibility are fully documented. With respect to proposed expenditures or obligations for procurement, this involves raising a Requisition which must be signed both by the Allotment Holder and by the Certifying Officer[237] and state the allotment code and object of expenditure, against which the proposed obligation is to be charged.

The Requesting Unit should assign a serial number to the Requisition and upon receipt and acceptance of the Requisition for processing, the Procurement Section should add a serial procurement reference number. A copy of the Requisition showing the date of acceptance by the Chief, Procurement Services, the serial procurement reference number and the name of the Procurement Officer assigned to the Requisition shall be transmitted to the Certifying Officer. These numbers shall be linked to the obligation number and serve to identify the Requisition and the steps taken to implement it through the procurement process.[238]

A Requisition may be raised for procurement either of work such as construction or only, or primarily, of goods or of services. For the procurement of goods a simple purchase order contract usually is suitable, while the procurement of services or of work will require a more elaborate contract format specifically adapted for each particular transaction. If a Requisition involves both goods and services or work, a purchase order contract should be used only when the services or work are uncomplicated tasks (such as installation and commissioning) and merely incidental to the delivery of the goods and only when the value of the goods clearly exceeds the value of the services or work. If multiple types of goods, services or work are needed, or if different suppliers can best meet the requirements, separate Requisitions for each category or group of requirements should be raised. In any event, upon receipt of a Requisition, the Chief, Pro-

---

[237] ST/SGB/Financial Rules/1/Rev.3 (1985), Financial Rule 110.3. ST/SGB/2003/7, Financial Rules 105.4 and 5.

[238] *See* ST/SGB/Financial Rules/1/Rev.3 (1985), Financial Rules 110.17(a) (i) and (ii).

curement Services, must review and approve it and determine the most appropriate contract format for its implementation.

Certain important information is generated in the Substantive (Technical) Unit concerned and must be forwarded to the Procurement Services, where it is needed for further processing of the procurement action. Therefore, the Requesting Officer raising a Requisition must ensure that the Requisition contains the following information:

a.) the name and address of the recipient and the place of delivery.

b.) the date(s) of delivery for goods and, if applicable, the commencement and completion date(s) for the performance of services or work. The date(s) must be realistic and allow adequate time for completion of the procurement process and any manufacturing or shipping involved.

c.) for goods, the preferred or required mode of shipment (air, land or sea) should be indicated.

d.) a list of recommended suppliers, stating their name, address, contact person and qualifications as well as any experience gained by the requisitioning officer from previous contracts with the potential suppliers, or, alternatively, identification of a single, potential supplier and justification of a negotiated contract in lieu of competition.

e.) indication of the allotment code and object of expenditure against which the proposed obligation is to be charged and an estimate of the amount that will be required.

f.) written confirmation by the Allotment Holder that the estimate is reasonable and in accordance with the purposes of the allotment.

g.) certification by the Certifying Officer that the proposed obligation is in accordance with the Financial Regulations and Rules and any applicable instruction, is reasonable, is in accordance with the purposes of the allotment and can be met from the available balance in the relevant allotment account. Should it subsequently become clear that the proposed obligation is insufficient to cover the requested procurement, then the Requisition must be resubmitted to the Certifying Officer and to the Allotment Holder for renewed certification and approval of the higher amount.

## 2. *Terms of Reference and Technical Specifications*

Attached to each Requisition also must be a succinct description[239] of the object that is to be procured, i.e. comprehensive and detailed Terms of Reference for services or work and succinct Technical Specifications for goods, as follows:

### a.) Terms of Reference

A document should describe the objective and function of the services or work, the methodology to be employed, the stages and timing of progress in implementation to be reached and the reports on the accomplished stages of progress to be submitted. The required quality of the services or work should be defined as well as the means of monitoring that performance is satisfactory. The outcome should be described in terms of services or of functionality and clearly state the procedure and criteria for any testing or commissioning involved. Where a contractor as part of his obligations under a contract for work, e.g. engineering, is required to procure equipment, it normally is not necessary to state the technical specifications of the equipment with the same degree of detail as when the equipment is purchased directly by the organisation; preferably, under such work contracts, the description should focus on functionality and performance criteria.

### b.) Technical Specifications

For goods the Technical Specifications should contain a generic but clear description and stating the required performance capability or capacity, the required compatibility or inter-operability of equipment with other equipment as well as any other technical or economic criteria that will be used to evaluate the eventual proposal. Brand names should not be used in the description. If testing or commissioning is required, the procedure and the criteria should be stated.

The Requesting Officer in the Substantive (Technical) Unit concerned should consult the Procurement Officer assigned to deal with the procurement action concerning the format, structure and non-technical aspects of Terms of Reference or Specifications in order to ensure that these technical documents are suitable to serve as integral parts of the eventual contract. The deliverables must be clearly stated (i.e. scope and timing of milestones or time, place and mode of

---

239 *See* Section 3.1 of the Common Guidelines.

delivery of equipment). Such consultations are particularly important for non-standard, complex or extensive procurement requirements.

The criteria to be used for the evaluation[240] of competitive bids or proposals must be stated in the Requisition, such as whether the "lowest cost, technically acceptable" bid or proposal is to be selected or whether the determining criteria are which bid or proposal "most effectively satisfies the technical and operational requirements".

## F. Authorized Procurement Officers

Only Procurement Officers are authorised to enter into contracts on behalf of the organisation for the purchase, rental or sale of goods, construction and/or services. The meaning of "enter into contracts" comprises award decisions and actual execution of contracts by signature as well as entering into contractual commitments in other forms, such as through negotiation with a potential contractor or the invitation of tenders, proposals or quotations.[241] These are functions that are reserved for the Procurement Officer and, accordingly, only a duly authorised Procurement Officer may make commitments to external parties concerning procurement procedures and proposed procurement contracts or obligations.

Upon receipt and acceptance of a Requisition, the Procurement Officer shall be responsible for ensuring that the procurement procedures set out in the Financial Rules and in any other applicable instruction are followed. The Procurement Officer shall maintain transparent official records that document each procurement transaction through written findings, contracts and purchase orders.[242]

From the time a Requisition has been transmitted to the Procurement Services and until the pertinent procurement contract has been concluded, all communications with the invited, potential suppliers must go through the Procurement Services. After the procurement contract has been concluded, the Substantive (Technical) Unit concerned may communicate directly with the contractor on purely substantive or technical aspects.

---

240 ST/SGB/Financial Rules/1/Rev.3 (1985), Financial Rule 110.21. ST/SGB/2003/7, Financial Rule 105.15.

241 ST/SGB/Financial Rules/1/Rev.3 (1985), 110.16(a).

242 ST/SGB/Financial Rules/1/Rev.3 (1985), Financial Rules 110.19(h), 22, 24 and 110.17(g). ST/SGB/2003/7, Financial Rules 105.15(c), 105.16(b) and 105.18.

## G. Sole Source Procurement

By Sole Source Procurement is meant the procedures for the negotiation, award and conclusion of procurement contracts in cases that constitute exceptions to the requirement of following a competitive procedure.[243] In these exceptional categories, contracts may be awarded by direct negotiation with a supplier.[244]

All such exceptions to competitive procedures must be submitted to an internal Committee on Contracts for its review. The Committee requires a justification of the grounds for the exception and identification of the specific Financial Rule being invoked.[245] Normally, such justification must be set out in a memorandum from the Allotment Holder and attached to the Requisition.

The exceptions to competitive procedures enumerated in the Financial Rules are the following:

a.) The proposed contract involves a solely available supplier of a particular good or service

b.) The prices or rates are fixed or other restrictions exist pursuant to national legislation or by regulatory bodies

c.) The goods or services are available only from a particular supplier for reasons of standardization and because of the need for compatibility with existing goods or services

d.) Special circumstances, when the exigencies of the Organisation do not permit the delay attendant upon calling for tenders or proposals

e.) A determination by the Director of Administration in consultation with technical experts on the Organisation's staff that competitive bidding or calling for proposals will not give satisfactory technical results, in which case appropriate reasons shall be recorded in writing.

As mentioned above, only Procurement Officers are authorized to "enter into contracts". In the context of sole source procurement, this rule ensures both transparency through the requirement of action by two officials, i.e. the Procurement Officer supported by the Substantive/Technical Officer preparing the requi-

---

243 *See* Section 4.5 of the Common Guidelines.

244 ST/SGB/Financial Rules/1/Rev.3 (1985), Financial Rule 110.19. ST/SGB/2003/7, 105.16(a).

245 ST/SGB/Financial Rules/1/Rev.3 (1985), Financial Rule 110.17(a)(iv). ST/SGB/2003/7, Financial Rule 105.13(b).

sition, and efficiency through the specific experience that a trained Procurement Officer can bring to bear, but which is not a core competence of a Substantive/Technical Officer. Conversely, the Procurement Officer normally will not have sufficient technical know-how and the Substantive/Technical Officer therefore must provide the necessary description in the form of Terms of Reference/ Technical Specifications so that the Procurement Services on this basis can invite tenders, proposals or quotations and undertake direct negotiations with the sole source.

The Procurement Officer reviews the Requisition, in particular the sole source justification and the Terms of Reference/Specifications for completeness and consistency as well as for conformity with the Financial Rules and other instructions. Upon approval of the Requisition, the Procurement Officer prepares a written request for a formal, comprehensive, technical and financial proposal from the sole source. The request normally shall consist of:

a.) the Terms of Reference/Specifications

b.) a Model of the intended Contract (including the General Terms and Conditions established by the Legal Services)

c.) a cover letter inviting a formal Proposal and setting out contractual and procedural points concerning the Proposal's format, its breakdown of contractor's cost, proposed payment conditions, etc.

The Terms of Reference/Specifications shall be prepared by the Requesting Officer and reviewed by the Procurement Officer, in order to ensure consistency with the Model Contract. The Model Contract and the cover Letter of Invitation shall be prepared by the Procurement Officer and be reviewed by the Requesting Officer to ensure consistency with the Terms of Reference/Specifications and other technical requirements.

After receipt by the Procurement Services of the formal Proposal from the sole source, a copy of the Proposal will be forwarded to the Substantive Unit for review of the substantive (technical) aspects by a technical team while the Procurement Officer reviews the contractual and financial aspects. Thereafter, the reviewers shall consult each other and agree on the points to be negotiated. Normally, the Procurement Officer who shall consult the Legal Services, as appropriate, shall conduct negotiations in writing. When negotiations are conducted verbally, the Procurement Officer shall ensure that the main issues and the outcome of the negotiations are put in writing and included in the file of Procurement Services.

When agreement has been reached with the sole source on all contractual, financial and technical points, the Procurement Officer shall prepare a written presentation to the Committee on Contracts setting out the ground(s) for making an exception to competitive procedures (sole source justification) and the negotiations and the outcome, including the cost of the proposed contract. Attached to the presentation shall be the memorandum containing the Allotment Holder's sole source justification and initial estimate as well as well as the Terms of Reference/Specifications and the technical team's evaluation. The presentation by Procurement Services shall analyse the proposed contractual terms, including the cost, and recommend whether to award to the sole source.

The Committee on Contracts[246] shall examine the justification for procurement from the sole source, the negotiations and the proposed contract, and recommend whether to approve, defer or reject award of the proposed contract to the sole source.

## H. Competitive Procedures

Normally – i.e. whenever procurement from a sole source cannot be justified – all procurement contracts shall be let after calling for competitive bids, i.e. Competitive Tenders, Competitive Proposals or Competitive Quotations.[247]

*Pre-qualification* of invitees can be a useful initial stage and may suitably be used for large or complex projects, in particular projects involving custom-made technology, for which there is no record of qualified, potential suppliers. The pre-qualification criteria should be advertised through the printed media or the organisations' homepage on the Internet well in advance of inviting formal Competitive Tenders or requesting formal Competitive Proposals from the pre-qualified suppliers. To avoid that a large number of potential suppliers incur the not insignificant cost involved in preparing formal tenders or proposals, normally no more than five should be short-listed through the pre-qualification process. When the procurement procedure is not initiated by a pre-qualification stage, the Procurement Services shall invite Competitive Tenders, Proposals or Quotations by advertising or distribution of formal invitations on as wide an international basis as possible, taking into account the known possible sources of procurement, including the data on potential suppliers registered in electronic databanks.

*Competitive Tenders* should be invited where the Technical Specifications or Terms of Reference contained in the solicitation documents provide a complete

---

246 ST/SGB/Financial Rules/1/Rev.3 (1985), Financial Rule 110.17(a).

247 ST/SGB/Financial Rules/1/Rev.3 (1985), Financial Rule 110.18. ST/SGB/2003/7, Financial Regulation 5.12, Financial Rule 105.14. *See also* Section 4 of the Common Guidelines.

and definitive description, quantitatively and qualitatively, that is not subject to modification or negotiation after receipt and opening of bids. It further may be required that an invitation of Competitive Tenders shall be preceded by advertising through the printed media or the organisation's homepage on the Internet for expressions of interest by potential bidders.

*Competitive Proposals* are requested more frequently, namely where more than one qualified, potential supplier are known to be available and/or where the Technical Specifications or Terms of Reference are intended to solicit additional information for the purpose of comparing different Competitive Proposals since the description in the solicitation documents is not yet complete and definitive but subject to modification and/or negotiation before the award will be made. Whenever feasible, Competitive Proposals should be requested from five to eight qualified, potential suppliers, selected on as wide an international basis as possible while taking into account the data registered in the electronic data banks.

For procurement actions where the estimated cost is above a relatively low and below a relatively high threshold, it may be a requirement that Competitive Tenders and Competitive Proposals are submitted in one sealed envelope. Where the cost is estimated to exceed the higher threshold, it may be required that the submission be made in two sealed envelopes, one of which shall contain the technical part of the bid while the other shall contain the contractual and financial parts.

*Competitive Quotations* may be requested where it is estimated that the cost will be below a modest threshold. Competitive Quotations should be requested from at least three qualified, potential suppliers, selected on as wide an international basis as possible. Normally, requests for Competitive Quotations are intended for requesting prices and commercial terms for goods, services or work that meet standard specifications and are readily available in the market.

## I. Solicitation Documents

The *Solicitation Documents*[248] are those used to invite Competitive Tenders or to request Competitive Proposals or Quotations. They must provide all the information necessary for an invited bidder to prepare a bid for the goods, services or work to be provided. In particular, they shall comprise:

a.) a cover letter from the Procurement Services inviting the Competitive Tender or requesting the Competitive Proposal or Quotation and stating

[248] *See* Section 3 of the Common Guidelines.

the procedure to be followed, including the required format of the tender, proposal or quotation, use of sealed envelopes, deadline for submission, breakdown of cost, evaluation criteria, award and payment terms

b.) the Technical Specifications or the Terms of Reference for the procurement object

c.) a Model of the intended contract including its General Terms and Conditions.

## J. Submission Deadline, Clarification of Solicitation Documents, Receipt and Opening of Bids[249]

If for reasons beyond its control, it is not possible for an invited bidder to meet the deadline for submission of competitive bids, the Procurement Services may extend the deadline by simultaneous written notifications to all invited bidders.[250]

If necessary for operational or technical reasons, the Procurement Services may, by simultaneous written notifications to all the invited bidders,[251] amend or correct the solicitation documents at any time before the deadline for submission of competitive bids. If the notification is issued close to the deadline, a reasonable extension of the deadline should be granted.

Upon written request of an invited bidder, the Procurement Services may provide written clarification of the solicitation documents. Such clarification shall be communicated simultaneously to all invited bidders and may not reveal the identity of the bidder who sought the clarification.[252]

A Competitive Tender or Proposal, or a Competitive Quotation, received after the deadline for submission may not be opened. A late Competitive Tender should be returned unopened to the bidder who submitted it and in case of a late Competitive Proposal or Quotation, the bidder should be notified of the lateness of the submission and the late proposal or quotation be retained for six months and thereafter destroyed, unless requested by the bidder or required as evidence by Procurement Services.

---

[249] *See* Section 5 of the Common Guidelines.

[250] ST/SGB/2003/7: Financial Regulation 5.12(b) and (c).

[251] *Ibid.*

[252] *Ibid.*

Sealed Competitive Tenders and sealed Competitive Proposals shall be addressed to Procurement Services where they must be date-stamped upon receipt and safeguarded until they have been opened. The opening[253] is done by a Tender Opening Panel composed of staff representing the Financial, Legal and Procurement Services. The time and place of the Opening, or, where two sealed envelopes are used, the initial Opening, should be stated in the Invitation to the bidders, as they should be invited to attend the Opening. The Tender Opening Panel will open the tenders or proposals and announce from which invitees tenders or proposals have been received in a good condition and within the deadline and then draw up and sign a protocol to record the proceedings and attendance. For tenders or proposals submitted in two sealed envelopes, only the envelope containing the technical part shall be opened at the initial opening session and, after completion of the technical evaluation, the Tender Opening Panel shall reconvene to open the second envelope containing the contractual and financial parts. Those invitees whose technical tenders or proposals have been found technically acceptable by the Technical Evaluation Team shall be invited to the Opening of the second envelope. At the opening of the second envelope, the Tender Opening Panel shall announce the names of invitees whose technical tenders or proposals have been found technically acceptable. A protocol on the second session shall be established following the same procedure as for the initial session.

The Tender Opening Panel shall be responsible for dealing with any complaint from the invitees concerning the competitive bidding procedure and any action governed by this procedure.

Unsealed tenders, proposals and quotations shall be addressed to the Procurement Services where they are date-stamped upon receipt and safeguarded until the deadline for their submission has passed. Immediately after the deadline has passed, they are forwarded to and opened by the Procurement Officer assigned to process the Requisition concerned.

---

[253] ST/SGB/Financial Rules/1/Rev.3 (1985), Financial Rule 110.20. ST/SGB/2003/7, Financial Rule 105.14 (e).

## K. Evaluation of Bids

### *1. Criteria*

Competitive bids received in time and in a good condition shall be evaluated in accordance with the criteria that were stated in the solicitation documents.[254] In this regard there may be a choice between the criteria traditionally used by the United Nations Procurement Services,[255] namely that

a.) normally, the contract shall be awarded to the bidder who submitted the least costly technically acceptable tender, proposal or quotation; and, alternatively, that

b.) exceptionally, the contract shall be awarded to the bidder who submitted the tender, proposal or quotation that most effectively satisfies the technical and operational requirements, but which is not necessarily the least costly technically acceptable bid, taking into account technical and operational considerations, price and life-cycle costs as well as the supplier's financial soundness and capacity to deliver the goods or to perform the services within the time required.

The applicable evaluation criteria must be clearly stated in the cover letter of invitation to bidders from Procurement Services.

### *2. Process*

After the opening of sealed bids, or after the deadline has passed for submission of unsealed bids, they must be evaluated. The evaluation of the substantive or technical aspects is carried out by a team of staff members from the Substantive (Technical) Unit concerned. The Procurement Officer assigned to process the Requisition undertakes the evaluation of the contractual and financial aspects. The following procedure governs the evaluation:

---

254 *See* Section 5.4 of the Common Guidelines.

255 ST/SGB/Financial Rules/1/Rev.3 (1985), Financial Rule 110.21. ST/SGB/2003/7, Financial Rule 105.15(a) and (b).

## a.) bids submitted in one sealed envelope and unsealed bids

i) Without delay after the opening of sealed bids or the deadline for submission of unsealed bids, and after appointment of the technical evaluation team, the Procurement Officer first transmits copies of the bids to the Substantive (Technical) Unit for its evaluation. Where the evaluation criteria are "least costly technically acceptable", the technical evaluation merely determines which bids meet the technical requirements stated in the Terms of Reference or Technical Specifications. Where, however, the evaluation criteria are "most effectively satisfies the technical and operational requirements", the technical evaluation consists in a comparative evaluation of the extent to which each of the bids meet the technical and operational requirements as stated in the solicitation documents and ranks the bids accordingly. The technical evaluation shall be carried out as soon as possible.

ii) Upon receipt of the signed technical evaluation, the Procurement Officer proceeds to undertake the financial and contractual evaluation. Where the evaluation criteria are "least costly technically acceptable", the evaluation compares the proposed contractual cost of the bids evaluated as technically acceptable and determines the least costly. Where, however, the exceptional evaluation criteria of "most effectively satisfies the technical and operational requirements" apply, the Procurement Officer is joined by the members of the technical evaluation team in order to evaluate whether it is advisable to alter the ranking order of the bids determined in the technical evaluation, when also taking into account the non-technical considerations, i.e. the price and life-cycle cost as well as the suppliers' financial soundness and capacity to deliver the goods and to perform the services within the time required.

## b.) bids submitted in two sealed envelopes

i) The evaluation of the technical bid in the *first envelope* to be opened is carried out after the opening and the appointment of the members of the technical evaluation team. Where the selection criteria are "least costly technically acceptable", the technical evaluation merely determines which bids meet the technical requirements as stated in the Technical Specifications or the Terms of Reference without establishing any order of preference or ranking. Where, however, the exceptional selection criteria "most effectively satisfies the technical and operational requirements" are applicable, the technical evaluation consists in a comparative evaluation of the degree or extent to which each bid meets the technical and operational requirements as stated in the solicitation documents and ranks the bids accordingly.

ii) Upon receipt by the Procurement Services of the signed technical evaluation, and after the *second envelope* has been opened, the Procurement Officer assigned to the Requisition proceeds with the contractual and financial evaluation. Where the evaluation criteria are "least costly technically acceptable", the financial evaluation compares the proposed contractual cost for each bid that has been evaluated as technically acceptable and determines the least costly bid. In case the exceptional evaluation criteria are "most effectively satisfies the technical and operational requirements", then the Procurement Officer is joined by the members of the technical evaluation team in order to evaluate whether it is advisable to alter the ranking order of the bids determined in the technical evaluation when also taking into account the non-technical considerations, e.g. price and life-cycle cost as well as the suppliers' financial soundness and capacity to deliver the goods and to perform the services within the time required.

## L. Clarification of Bids and Negotiations[256]

If, in order to carry out the evaluation of one or more bids, it is necessary to seek clarification of any technical, financial or contractual aspect, the questions should be transmitted to the bidder in writing by the Procurement Officer and a written reply be requested.[257] Whenever the question or reply is verbal, the content shall be put in writing as soon as possible and placed in the file. The Procurement Officer also must examine the contractual aspects of the preferred bid and communicate in writing with the bidder to seek clarification of any aspect that does not fully conform to the model contract that was included with the solicitation documents.

With the assistance of the Legal Service as appropriate, the Procurement Officer may, in the case of competitive proposals or quotations, negotiate such aspects of the contract as is necessary in order to implement the intent of the solicitation documents. In any event, the formulation of all material aspects of the procurement contract should be agreed, *ad referendum*, before the case is presented to the Committee on Contracts.

Under the procedure for inviting Competitive Tenders, the Model Contract included among the Solicitation Documents should be accepted without change and not be altered by negotiation.

## M. Review by the Committee on Contracts and the Award Decision

The Procurement Officer will, in written form, present the outcome of the technical, contractual and financial evaluation and of any negotiation to an internal, collegial body, the Committee on Contracts, proposing the action to be taken or

---

256 *See* Section 5.4.3 of the Common Guidelines.

257 ST/SGB/2003/7, Financial Regulation 5.12(b).

the recommendation to be made by the Committee. The presentation shall include:

a.) the Terms of Reference/Technical Specifications

b.) the technical, financial and contractual evaluation; and

c.) the Requisition with certification of availability of required funds.

The Committee on Contracts examines the case as presented and recommends to the Senior Official responsible for the organisation's procurement activities to approve, defer or reject the award of the contract.[258] When the Senior Official does not accept a recommendation of the Committee, he/she will record the reasons in writing.[259]

The Senior Official's decision to award remains an internal decision that cannot be relied on by any external party, except the successful bidder upon being notified thereof.

No procedure is foreseen for any invitee to formally challenge the award or the procedural steps followed to arrive at the award and communicate it to the successful bidder.

---

[258] ST/SGB/Financial Rules/1/Rev.3 (1985), Financial Rule 110.17(a). ST/SGB/2003/7, Financial Rule 105.13(c).

[259] *Ibid.*

# IV. THE WORLD TRADE ORGANIZATION'S PROCUREMENT REGIME COMPARED TO THE UNITED NATIONS REGIME[260]

## A. Legal Framework

### *1. The WTO Agreement*

The Marrakesh Agreement establishing[261] the World Trade Organization[262] (hereinafter the "WTO" and the "WTO Agreement") was concluded on 15 April 1994 at the end of the so-called Uruguay Round of Multilateral Trade Negotiations, held in Marrakesh, Morocco.[263]

The WTO was established on 1 January 1995, the date of entry into force of the WTO Agreement,[264] as confirmed by the Preparatory Committee for the WTO on 8 December 1994.[265] The WTO was considered to be legally distinct from GATT 1947,[266] not its legal successor, and therefore the coexistence of two organisations for a period after 1 January 1995 gave rise to decisions to coordinate the respective obligations of Member States. For practical intents and

260 A comprehensive description is provided by S. Arrowsmith, *Government Procurement in the WTO* (2003).

261 WTO Agreement art. I.

262 1867 *UNTS*, 1868 *UNTS* and 1869 *UNTS*, No. I: 31874, and Ann. A in 1890 *UNTS* and 1895 *UNTS*.

263 The Final Act of the Uruguay Round of Multilateral Trade Negotiations and the WTO Agreement are reproduced at 33 *ILM* 1143–1153 (1994). The adjustments to GATT (1947), amending it to become GATT (1994), also are listed at 1154-1156. For the consolidated text of GATT (1994) available at http://www.WTO.org.

264 Interpretation and Application of art. XIV.2 of the WTO Agreement. WTO Analytical Index – Guide to WTO Law and Practice.

265 WTO document PC/M/10, para. 4: The Preparatory Committee for the WTO, on 8 December 1994, "confirmed 1 January as the date of entry into force of the WTO Agreement." *Ibid.*, explanatory footnote 364 to the WTO Agreement.

266 55 *UNTS* 187 GATT (1947) entered into force provisionally on 1 January 1948.

purposes such as functions and membership, however, the WTO was intended as and did become the successor to GATT (1947).[267]

The WTO Agreement itself is brief. According to its Article II.1, the WTO "shall provide the common institutional framework for the conduct of trade relations among its Members in matters related to the agreements and associated legal instruments included in the Annexes to this Agreement." The text of the WTO Agreement accordingly limits itself to addressing such organisational matters as the organisation's legal status, functions, structure of organs, decision-making, budget and contributions, membership and relations with other organisations, while substantive trade policies and obligations are dealt with in the annexed agreements (and associated legal instruments), of which there are two categories: multilateral and plurilateral. The WTO Agreement provides in its Article II.2, that the multilateral trade agreements included in annexes 1, 2 and 3 shall constitute integral parts of the WTO Agreement and be binding on all Member States of WTO. Annex 1 includes the General Agreement on Tariffs and Trade in the version approved in 1994 (hereinafter "GATT (1994)"),[268] which incorporates the 1947 version ("GATT (1947)"). Annex 1 further includes the General Agreement on Trade in Services (referred to as "GATS")[269] and the Agreement on Trade-Related Aspects of Intellectual Property Rights (referred as "TRIPS").[270]

The overall objectives of these agreements, and thus of the WTO, are "the substantial reduction of tariffs and other barriers to trade" and "the elimination of discriminatory treatment in international commerce", to be obtained through "reciprocal and mutually advantageous arrangements" that are conducive to "raising standards of living, ensuring full employment and a large and steadily growing volume of real income and effective demand, developing the full use of the resources of the world and expanding the production and exchange of goods".[271] Consonant with these objectives laid down in the preamble, the operative provisions of GATT (1994) define the fundamental principles guiding the rights and obligations of the Member States – referred to by GATT (1994) as

---

[267] On the establishment of the GATT, *see* P. Neumann, "The Relationship Between GATT and the United Nations", 3 *Cor. Int. L. J.*, 63-78 (1970), and *id.*, "Build, Operate, Transfer Project Financing in Emerging Countries", in F. Scott/C.- P. Martens (eds.), *International Project Finance*, at 140-141 (2001).

[268] 1867 *UNTS* 190, I:31874.

[269] 33 *ILM* 1167 (1994).

[270] *Ibid.*, at 1197.

[271] *See* preamble to GATT (1994).

"contracting parties" – to be those of "Most-Favoured-Nation Treatment" and "National Treatment".

## 2. *The GATT (1994)*

Article I.1 of GATT (1994) establishes the principle of most-favoured-nation treatment by requiring that

> "... any advantage, favour, privilege or immunity granted by any contracting party to any product originating in or destined for any other country shall be accorded immediately and unconditionally to the like product originating in or destined for the territories of all other contracting parties."

This obligation covers "customs duties and charges of any kind imposed on or in connection with importation or exportation" or "on the international transfer of payments for imports or exports" and even with respect to "the method of levying such duties and charges and ....all rules and formalities in connection with importation and exportation". By virtue of a cross-reference to Article III.2 and III.4, the principle extends to internal taxes and other internal charges that are imposed on imported or domestic goods.

The principle of national treatment is set out in Article III of GATT (1994), which prohibits the application of internal taxes or charges, laws, regulations and requirements to imported or domestic goods "so as to afford protection to domestic production." Moreover, imported products may not be subjected to internal taxes or charges in excess of those applied to like domestic products, and products imported from another contracting party

> "shall be accorded treatment no less favourable than that accorded to like products of national origin in respect of all laws, regulations and requirements affecting their internal sale, offering for sale, purchase, transportation, distribution or use."

Also the multilateral trade agreements on services and on intellectual property rights incorporate the principles of most-favoured-nation and national treatment.

## 3. *The GATS*

In international trade the aggregate value of trade in services clearly exceeds that of goods and is increasing at a faster rate. The General Agreement on Trade in Services, referred to as "GATS" and contained in Annex 2 to the WTO Agree ment, sets out a most-favoured-nation obligation in its Article II.1 requiring that contracting parties

> "shall accord immediately and unconditionally to services and service providers of any other Member treatment no less favourable than that it accords to like services and service providers of any other country."

However, each contracting party may reserve specific exemptions that are listed in a schedule annexed to GATS and reviewed after five years.

Part III of GATS requires national treatment in connection with those sectors where a contracting party has undertaken market access commitments as stated in the schedule for the contracting party concerned. The national market in government procurement is thereby opened to suppliers from other Member States. Specifically, pursuant to Article XVI.1,

> "each Member shall accord services and service suppliers of any other Member treatment no less favourable than that provided for under the terms, limitations and conditions agreed and specified in its Schedule"

and, pursuant to Article XVII.1,

> "In the sectors inscribed in its Schedule, and subject to any conditions and qualifications set out therein, each Member shall accord to services and service suppliers of any other Member, in respect of all measures affecting the supply of services, treatment no less favourable than it accords to its own like services and service suppliers."

This means that the treatment accorded to domestic services or service suppliers, whether identical to or different from that accorded to services or suppliers of any other Member, must not result in a modification of the conditions of competition in favour of the domestic services or service suppliers.

## *4. The TRIPS*

The significance and value of intellectual property rights in international trade have been increasing at an accelerating rate during the last decades. The Agreement on Trade-Related Aspects of Intellectual Property Rights, referred to as "TRIPS" and contained in Annex 3 to the WTO Agreement, provides for the applicability of the fundamental trade liberalisation principles – as well as of the widely accepted international agreements regarding intellectual property rights – to trade in goods and services involving intellectual property rights. Part I of TRIPS sets out both a national treatment obligation and a most-favoured nation clause. Thus, Article 3.1 of TRIPS requires that each Member shall accord to natural and legal persons who are nationals of other Members

> "treatment no less favourable than that it accords to its own nationals with regard to the protection of intellectual property, ...",

while Article 4 provides that

> "With regard to the protection of intellectual property, any advantage, favour, privilege or immunity granted by a Member to the nationals of any other country shall be accorded immediately and unconditionally to the nationals of all other Members."

## *5. Coverage of Government Procurement*

Considering the high value of goods and services procured by governments,[272] which is estimated to typically represent 10-15% of the gross domestic product, it is from an economic viewpoint a very significant fact that the fundamental trade liberalisation rules of WTO's multilateral trade agreements do not apply to government procurement.

### a.) GATT (1994)

As Article I of GATT (1994), which requires the observance of the principle of most-favoured-nation treatment in the conduct of international trade, does not expressly mention government procurement, differing views have been expressed on whether the article nonetheless is applicable to government procurement.[273] As documented by Annet Blank and Gabrielle Marceau,[274]

---

[272] The world market for government procurement has been estimated to be well over US $ 1.000 billion annually. G. de Graaf/M. King, "Towards a More Global Government Procurement Market: The Expansion of the GATT Government Procurement Agreement in the Context of the Uruguay Round", 29 *Int'l L.* 2 (1995).

[273] S. Arrowsmith, "Towards a Multilateral Agreement on Transparency in Government Procurement" 47 *ICLQ* 793 (1998); and *id.*, *Government Procurement in the WTO*, at 61-63 (2003) is inclined to exclude applicability. A. Reich, "The New GATT Agreement on Government Procurement: The Pitfalls of Plurilateralism and Strict Reciprocity", 31 *J. World Trade* 125 (1997); and *id.*, *International Public Procurement Law: The Evolution of International Regimes on Public Purchasing* 104 (1999), cites arguments in favour of applicability.

[274] A. Blank/G. Marceau, "The History of the Government Procurement Negotiations Since 1945", 5 *Pub. Proc. L. R.* 77-147, at 77-88, 120 (1996).

however, the drafting history of Article I of GATT unambiguously indicates the intent to exclude imports for government procurement from the applicability of the most-favoured-nation rule. In particular, it was decided during the negotiations of the Charter for the proposed International Trade Organization,[275] from which the pertinent provisions were transposed into the GATT, to delete the references to government procurement contained in the initial text proposed by the United States.[276] Thus, from the draft provision that became Article I of GATT, the delegates deleted the proposed last sentence that read "The principle underlying this paragraph shall also extend to the awarding by Members of governmental contracts for public works, in respect of which each Member shall accord fair and equitable treatment to the commerce of the other Members".[277] Even though the interpretative value of preparatory works, according to Article 32 of the Vienna Convention on the Law of Treaties,[278] is merely supplementary, it may be relied on to remove ambiguity or obscurity left after application of the principal criteria of interpretation. In the present case the conclusion that government procurement, as mandated by the preparatory works, is not made subject to most-favoured-nation treatment seems permissible, since it does not conflict with the ordinary meaning of the terms of GATT whether seen in their context or in the light of the object and purpose of GATT.

---

[275] The ITO Charter was approved in 1948 by the Conference in International Trade and Employment convened by ECOSOC at Havana. The entry into effect of the Charter was subject to ratification. Only Australia and Liberia did ratify and on 6 December 1950 the United States Government published its decision not to resubmit the Charter, which had met with domestic opposition, to ratification by the Senate. P. Neumann, "The Relationship Between GATT and the United Nations" 3 *Cor. Int. L. J.*, at 67-68, 77-78 (1970).

[276] The initial United States proposal during the ITO negotiations was that governmental purchases and contracts should be treated as any other measures relating to trade in goods and be subject to the general obligations of National and Most Favoured Nation treatment. A. Blank/G. Marceau, *supra* note 274, at 1.

[277] *Ibid.*, at 79.

[278] After referring in art. 31, entitled "General rule of interpretation," to principal other criteria such as "the ordinary meaning to be given to the terms of the treaty in their context and in the light of its object and purpose", the Convention in art. 31, entitled "Supplementary means of interpretation" provides: "Recourse may be had to supplementary means of interpretation, including the preparatory work of the treaty and the circumstances of its conclusion, in order to confirm the meaning resulting from the application of art. 31, or to determine the meaning when the interpretation according to art. 31:
leaves the meaning ambiguous or obscure; or
leads to a result which is manifestly absurd or unreasonable."

Similarly, from the proposed provision on national treatment that became Article III.1 of GATT, the negotiators decided to delete the phrase reading "including laws and regulations governing the procurement by governmental agencies of supplies for public use other than by or for the military establishment".[279] The deletion must be interpreted in the same way as the above mentioned deletion of government procurement from the ambit of most-favoured-nation treatment. In addition, procurement by governmental agencies was expressly excluded[280] from the national treatment principle by the insertion into the provision that became Article III of GATT of section 8(a) providing as follows:

> "The provisions of this Article shall not apply to laws, regulations or requirements governing the procurement by governmental agencies of products purchased for governmental purposes and not with a view to commercial resale or with a view to use in the production of goods for commercial sale."

Considering that the acquisition by governmental agencies of products intended for consumption or use by the government concerned clearly falls under the definition of government procurement, GATT explicitly exempts government procurement of products from any obligation stemming from the national treatment principle.

Purchases and sales done by a State enterprise of a Contracting Party are, however, subject to the obligations set out by GATT in its Article XVII concerning State Trading Enterprises, a term that includes both enterprises established or maintained by a Contracting Party and enterprises enjoying, whether formally or *de facto*, exclusive or special privileges granted by a Contracting Party. According to GATT Article XVII.1, a State Trading Enterprise shall act in accordance with GATT's general principles of non-discriminatory treatment which might appear to allude to the principles of most-favoured-nation and national treatment and be supported by the provision that purchases and sales shall be made "solely in accordance with commercial principles". However, when a State Trading Enterprise imports "products for immediate or ultimate consumption in governmental use and not otherwise for resale or use in the production of goods for sale," the Contracting Party merely shall accord "fair and equitable treatment" to the trade of the other contracting parties: thus, the

---

279 *Ibid.*, at 79.

280 M. A. Kinsey, "Transparency in Government Procurement: An International Consensus?", 34 *Pub. Cont. L. J.*, at 156 (2004-2005). For a detailed analysis, *see* S. Arrowsmith, *Government Procurement in the WTO*, at 49-61 (2003).

stricter principles of non-discriminatory treatment are not applicable here. It follows, therefore, that government procurement effected by a State Trading Enterprise is neither subject to the requirement of most-favoured-nation treatment nor to the principle of national treatment.

### b.) GATS

GATS is applicable to the supply of services (i) from the territory of one Member into the territory of another Member, (ii) in the territory of one Member to the service consumer of any other Member, or (iii) by a service supplier of one Member through either commercial presence or presence through a natural person of a Member in the territory of another Member.[281] A "service supplied in the exercise of governmental authority", i.e. any service supplied neither on a commercial basis nor in competition with one or more service suppliers, is excluded from the field of applicability of GATS.[282]

Article XIII.1 of GATS exempts government procurement[283] both from the application of Article II concerning most-favoured-nation treatment and from Articles XVI and XVII regarding market access and the requirement of national treatment in the context of the market access commitments extended by the Member State concerned.[284]

Arguably the exemption does not apply in the case of a government's procurement of the general contractor for implementation of the so-called BOT (build, operate, transfer) concessions, also referred to as public-private-partnership projects, i.e. infrastructure investment projects undertaken for purposes such as the construction and operation of an electric power station or of a toll road, where the general contractor is a consortium of the constructing and/or operating companies, that undertakes to obtain financing and to implement. In turn, the consortium receives a concession for a specified number of years to collect fees from the consumers of the electricity or the users of the toll road. The output or benefit resulting from the project thus will meet a public need without burdening the financing capacity of the public treasury. If the output is considered a product, the concession contract may appropriately be subsumed under GATT Article

---

281 GATS art. I.2.

282 GATS art. I.3(c).

283 M. A. Kinsey, *supra* note 280.

284 For a detailed analysis *see* S. Arrowsmith, *Government Procurement in the WTO*, at 78-84 (2003).

III.8(a) as a procurement of products "for governmental purposes" with a view to "use in the production of goods for commercial resale." Similarly, should the output or benefit be considered services, the reference in GATS Article III.1 to "services purchased for governmental purposes.....with a view to use in the supply of services for commercial sale" would appear to be applicable. In either case, the result is that the procurement leading to the award of the concession contract does not fall under the exception, but is required to be conducted in compliance with the national treatment obligation.[285] Moreover, since it would be reasonable[286] to adopt a uniform interpretation of the term "procurement" in the GATT, GATS and GPA,[287] it follows that the GPA appears to be applicable to such procurement. Such an interpretation would seem to be desirable due to the high value of concession contracts and significant foreign interest in the market, as well as feasible in view of the flexibility of GPA's procedures.[288] A difficulty may lie in the contrary practice in EC law, however.[289]

### c.) TRIPS

That no express provision referring to government procurement is found in TRIPS, may be less significant when one considers the nature of the intellectual rights addressed by TRIPS, in particular that they normally are traded as attributes of or in conjunction with a product or service.

---

285 This position was expressed by P. Neumann, "Build, Operate, Transfer Project Financing in Emerging Countries", in F. Scott/C.-P. Martens (eds.), *International Project Finance*, 142-143 (2001). S. Arrowsmith discusses the arguments *pro et con* in *supra* note 284, at 55, 80 and 100-103.

286 S. Arrowsmith, *supra* note 284, at 101 (2003).

287 GPA art. I.1 provides that "This Agreement applies to procurement by any contractual means, including through such methods as purchase or lease, rental or hire purchase, with or without an option to buy, including any combination of products and services."

288 Examples of national legislation requiring public bidding for awarding BOT projects are mentioned on pp. 98-99 in the publication: UNIDO BOT Guidelines. United Nations Industrial Development Organization, Vienna (1996). *See also* D. A. Levy "BOT and Public Procurement: A Conceptual Framework", 7 *Ind. ICLQ. L. Rev*. 95-109 (1995-1996).

289 *Telaustria Verlags GmbH und Telefonadress GmbH* v. *Telekom Austria* and *Herold Business Data AG, ECJ case* C-324/98.

## 6. *The Government Procurement Agreement*

The importance of the Government Procurement Agreement (hereinafter the "GPA")[290] is evident when one considers the exclusion of national laws and regulations concerning government procurement from most of the obligations imposed on WTO Member States by the multilateral trade agreements GATT(1994) and GATS. The resulting lacuna in international regulation of international trade has to a large extent, i.e. among the major trading nations Parties to the GPA, been filled by the mutually agreed norms of that instrument, including its principle of non-discrimination, buttressed by detailed procedural provisions on the conduct of government procurement and on the settlement of related disputes.[291] This dual reflection of the principles of non-discrimination and transparency through procedural as well as substantive obligations goes back to the initial discussions on government procurement in the framework of a working group of the OECD's Trade Committee, established in 1964.[292]

### a.) plurilateral agreement

The GPA belongs to the category of so-called plurilateral trade agreements, which must be distinguished from the multilateral trade agreements. Pursuant to Article II.3 of the WTO Agreement, the plurilateral agreements are included in its annex 4 and are also part of the WTO Agreement, but they are binding only on the Member States that have accepted the plurilateral agreements and they create no rights or obligations for Members that have not accepted them. Notwithstanding this plurilateral feature, the GPA has been widely accepted and therefore covers relations in the field of government procurement between all the

---

290 1915 *UNTS*, I:A-31874.

291 The United States delegation to a Working Party of the OECD Trade Committee in June 1968 proposed the drafting of non-discriminatory guidelines on procurement, intended initially for the heavy electrical equipment sector, and on 19 February 1969 submitted a draft of procurement guidelines to this effect. After eight years, the negotiations were moved to the broader forum of the Multilateral Trade Negotiations *inter alia* in order to include the developing countries. M. Pomerantz, "Toward a New International Order in Government Procurement", 132 *Pub. Cont. L. J.*, at 139-140 and 143 (1981-1982) and A. Blank/G. Marceau, *supra* note 274, at 89.

292 A. Blank/G. Marceau, *supra* note 274, at 90.

major economies engaged in world trade, such as the European Union, the United States and Japan, but not China.[293]

Notwithstanding the prior existence of several directives of the European Community on the conduct of government procurement, in accordance with the precedent established by the European Court of Justice's judgement in the *Haegeman case*,[294] the GPA automatically became an integral part of the law of the European Community upon its entry into force since the Community and its Member States had become Parties. While the EC and the GPA procedures are largely compatible, in the case of procurement by entities in the public utilities sector, to ensure compatibility with the GPA, the Council of the European Community on 16 February 1998 issued Directive 98/4 modifying its Directive 93/38 of 14 June 1993 on the coordination of procurement procedures of entities operating in the water, energy, transport and telecommunication sectors. Potential differences in coverage between the GPA and EC Directive 93/38 were overcome through the listing in Appendix I, Annex 3, of the entities subject to the GPA and through application of conditions of reciprocity.[295]

The first version of the GPA was signed in 1979 and entered into force in 1981.[296] A Protocol of Amendments thereto was agreed in 1987 and these amendments entered into force on 14 February 1988.[297] In parallel with the

---

293 The following are Parties to the GPA: Canada, European Communities (including its 27 Member States: Austria, Belgium, Bulgaria, Cyprus, Czech Republic, Denmark, Estonia, Finland, France, Germany, Greece, Hungary, Ireland, Italy, Latvia, Lithuania, Luxembourg, Malta, Netherlands, Poland, Portugal, Romania, Slovakia, Slovenia, Spain, Sweden, United Kingdom), Hong Kong, China; Iceland; Israel; Japan; Korea; Liechtenstein; Netherlands with respect to Aruba; Norway; Singapore; Switzerland; United States. Twenty other WTO member States and the IMF, OECD and UNCTAD are observers. WTO documents GPA/89 and GPA/90 of 11 December 2006.

294 *Haegeman* v. *Belgian State, ECJ* Case 181/73 (1974).

295 These techniques, which are explained by S. Arrowsmith, *supra* note 284, at 117-121, appear to effectively avoid any ambiguity. Therefore there appears to be little justification for the concerns in this regard voiced by M. Echégut-Vigroux, "The International Government Procurement Agreement and the EC Legal Order", in V. Kronenberger (ed.), *The EU and the International Legal Order: "Discord or Harmony?"*, 225-227 (2001).

296 For a description of the historical background represented by the protectionist "buy national legislation" in the United States since the 1930ies, especially the federal "Buy American Act", followed by liberalisation of trade through OECD, EEC and EFTA during the 1960ies, *see* M. Pomerantz, *supra* note 291, at 130-143 (1981-1982).

297 S. Arrowsmith, *supra* note 284, at 36.

Uruguay round,[298] negotiations were held on the extension of the scope and coverage of the GPA, which led to the conclusion of the presently applicable version on 15 April 1994 at Marrakesh simultaneously with the signing of the WTO Agreement.[299] The new version entered into force on 1 January 1996.[300]

The relatively limited participation of WTO member states in the GPA may be due to reluctance to abandon the option of supporting national industrial or regional development through procurement and to the cost of implementing the detailed procedural rules of the GPA and the need to undertake extensive bilateral negotiations on coverage with other Parties.[301]

### b.) purposes

According to its preamble, the underlying aims of the GPA are to achieve greater liberalisation and expansion of world trade and to improve the framework for the conduct of world trade. To further these aims, the Parties recognize the need for an effective, non-discriminatory and transparent multilateral framework of laws, regulations, procedures and practices regarding government procurement, as well as the need to establish international procedures on notification, consultation and surveillance, and also dispute settlement in order to ensure a fair, prompt and effective enforcement of these provisions.

---

298 The negotiations were held in an Informal Working Group of the Parties to the GPA, who declined the wish of developing countries to negotiate in the wider framework of the Uruguay round of the multilateral trade negotiations. The negotiations were concluded on 13 December 1993 in parallel with the successful conclusion of the Uruguay Round of multilateral trade negotiations on 15 December 1993. A. Blank/G. Marceau, *supra* note 274, at 109-110 and 118.

299 The new GPA has been estimated to open up government contracts worth ca. US $ 350 billion annually to international bidding. G. de Graaf/M. King, *supra* note 272, at 435 (1995). The same authors find that "the key elements of the new GPA are derived largely from the European Union's directives on public procurement". *Ibid.*, at 437.

300 A. Blank/G. Marceau, *supra* note 274, at 122.

301 S. Arrowsmith, "Towards a Multilateral Agreement on Transparency in Government Procurement", 47 *ICLQ* 799 (1998). To increase participation, the author favours an agreement on transparency that would dispense with detailed procedural prescriptions but require publication of national general procurement rules, demand advance disclosure of the rules and criteria for specific procurements and provide for publicity for procurement opportunities. The Dispute Settlement Mechanism should only be used to enforce the obligation to develop and implement such national procedures, while participating States should be required to establish review procedures to address the handling of specific procurements, including the provision of an independent authority to hear complaints by suppliers.

Although the purposes of the GPA are not expressed in the same terms as those employed by the revised Financial Regulations[302] of the United Nations, which list the general principles to be given due consideration when exercising the procurement functions of the United Nations, most of the purposes are shared. The economical use of resources, or value for money, is a common objective which in the case of the GPA is encompassed by the goal of greater liberalization and expansion of world trade.[303] The same applies for transparency, fairness and effectiveness, which are expressly referred to in both instruments.[304] A factor specifically listed only for the United Nations is the purpose of safeguarding the interests of the United Nations and the special weight given to this purpose. International competition is referred to expressly as an objective in the United Nations Financial Regulations, while it is merely implied in the GPA. The GPA, moreover, is different in that it rests on the principle of reciprocity, which is referred to in the preamble[305] and manifested through the mutual offering and accepting of sectors of the national markets for government procurement to be covered by the GPA as detailed in the national annexes,[306] but not otherwise reflected in the procedures for procurement actions. As will be further discussed below, the GPA also differs from the United Nations procurement regime by calling on the Parties to establish procedures for suppliers to challenge decisions of the procuring entity and through the applicability of the procedures of the Dispute Settlement Understanding under the WTO Agreement[307] to disputes between the Parties regarding benefits and obligations under the GPA.

---

302 ST/SGB/2003/7, Regulation 5.12: "(a) Best value for money; (b) Fairness, integrity and transparency; (c) Effective international competition; (d) The interest of the United Nations." *See also* Section 1, Preamble, of the Common Guidelines for a similar enumeration.

303 GPA preamble, 1st recital.

304 United Nations Financial Regulation 5.12 (b) and GPA preamble, 3rd and 4th recitals.

305 GPA preamble, 4th recital *in fine*:..."to maintain the balance of rights and obligations at the highest possible level."

306 Concerning the negotiations between the European Union and the United States regarding the balance of their offers of markets to be included in the expanded coverage of the new GPA of 15 April 1994, *see* G. de Graaf/M. King, *supra* note 272, at 441-452.

307 Dispute Settlement Understanding art. 1.1 and App. 1. 33 *ILM* 1226 and 1244 (1994).

### c.) applicability and coverage

The scope of applicability of the GPA comprises, according to its Article I.2,

> "procurement by any contractual means, including through such methods as purchase or lease, rental or hire purchase, with or with or without an option to buy, including any combination of products and services."

This comprehensive formulation – which includes service contracts – dates from the Uruguay round of negotiations.[308] Moreover, Article I.1 provides the GPA shall apply

> "to any law, regulation, procedure or practice regarding any procurement by any entities covered by this Agreement, as specified in Appendix I."

As covered entities, Appendix I lists in its Annexes 1-3, respectively, the central government entities, the sub-central government entities and all other entities that shall procure in accordance with the GPA. Annex 4 specifies the services and Annex 5 the construction services covered by the GPA. Since an Appendix I is established for each Party, the relevant monetary thresholds above which procurement of goods and services shall be covered are stated individually in each Party's Annex. All Parties maintain the same threshold of SDR[309] 130.000 for procurement of goods and services under Annex 1 by central government entities, while for sub-central government entities most Parties have a threshold of SDR 200.000. For other covered entities in Annex 3, which includes utilities, the threshold tends to be higher, often set at SDR 400.000. The highest thresholds are found for construction services: it is SDR 5 million for most Parties and in some cases considerably higher.

The technique of letting Parties designate covered entities and set minimum monetary thresholds serves to implement the principle of reciprocity, e.g. in connexion with the accession of new Members. Article XXIV.2 of the GPA provides that accession by a new Member is subject to "terms to be agreed between that government and the Parties", which means that a candidate for membership will present an offer of the share of its market for government procurement that it is willing to open to products, services and suppliers from the other Members. The offer is considered by the other Members and negotiations regarding the terms may well ensue before a revised offer is accepted. Moreover,

---

308 GPA preamble, 6th recital.

309 SDR, a Special Drawing Right is the unit of account of the International Monetary Fund. On 27 June 2007, the exchange value of one SDR was 1,51355 US$.

should a Member wish to modify the coverage, to which it is committed under the Annexes in force, it must notify the intended modifications to the Committee on Government Procurement, composed of representatives of all Member States. Unless the modifications are of a purely formal or minor nature, the Committee shall meet "to consider the proposal and any claim for compensatory adjustments, with a view to maintaining a balance of rights and obligations and a comparable level of mutually agreed coverage provided in this Agreement prior to such notification".[310]

A consequence of the monetary thresholds is to limit the scope of applicability of the GPA to procurement actions of substantial value. This presents a difference from the United Nations procurement procedures as the latter also apply to actions with a modest value. The regimes are similar, however, in not having any monetary ceiling for the actions or the items to be procured in accordance with their procedures.

Developing countries may benefit from "special and differential treatment", as provided in Article V, in particular with respect to the coverage of procurement under the GPA. Article V.1 and 2 state that when implementing and administering the GPA, the Parties shall take into account the development, financial and trade needs of developing and, in particular, of the least developed countries. Consistently with the GPA, the Parties also shall facilitate increased imports from developing countries when preparing or applying laws, regulations and procedures affecting government procurement. It is doubtful that these provisions in Article V.1 and 2 permit outright preferential treatment of products, services or suppliers of developing countries in the course of a competitive procurement action: what is permitted and encouraged, however, are the forms of differential treatment referred to in Article V. Specifically, Article V.3 requires that the needs of the developing countries be taken into account when drawing up the coverage lists to be included in the Annexes, e.g. in the way that developed countries include in their Annexes entities that procure products and services exported by developing countries. Further, Article V.4 and 5 enable a developing country to negotiate exclusions from the national treatment rules regarding certain entities, products or services and, after becoming a Party, to modify its coverage to take into account its needs and to request the Committee on Government Procurement to grant exclusions from the national treatment rules.

---

310 GPA art. XXIV.6(a).

## B. Comparison between the GPA's and the United Nations Procedures

### *1. General Comparison*

The description above of the WTO agreements has identified features that are shared by the multilateral agreements and some that are unique for the plurilateral GPA. A comparison with the regulatory framework for the procurement procedures of the United Nations shows that the legal framework of the GPA differs with regard to the form of the legal instruments and to some, but not the most essential of the purposes. Consequently, apart from the implications flowing from the principle of reciprocity between States Parties, which arise only under the GPA, the differences between the legal frameworks appear to be related primarily to questions of legal form and not to constitute material, substantive discrepancies. In both regimes, the subject matter is essentially the same. When taking these considerations into account, it would seem fully justified when describing the main features of the detailed procurement procedure under the GPA to make use of comparisons, when appropriate, with the procurement procedure of the United Nations.

### *2. Specific Comparisons*

#### a.) technical specifications

As the GPA is intended for implementation by a substantial number of procurement entities in the government bureaucracies of different Member States, it understandably differs from the United Nations Financial Regulations and Rules by not addressing such administrative or institutional questions as which officials have authority to obligate funds or to conclude procurement contracts. On the other hand, the GPA in its Article VI lays down detailed requirements regarding the contents and source of the technical specifications that shall form part of the solicitation documents, while this important subject is dealt with by the United Nations only at the level of manuals or administrative instructions but not in the Financial Regulations and Rules. That United Nations practice generally may be in conformity with the GPA requirements can be deduced from Section 3.1.1-3 of the Common Guidelines, however.

GPA Article VI.1 lists characteristics of the products or services to be procured, or of their production, or of conformity assessment procedures of the procuring entity, which should form part of the technical specifications, but also states that this shall not be done with a view to, or with the effect of, creating unnecessary obstacles to international trade. Article VI.2 provides that, where appropriate, the technical specifications shall be "in terms of performance rather than design or descriptive characteristics" and be based on international, rather than national standards, where the former exist. According to Article VI.3, no mention may be made of "a particular trademark or trade name, patent, design or type, specific origin, producer or supplier", unless necessary to describe the requirements intelligibly and in that event words such as "or equivalent" must be added.

Clearly, the purpose of these requirements is to enhance the objectivity and impartiality of the description of the technical requirements while avoiding the pitfall of narrowing the range of suppliers by stating overly detailed specifications. The requirements fully correspond to good public procurement practice and are normally observed by the United Nations.[311] Their inclusion in the United Nations Financial Rules therefore would not modify existing practice but would be a desirable step to enhance the level of transparency

The same purposes of objectivity and impartiality are pursued by the GPA's Article VI.4, which prohibits that advice on the preparation of the specifications for a specific procurement is sought or accepted from a firm that may have a commercial interest in the procurement, whenever this is done in a manner that would have the effect of precluding competition.

In the United Nations practice the same concern normally is met by excluding a firm that has assisted in the preparation of the technical terms of reference or specifications, e.g. under a separate prior contract, from being invited to participate in the competition. Nevertheless, to forbid that technical officers informally consult firms on technical issues, including on the technical know-how of one or more firms, is seen to be counterproductive as well as unrealistic and unlikely to succeed. Also in these respects, the transparency of the United Nations regime would be enhanced by the inclusion of appropriately formulated provisions in the Financial Rules.

### b.) the three tendering procedures

Article VII of the GPA defines three tendering procedures, one of which must be used in a non-discriminatory manner. Under the open tendering procedure all

---

[311] *See* Section 3.1.2 of the Common Guidelines for the same rules in this regard.

interested suppliers may submit a tender.[312] A selective tendering procedure refers to a procedure, under which those suppliers invited to do so may submit a tender. In the non-competitive limited tendering procedure the procuring entity contacts suppliers individually.

In defining three clearly distinguishable, basic tendering procedures, and by presenting a detailed description of each of the basic procedures and defining the conditions for their use, the GPA achieves a clarity, and thus transparency, that escapes the corresponding United Nations Financial Regulations and Rules.[313] That the corresponding Section 3.2 of the Common Guidelines on "Types of Solicitation Documents" employs a terminology and states award criteria that deviate from those in the binding Financial Rules does not assist in reducing the lack of clarity, either.

### c.) qualification of suppliers

Under the GPA, it is not mandatory for procuring entities to establish or maintain permanent lists[314] of qualified suppliers, but its Article VIII lays down detailed rules for procuring entities to follow whenever such pre-selection of qualified potential suppliers is undertaken.

GPA Article VIII requires qualification procedures that do not discriminate among suppliers of other Parties or between suppliers that are domestic and those of other Parties. Conditions that constitute a condition for participation in tendering must be published in adequate time both to enable interested suppliers to participate and, to the extent compatible with efficient operation of the procurement process, also to complete the qualification procedures. Conditions for participation must, in any event, be non-discriminatory and limited to those that are essential to ensure the financial, commercial and technical capacity of a firm to fulfil the contract in question. The list of conditions that may be posed is extensive, however, as it ranges from financial guarantees and technical qualifications to information establishing the financial, commercial and technical capacity of suppliers as well as to verification of qualifications.

Whenever permanent lists of suppliers are maintained, suppliers must be allowed to apply to be included at any time and all qualified suppliers requesting

---

312 When used as a noun, "tender" refers to a bid, offer or proposal by an interested supplier.

313 ST/SGB/2003/7, Financial Rules 105.14 – 105.16.

314 A "permanent list" appears to refer to any list not drawn up only for a particular procurement action, but for repeated use.

to be on the lists shall be included within a reasonably short time. In the same vein, if after publication of a notice of an intended or proposed procurement a supplier – who has not yet been listed – requests to participate, the procuring entity immediately shall start the procedures for qualification. The procuring entity shall notify suppliers of the outcome of their requests to become qualified suppliers and it also shall inform suppliers, should they be removed from the relevant list, and of the termination of such lists.

Where permanent lists of qualified suppliers are used for selective tendering – the main purpose of maintaining such lists – the procuring entity shall, in accordance with Article IX.9, annually publish a notice in one of the publications listed in Appendix III to the GPA providing information on the lists maintained, the products or services to be procured through the lists, and on the conditions to be met by suppliers in order to be inscribed on the lists.

On all the foregoing points, the detailed provisions of Article VIII of the GPA indisputably impose a higher standard of transparency than the Financial Regulations and Rules of the United Nations, considering the latter are silent on the subject in spite of the long standing and influential practice of establishing data banks to register potential suppliers of goods, services or work to the United Nations and to make use of the data to select a limited number of suppliers to be invited to submit bids or proposals. The information published in Section 2 of the Common Guidelines merely serves to facilitate the collection of data on potential suppliers. There is no reference to any procedural or substantive duty or obligation of the procuring organisation towards potential or qualified suppliers.

### d.) invitation to participate: intended procurement

Except for the instances of limited tendering, for which a formal competitive procedure is not required, it is under Article IX of the GPA for all cases of intended procurement mandatory for procuring entities to publish an invitation to participate. The invitation must be published in the appropriate publication listed in Appendix II to the GPA. The invitation may contain the information enumerated in Article IX.6.(a) to (h),[315] and for central government procuring entities

---

[315] GPA art. IX.6, indents (a) to (h), reads:

"(a) the nature and quantity, including any options for further procurement and, if possible, an estimate of the timing when such options may be exercised; in the case of recurring contracts the nature and quantity and, if possible, an estimate of the timing of the subsequent tender notices for the products or services to be procured;

shall be in the form of a notice of proposed procurement containing this information. This taxonomic listing is sufficiently detailed to ensure a high level of information is available to potentially interested suppliers and thereby also provides a high degree of transparency. Sub-central government and other procuring entities may use a notice of planned procurement, or a notice regarding a qualification system, as an invitation to participate. Each notice of planned procurement shall contain as much of the information required for a notice of a proposed procurement as is possible, but in any event information on

a) the subject matter of the contract

b) the time limits

d) the address for requesting documents

e) a statement that interested suppliers should express their interest in the procurement to the procuring entity and

f) a contact point for obtaining further information.[316]

Further provisions concerning the selective tendering procedure are set out in GPA Article X, namely that to ensure "optimum effective international competition", tenders shall be invited from "the maximum number of domestic suppliers and suppliers of other Parties consistent with the efficient operation of the procurement system." Their selection shall be done in a "fair and non-discriminatory manner" and, by entities maintaining lists of permanent suppliers, selections may be made from among those listed, provided that "any selection

---

(b) whether the procedure is open or selective or will involve negotiation;
(c) any date for starting delivery or completion of delivery of goods or services;
(d) the address and final date for submitting an application to be invited to tender or for qualifying for the suppliers' lists, or for receiving tenders, as well as the language or the languages in which they must be submitted;
(e) the address of the entity awarding the contract and providing any information necessary for obtaining specifications and other documents;
(f) any economic and technical requirements, financial guarantees and information required from suppliers;
(g) the amount and terms of payment of any sum payable for the tender documentation; and
(h) whether the entity is inviting offers for purchase, lease, rental, or hire purchase, or more than one of these methods".

316 GPA art. IX.7 and 8.

shall allow for equitable opportunities for suppliers in the lists".[317] [318] A supplier that requests to participate in an intended procurement shall be permitted to submit a tender, provided, in case the supplier is not yet qualified, there is sufficient time to complete the qualification procedure.[319] [320]

When in case of the selective tendering procedure, an invitation to participate is issued in the form of a notice regarding a system for listing qualified suppliers, the notice also shall provide information on "the nature of the products or services concerned"[321] and a "statement that the notice constitutes an invitation to participate".[322]

According to Article IX.10, if after the issuance of an invitation to participate, but before the date for opening or receiving tenders, it should become necessary to amend or reissue the notice, the new notice shall be given the same circulation as the original. Moreover, any significant information given to one interested supplier also shall be provided in a non-discriminatory manner to the other interested suppliers.

The foregoing provisions on invitations have no counterpart in the United Nations Financial Regulations and Rules. Notwithstanding that similar procedures may be practiced by the United Nations in accordance with internal directives, the absence of externally available, binding rules result in lack of transparency and diminished legal certainty. An indication of the global reach of procurement by the United Nations is noticeable from Section 2.1 of the Common Guidelines, according to which "suppliers participate, as a general rule, in

---

317 GPA art. X.2

318 According to M. Pomerantz, considering the GPA recognizes that there frequently are too many suppliers listed to permit all of them to be invited, the underlying rationale of this provision is that over a series of invitations all qualified suppliers should have a chance to compete for one or more contracts. M. Pomerantz, *supra* note 291, at 146.

319 GPA art. X.3.

320 In comparing the procedures for selection of invitees under EC Directive 93/38 with those of art. X of the GPA, it has erroneously been stated that "the GPA allows non-selected candidates and even non-qualified candidates to tender" while "in contrast, Directive 93/38 allows only qualified and selected candidates to tender". GPA art. X.3 does provide the opportunity for interested suppliers to request to be invited to participate, but it is a condition for selection that the regular qualification procedure is first completed. For the cited viewpoint, *see* M. Echégut-Vigroux, *supra* note 295, at 230.

321 Apparently a reference to the products or services to be procured through the intended procurement.

322 GPA art. IX.9.

procurement proceedings without regard to country of origin, unless the UN General Assembly or the Security Council decides otherwise." Decisions on eligibility for participation in procurement proceedings or whether to register a supplier are, according to the Common Guidelines, made by the procuring entity which may deem any supplier ineligible, if the supplier has "intentionally submitted false, materially inaccurate or materially incomplete information." Similar to the provision of Article X.1 of the GPA, Section 4.1.1 of the Common Guidelines states that in competitive procedures "as many Suppliers as is practicable will be given the opportunity to offer the required goods, works or services."

#### e.) time-limits for tendering and delivery

GPA Article XI lays down the general rule that prescribed time limits shall be adequate to allow for the preparation and submission of tenders. In determining the time limits, the procuring entity, in addition to its own needs, shall take into account such factors as the complexity of the intended procurement, the extent of sub-contracting anticipated and the normal time for transmission of tenders from foreign and domestic points.

Normally, in open procedures, the period for receipt of tenders shall be not less than 40 days from the date of publication of the intended procurement. In selective procedures, the period for submitting an application to be invited to tender shall not be less than 25 days from the date of publication of the intended procurement and, if permanent lists of permanent suppliers are used, the period for receipt of tenders shall not be less than 40 days from the initial date of issuance of invitations to tender.

Only under specifically indicated circumstances may the above-mentioned timelines of 25 and 40 days be reduced, according to GPA Article XI.2 and 3.

Through this detailed regulation, the GPA ensures legal certainty and transparency in an important area addressed neither by the United Nations Financial Regulations and Rules nor by the Common Guidelines. While at the level of internal administrative instructions, manuals and sheer practice, similar time periods typically may be observed by the United Nations, neither the norm nor exceptions from the norm are regulated in a manner that ensures legal certainty for external entities through transparency and predictability.

### f.) tender documentation and award criteria

The term "tender documentation", as used in the GPA, refers to the information provided to interested suppliers and its Article XII.2 clearly states the general rule that such tender documentation shall

> "contain all information necessary to permit them to submit responsive tenders, including..."

Article XII.2 further specifies in detail the information it is mandatory to include: in addition to the information required to have been included in a notice of intended procurement,[323] referred to in Article IX and section (d) above, the suppliers also must receive information on (i) procedural requirements such as e.g. the language or languages in which the tender must be submitted, the closing date and time for receipt of tenders and the length of time during which a tender should be open for acceptance, the date, place and time of the opening of the tenders and the persons authorized to be present at this opening, (ii) any economic and technical requirement, financial guarantees and required documents required from suppliers as well as a complete description of the products or services required including technical specifications, any conformity certification and necessary plans, drawings and instructional materials, (iii) the criteria for awarding the contract, including any factors other than price that are to be considered in the evaluation (iv) the terms of payment and (v) any other conditions.

When compared to the United Nations procedure, it is noted that while the Financial Regulations and Rules are silent on the subject of mandatory tender documentation, the practice of the United Nations generally conforms to the requirements in the GPA in this respect.[324] The Common Guidelines in Section 3.1.1 state that solicitation documents "will contain all information necessary to prepare a suitable Offer" and then lists certain elements, including "evaluation criteria", that will be included "as appropriate", but the listing is far from as comprehensive and detailed as the enumerations in Articles IX and XII.2 of the GPA. Transparency and legal certainty no doubt are strengthened by comprehensive normative requirements such as those found in the GPA. An illustrative example is offered by GPA Article XII.2 (h) regarding the information to be

---

[323] Except for information on the amount and terms of payment of any sum payable for the tender documentation. The time for meeting this condition will have passed already.

[324] Compare summary above in Chapter III, Section E: Requisitions, Terms of Reference and Technical Specifications, and Section I: Solicitation Documents.

provided in the solicitation documents on the criteria for deciding on the award, which must include, *inter alia*

> "...any factors other than price that are to be considered in the evaluation of tenders and the cost elements to be included in evaluating tender prices, such as transport, insurance and inspection costs, and [for imports] customs duties and other import charges, taxes and currency of payment."

That the GPA expressly lists these details as required information, contrasts with the absence of any indication in United Nations Financial Rule 105.15 of these elements which form crucial parts of the evaluation process. The room for arbitrary evaluations undoubtedly is substantially widened when the conduct of the evaluation is left unregulated and when the award criteria are described only in non-specific terms in the solicitation documents. Even when the procuring entity acts without arbitrariness, suppliers are left without precise guidance on how to compose the most responsive, competitive bids or proposals possible, which further implies a potentially reduced quality of the eventual acquisition.

The GPA in Article XIII.4(b) defines the possible award criteria in a manner similar to the criteria in the current Financial Rule 105.15. Accordingly, unless it is decided in the public interest not to issue the contract, the award shall go to the tenderer who has been determined to be fully capable of undertaking the contract and whose tender is

> "either the lowest tender or the tender which in terms of the specific evaluation criteria set forth in the notices or tender documentation is determined to be the most advantageous."

Considering the great variety of contract types covered by the GPA, it is understandable that a more comprehensive, detailed description of the permissible award criteria was not agreed among the WTO Member States when drafting the GPA. Although the GPA avoids some of the obscurity found in United Nations Financial Rule 105.15, which is compounded by the nexus between the choice of award criteria and the use of either a "formal invitation to bid" or a "formal request for proposals", both regimes leave it to the solicitation or tendering documents to disclose a complete statement of the criteria, or even, in case of the United Nations procedures, whether or not to accomplish a full disclosure. In the absence of full disclosure in the documents provided to the invited suppliers, there is a risk that potentially determining criteria will be stated only in internal manuals or administrative instructions, or even be established by internal *ad hoc* decisions made subsequent to the issuance of invitations, and thus not be available, *de facto* or *de jure* to external entities. The GPA is comparatively more transparent in that it requires full disclosure in the tender documents of the determining criteria for awarding the contract, be they related or un-related to the price or consist in cost elements to be included in the price.[325] Also Section 5.4.1-2 of the Common Guidelines indicate it is the normal practice to disclose the evaluation criteria in the solicitation documents.[326]

### g.) submission, receipt and opening of tenders

Certain rules of an administrative or procedural nature, contained in Article XIII.1-3 of the GPA, have the effect of further strengthening the transparency requirements. Importantly, all tenders and documents must be submitted in writing, normally directly or by mail, but submission by facsimile or – by the less common methods: telex or telegram – may be permitted. Tenders presented by telephone are not permitted. A tender must contain all information necessary to perform the evaluation and it must accept and conform to all conditions and terms of the invitation to tender. While the deadline for submission generally must be observed, the tendering procedures may allow exceptions and if the delay in submission is "due solely to mishandling on the part of the entity" undertaking the procurement, the supplier shall not be penalized by the late submission. Presumably this implies that such late tenders must be considered whenever practically possible.

In the open or selective procedures, regularity of the receipt and opening of tenders, including consistency with the national treatment and non-discrimination requirements of the GPA, shall be guaranteed by the applicable procedures and conditions. The procuring entity also shall keep information on the opening of tenders and hold it available for eventual use by the procuring entity in the event it should be required under the challenge and dispute settle

---

325 M. Pomerantz in commenting on the first GPA (1979) opined that "In the past, perhaps no one aspect of procurement has lent itself more to discrimination than the failure of procuring agencies to establish the criteria of awards at the time of the original invitation for bids". M. Pomerantz, *supra* note 291, at 147.

326 S. Arrowsmith has convincingly argued that, for a possible future Transparency Agreement among WTO Member States, a requirement to fully disclose the award criteria in the solicitation documents for each procurement action (if not already contained in the national procurement legislation) would suffice to retain the essence, even if uniform national award criteria were not to be required. S. Arrowsmith, *supra* note 301, at 793.

ments procedures or to meet the obligations of a Party to provide information on its procurement activities.

In this respect, while the United Nations Financial Regulations and Rules require procurement contracts to be in writing,[327] and that written records must be made of the reasons for rejecting all bids or proposals[328] or for following a non-competitive procedure,[329] they are silent on the detailed conditions for receipt and opening of proposals or tenders set out in the GPA. Also the related Sections 5.1-3 of the Common Guidelines are barely informative. Although observance of the procedures referred to in the Financial Rules for practical reasons implies timely submissions and written exchanges between the procuring entity and the suppliers, the pertinent detailed instructions are internal and, as such, lack transparency.

### h.) negotiations

In the context of the competitive procedures, open or selective, Article XIV of the GPA addresses the conditions for the conduct of negotiations preceding the award of the procurement contract with suppliers participating in the procurement procedure. Negotiations, accordingly, shall primarily be used to identify the strengths and weaknesses in tenders and are permitted in two situations, namely when the intent to conduct negotiations has been indicated in the notice of a proposed procurement inviting suppliers to participate and when, at a later stage, the evaluation of tenders indicates that "no one tender is obviously the most advantageous in the terms of the specific evaluation criteria set forth in the notices or tender documentation".[330]

Article XIV further states that during negotiations the tenders shall be treated in confidence and that no information shall be provided, which might "assist particular participants to bring their tenders up to the level of other participants".[331] The confidentiality requirement therefore comprises not only the information in the original tender, but also such additional, clarifying information as may be forthcoming during a negotiation. Moreover, pursuant to Article XIV.4, negotiations shall not cause any discriminatory treatment of a participa-

---

[327] Financial Rule 105.18.

[328] Financial Rules 105.15(c).

[329] Financial Rule 105.16(b).

[330] GPA art. XIV.1(b).

[331] GPA art. XIV.3.

ting tenderer and, accordingly, it is prohibited to invoke other selection criteria to eliminate a tender than the original selection criteria set forth in the notices or tender documentation. Should it be found necessary to modify the criteria, all participating suppliers must be informed thereof in writing and invited to submit revised tenders on the basis of the revised requirements. In any event, upon conclusion of the negotiations, all participants that have not been eliminated during the negotiations must be invited to "submit final tenders in accordance with a common deadline" – in practice often referred to as the "best and final offer".

As can be seen, also with respect to negotiations, there is a marked difference between the fairly detailed statement of principles and rules in the GPA and the absence of any specific guidance in the United Nations Financial Regulations and Rules. The absence of such guidance may have facilitated the introduction of the so-called "Best And Final Offer" (BAFO)[332] in connexion with the Request for Proposals modality. In this regard, the non-binding Common Guidelines in Section 3.2.2 provide that authorization of negotiations in respect of one or more proposals may be given in Requests for Proposals. Such authorization, however, seems not to be permissible under a formal competitive bidding procedure, i.e. when a formal Invitation to Bid has been issued. Likewise, according Section 5.4.3, authorization by the Procuring Entity[333] is necessary in order for a proposal to be altered after the deadline for its submission has passed. It results that, to achieve transparency, publication of comprehensive mandatory norms on negotiations, e.g. in the Financial Regulations or Rules would be necessary.

### i.) limited tendering

Both Article XV of the GPA and United Nations Financial Rule 105.16 enumerate in an almost casuistic manner the concrete circumstances, in which no formally competitive procedure is required. To a considerable extent, the circumstances enumerated in the two instruments are identical, similar or overlap.[334]

---

[332] *See* Chapter V.G.1 *in fine* and fn. 525.

[333] The manner of authorization is not indicated, however.

[334] *See also* Section 4.5 of the Common Guidelines for examples of grounds for direct negotiations in lieu of a competitive procedure.

Thus, the situation where no tender or only unresponsive ones[335] have been received in a competitive procedure is mentioned in GPA Article XV(a) as well as by United Nations Financial Rule 105.16(a)(v).

The examples in GPA Article XV(b) of instances where only one supplier can be expected to meet the requirements (works of art, exclusive rights, patents and copy rights, technical reasons) are strongly reminiscent of United Nations Financial Rule 105.16(a)(i) referring to the absence of a competitive marketplace as in case of monopolies, government regulation or proprietary products or services.

Both GPA Article XV(c) and United Nations Financial Rule 105.16(a)(vii) refer to urgent and unforeseeable requirements that should not be delayed by a competitive procedure which presumably is more lengthy than a non-competitive one.

GPA Article XV(d) corresponds to United Nations Financial Rule 105.16(a)(ii) concerning the need to ensure compatibility with existing equipment and/or previous deliveries. The rational of ensuring compatibility also is pursued by GPA Article XV(f) concerning additional construction services that were not included in the initial contract but are required for the same objectives, and by GPA Article XV(g) regarding new construction services quite similar to those for which an initial contract has been awarded in a competitive procedure.

GPA Article XV(e) takes up the ground of proprietary products or services, also addressed by United Nations Financial Rule 105.16(a)(i), by referring to prototypes developed under contracts specifically for research, experiment, study or original development.

Certain specific situations, e.g. contracts to be awarded to the winner of a design contest (GPA Art. XV(j)), products purchased on a commodity market (GPA Art. XV(h)) or exceptionally advantageous short-term opportunities (GPA Art. XV(i)) are not referred to expressly in the United Nations Financial Rules, although at the practical level there are several examples of the United Nations arranging an architectural design contest as forerunner for the construction of office complexes and of the purchase of large quantities of vaccines or of foodstuff commodities by the subsidiary organs UNICEF and the World Food Programme, respectively.

335 GPA art. XV(a) expands the ground to expressly include collusive tenders and tenders from unqualified suppliers.

Both under the GPA[336] and the United Nations Financial Regulations and Rules,[337] it is a requirement that written records of each transaction be kept, whenever the procurement is done without formal competition. This is required to ensure transparency and acts as a safeguard against any misuse of the informal procedure. GPA Article XV.2 demands that such written reports shall be at the disposal of the responsible government entities for their use in meeting their obligation to provide information or to engage in the challenge or dispute settlement procedures, referred to below.

### j.) transparency, provision of information and review

A large number of the GPA's provisions on the procurement procedure concern requirements enhancing the transparency of the procurement activities with a view, in particular, to ensure observance of the fundamental principles of most-favoured nation treatment, non-discrimination and effectiveness.[338] As mentioned above, in general, transparency-related requirements are considerably more prevalent in the GPA than in the United Nations Financial Regulations and Rules and no obligation to provide any information on procurement is stated in the latter.

#### *(1) transparency for non-Parties*

Article XVII of the GPA is entitled transparency, but hardly expands the transparency requirements found in other GPA provisions, since it is concerned with the definition of the minimum level of transparency required of government procuring entities in States not Parties to the GPA in order for tenders from suppliers in these non-member States to be entertained and for these Governments to be entitled to participate in the capacity of observers in the Committee on Government Procurement, established pursuant to Article XXI of the GPA.

---

[336] GPA art. XV.2.

[337] Financial Rule 105.16(b).

[338] S. Arrowsmith has suggested that a new agreement on government procurement limited to requiring transparency could be acceptable to a greater number of member states than the Parties to the GPA. S. Arrowsmith, *supra* note 301, at 793. M. A. Kinsey has referred to the reluctance of some member States during negotiations within the WTO to make binding commitments on transparency because of a concern transparency might increase access to their markets for government procurement. M. A. Kinsey, *supra* note 280, at 155 (2004-2005).

The Committee's membership is composed of representatives of all the Parties. The Committee facilitates consultations on matters relating to the GPA and also serves as a forum for negotiation of the terms for accession by new Members.

### *(2) information by procuring entities*

The GPA imposes certain obligations to publish post-award information on procurement matters. Thus, Article XVIII requires procuring entities within 72 days of the award of each contract to publish data relating to the contract on:

a.) the nature of the products and services in the award

b.) the name and address of the awarding entity

c.) the date of the award

d.) the name and address of the winning tenderer

e.) the value of the award or the highest and lowest offer taken into account in the award

f.) where appropriate, either means of identifying the notice of invitation to participate in the procurement, or the ground justifying limited tendering

g.) the type of procedure used.

In addition, at the request of a supplier from a State Party, a procuring entity shall promptly provide:

a.) an explanation of its procurement practices and procedures,

b.) pertinent information concerning the reasons (i) for rejecting the supplier's application to qualify or (ii) why the supplier's existing qualification was discontinued and (iii) why it was not selected,

c.) where the supplier is an unsuccessful tenderer, pertinent information (i) concerning the reasons for not selecting the supplier's tender, (ii) on the characteristics and relative advantages of the tender selected and also (iii) the name of the winning tenderer.

In general, the procuring entity shall promptly inform the suppliers participating in a procurement action of the award decision and, upon request, provide this information in writing. On certain grounds, however, the information referred to above may be withheld, namely if it's release would impede law enforcement, otherwise be contrary to the public interest, prejudice the legitimate commercial interests of a particular enterprise or when it might prejudice fair competition between suppliers.

The importance of the obligation to provide post-award information to participating suppliers can best be appreciated in the context of the challenge procedure for suppliers, required under Article XX and discussed below.

### *(3) information by Parties*

Also Article XIX imposes post-award information and review obligations, but on the States Parties to the GPA, while Article XVIII, as mentioned above, places obligations on the procuring entities. Each Party must promptly publish any law, regulation, judicial decision, general administrative ruling and any procedure regarding government procurement. Upon request of any other Party, each Party shall explain its procedures for government procurement. The government of an unsuccessful tenderer may seek such additional information on the award "as may be necessary to ensure that the procurement was made fairly and impartially." Similar to requests from unsuccessful bidders, information shall be provided on "both the characteristics and relative advantages of the winning tender and the contract price." This information normally may be disclosed by the government of the unsuccessful tenderer, provided it is done with due discretion. Where, however, "release of this information would prejudice competition in future tenders," it shall not be disclosed, except after consultation with and agreement of the Party that gave the information to the Government of the unsuccessful tenderer.

In general, all available information concerning procurement shall be provided to another Party upon its request. Corresponding to the provisions on information requested by a supplier, confidential information requested by a Party shall not be released where it would impede law enforcement or otherwise be contrary to the public interest, or would prejudice the legitimate commercial interests of a particular enterprise or might prejudice fair competition between suppliers.

An important, and most likely the essential, purpose of requiring the procuring entities and the Parties to provide the above mentioned information on actually performed procurement actions is the usefulness of such information in the challenge and the dispute settlement procedures that are available, respectively, to the participants in tendering procedures under Article XX and to the Parties under Article XXII of the GPA.

In addition, specific obligations to collect and to provide annual statistical data to the Committee on Government Procurement are set out in Article XIX.5. The data concerns the value and number of contracts awarded as well as similar information relevant for evaluation of the government procurement markets open to firms from all the Parties and thus of interest for the efforts of the Parties to expand foreign trade.

#### *(4) United Nations procurement regime*

The United Nations Financial Rules do not regulate which information must be provided to suppliers or to Member States on the procurement awards. While information may be provided from time to time, this is a discretionary *ad hoc* measure, as found expedient in order to accommodate expectations of suppliers and Member States. The Common Guidelines reflect a general reluctance on behalf of the United Nations system to provide information on the reasons for award decisions. Thus, while Section 6.1.2 provides that unsuccessful offerors "normally will be sent a formal letter of regret", Section 6.1.3 restrictively states that the procuring entity will not disclose:

- "information that may prejudice legitimate commercial interests of the parties or inhibit fair competition," – which is similar to the GPA -, and
- "information relating to the examination, evaluation or comparison of offers," – which is contrary to the information obligations in GPA Articles XVIII and IXX referred to above.

While the first point is an obvious consequence of the duty of confidentiality, the second represents a material contrast to the disclosure requirements of the GPA. Disappointed bidders are clearly disadvantaged under the United Nations procedures when compared to their position under the GPA. As they are not entitled to claim the relevant documentation and in practice left without any access, no meaningful remedy is practically feasible.

### k.) challenge procedures

#### *(1) complaint and consultation*

The Uruguay Round of Multilateral Trade Negotiations that led to the conclusion of the WTO Agreement in 1994 was, during 1985-1994, shadowed by parallel negotiations in the Committee on Government Procurement to amend the GPA.[339]

Among the amendments[340] which have been included in the current version, GPA (1994),[341] is the obligation of the Parties to provide procedures enabling suppliers, failing settlement through consultation, to launch a complaint directly against the procuring entity for the purpose of alleging, as formulated by Article XX.1 "a breach of this Agreement in the context of a procurement".[342] The contention of the complaint therefore should concern the international obligations assumed by the Party of the procuring entity to conduct the procurement in accordance with the GPA, rather than any obligation that may arise under the national legislation of the Party of the procuring entity.[343]

---

339 33 *ILM* 1127 (1994).

340 In the United States, the host country to the United Nations main headquarters, administrative and judicial venues are available under federal law for bidders to file "bid protests" against procurement decisions. The General Accounting Office's Comptroller General may settle claims and stay performance in pre- and post-award claims. Claims may also be filed before the centralized Court of Federal Claims and the decentralized federal District Courts. Judicial jurisdiction was accepted in 1956 by the Court of Claims which held that the Government has an implied-in-fact contract to act in good faith when it solicits bids and that this duty was breached when the Government failed to fairly consider the bid of the protesting firm (*Heyer Products Co. v. United States,* 140 F. Supp. 409 Ct.Cl. (1956), *modified,* 177 F. Supp. 251 Ct.Cl. (1959). *See* J. R. Cantor, *supra* note 118, at 155.

341 Procedures for bidders' protests are also required under European Union directive 89/665/EEC and suggested by UNCITRAL's Model Law on Procurement of Goods and Construction, Chapter V (adopted 9 December 1993), *see* 33 ILM 445 (1994), and Model Law on Procurement of Goods, Construction and Services, Chapter VI (adopted 15 June 1994) 34 ILM 718 (1995).

342 The procedures normally would take place in the national courts of the Party concerned, according to G. de Graaf/M. King, *supra* note 272, at 440.

343 "Article XX requires each party to make provision for suppliers to challenge breaches of the GPA, by that party or its regulated entities before an independent body in the procuring state." S. Arrowsmith, *supra* note 284, at 384-385, where it is further pointed out that while "these challenge procedures must meet certain minimum standards concerning the nature of the review body, the procedure for hearing the challenge, and the remedies available," the States are "free to design their own challenge mechanisms" within this basic framework. A similar position is argued by I. Dendauw, "New WTO Agreement on Government Procurement: an Analysis of the Framework for Bid Challenge Procedures and the Question of Direct Effect", 18 *J. Energy Nat. Resources L.*, at 263-266 (2000). In the light of the doctrine of the ECJ, the author finds the GPA is directly applicable in that it forms an integral part of EC law, but that it does not have direct effect since its norms, apart from the provision conferring on private parties the right to bring procuring entities before national courts, are not sufficiently clear, precise and unconditional.

As a first step in the event of such a complaint, Article XX.1 requires the Party concerned to encourage the supplier to seek a resolution of its complaint in consultation with the procuring entity, while the procuring entity is required to accord timely and impartial consideration to the complaint "in a manner that is not prejudicial to obtaining corrective measures under the challenge system", thus keeping this option open in the event the consultation stage does not result in an amicable settlement of all aspects of the complaint.

### *(2) procedural standards*

Article XX of the GPA does not establish a challenge procedure at the international level, but requires each of the States Parties to "provide non-discriminatory, timely, transparent and effective procedures enabling suppliers to challenge alleged breaches of the Agreement arising in the context of procurements in which they have, or had, an interest"[344] The procedures must meet the standards and specific requirements stipulated by Article XX. Accordingly, each Party shall provide its challenge procedures in writing and make them generally available. Moreover, as a corollary to its information obligations, each Party shall ensure the retention of documentation relating to "all aspects of the process concerning procurements" covered by the GPA for three years (Article XX.8).

The phrase in Article XX.2 of the GPA that the procedures shall be provided for suppliers to deal with "breaches of the Agreement arising in the context of procurements in which they have, or have had, an interest" must be understood as criteria for the receivability of the complaint and for the legal standing of the complainant, respectively. A supplier also may be required to observe certain timelines for the initiation of a challenge, which shall not be less than ten days from the time the basis, or ground, of the complaint was known or reasonably should have been known.

Article XX.6 of the GPA establishes a high standard for due process requirements to be met by the challenge procedures of a Party. Challenges must be heard either by a court of law or by an impartial and independent review body with no interest in the outcome, the members of which shall be secure from external influence during their term of appointment. Interestingly, but not devoid of reason, the formulation of these specific requirements seems also to refer to

---

344 GPA art. X.2.

courts. Moreover, when the review body is not a court, it either shall be subject to review by a court or, if not, its procedures shall provide that:

a.) Participants can be heard before an opinion is given or a decision is reached

b.) Participants can be represented and accompanied

c.) Participants shall have access to all proceedings

d.) Proceedings can take place in public

e.) Opinions or decisions are given in writing with a statement describing the basis for the opinions or decisions

f.) Witnesses can be presented

g.) Documents are disclosed to the review body.

The procedural requirements for a review body whose decisions are not reviewable by a court clearly are such as to cause the review body to offer due process guarantees that approximate those of a court. There may be good reasons for establishing a special review body to hear challenges, rather than to make use of an ordinary court, among which would be the need for speedy consideration by a body possessing specialized expertise in procurement matters.

### *(3) procedure*

According to Article X.5, the challenge procedure may require challenges to be notified to the procuring entity within specific time-limits, but not sooner than 10 days from the time the basis of the complaint became known or reasonably should have been known by the interested supplier. A short deadline will enhance the possibility of resolving the matter while the procurement process is still pending.

With a view to attaining an objective, which is given major importance by the GPA – in contrast to its absence from the United Nations procurement regime – namely "the preservation of the commercial and other interests involved," Article XX.8 requires that "the challenge procedure normally shall be completed in a timely fashion." The central commercial interest of a tenderer challenging a procurement process clearly is the opportunity, without delay, to be awarded the contract, either through implementation of a correct procedure or through correction of any breach of the procedure. Beyond this general guidance, the setting of detailed time-limits is left to the implementing Governments. This question should be considered in conjunction with the analysis of rules on interim remedies.[345]

### *(4) remedies*

The remedies which, according to the GPA, must be available in the challenge procedures represent truly novel features. The first remedy expressly required in Article XX.7(a) consists in "rapid interim measures to correct breaches of the Agreement and to preserve commercial opportunities." It is quite conceivable that a supplier who during an early phase of the procurement procedure becomes aware of an irregularity and raises a challenge without delay, thereby will be intervening at an early stage where the irregularity can still be corrected with no or only a minor delay in completing the procedure. This outcome is implied by the following sentence, which allows a further sanction, namely suspension: "Such action may result in suspension of the procurement process." The intent here must be that the procurement process is suspended by an interim measure for the period required to effect the correction and (thereby also) to preserve commercial opportunities. Normally, the procurement process would thereafter be resumed, but, depending on the circumstances of the procurement case at hand, effectuation of the correction through suspension may be so time-consuming, or the correction may otherwise affect the purpose or integrity of the procurement process in such a way, that the process cannot legitimately be resumed. Some likely examples would be where delivery of essential medical supplies in an emergency or execution of repairs to a public power station are urgent, or where another tenderer or the government of the procuring entity would sustain disproportionately large economic losses by a suspension. With such situations apparently in view, Article XX.7(a) further provides: "However, procedures may provide that overriding adverse consequences for the interests concerned, including the public interest, may be taken into account in deciding whether such measures should be applied. In such circumstances, just cause for not acting shall be provided in writing."

The GPA provides that the procurement process may be suspended for the purpose of correction, but does not define whether the procurement process ends already with the recording of the internal award decision, or thereafter with the communication of the award decision to the tenderers – whether successful or

---

345 D. I. Gordon, "Constructing a Bid Protest Process: Choices Every Procurement Challenge System Must Make", 35 *Pub. Cont. L. J.*, 10-11 (2006) available at http://papers.ssrn.com/sol3/papers.cfm?abstract_id=892781 (last visited 15 February 2008).

unsuccessful -, or first with the conclusion of the detailed contract following the award. It therefore seems to be left to legislation or regulation by each Party to determine whether also an award can be reversed under the challenge procedure. If, however, one contemplates the interests that must be taken into account, i.e. the reference in Article XX.7(a) to the "overriding adverse consequences for the interests concerned, including the public interest", it is arguable that the successful tenderer may have a commercial interest in retaining the awarded contract, the magnitude and weight of which equals that of the unsuccessful tenderer, even if the latter has been wrongfully passed over, and that therefore the public interest should be decisive for the determination of which interim measures, including suspension, are appropriate.[346]

A further remedy that must be offered under the challenge procedure is "an assessment and a possibility for a decision on the justification of the challenge". The assessment appears to be a part of interim measures in as much as it may constitute the basis for deciding on whether to pursue further measures, including "a decision on the justification of the challenge." In all events, the remedies must comprise either "correction of the breach of the Agreement" or in the alternative "compensation for the loss or damages suffered." In this connexion, there is no definition in the GPA of the method or criteria for calculating the compensation due, except the rule that the compensation "may be limited to costs for tender preparation or protest". It is apparent, however, that compensation covering only the cost for tender preparation or protest represents the minimum permissible compensation. Such minimum compensation may be appropriate, for instance where faulty tender documents have caused a supplier to participate while correct tender documents would have caused the supplier not to do so,[347] but where the challenge has not proven that the award decision was

---

[346] The GPA does not refer to the calculation or quantification of the commercial interest. A generally acceptable international standard may be derived from the definition of damages for breach of contract in art. 74 of the United Nations Convention on Contracts for the International Sale of Goods, adopted on 11 April 1980, which reads: "Damages for breach of contract by one party consist of a sum equal to the loss, including loss of profit, suffered by the other party as a consequence of the breach. Such damages may not exceed the loss which the party in breach foresaw or ought to have foreseen at the time of the conclusion of the contract, in the light of the facts and matters of which he then knew or ought to have known, as a possible consequence of the breach of contract." For the party in breach one would substitute the procuring entity and for breach of contract, breach of the GPA. 1489 *UNTS* 3, I: 25567.

[347] UNCITRAL's Model Law on Procurement of Goods, Construction and Services, art. 54.3(f), suggests this solution as one option, and as another option compensation for (all) "loss or injury suffered by the supplier or contractor submitting the complaint in connexion the procurement proceedings." 34 *ILM* 718 (1995).

wrongfully denied to the supplier launching the challenge. Conversely, it would be appropriate to compensate a supplier fully for the loss, including any loss of profit, sustained due to having been passed over in favour of a competitor that submitted a less competitive tender. Considering that compensation including compensation for loss of profit is not required in all cases and that it normally would be a heavy burden for a supplier to prove that its tender was the most competitive and should have won the award, the instances where an award will be quashed are likely to be rare.[348]

## *3. Dispute Settlement Understanding*

### a.) applicability of the Dispute Settlement Understanding[349]

Article XXII of the GPA, entitled "Consultations and Dispute Settlement" refers to procedures among the Parties to the GPA, as distinguished from the above-mentioned challenge procedures, under which suppliers may pursue their complaints against the procuring entity. Article XXII is a supplement to the elaborate procedure set out in the "Understanding on Rules and Procedures Governing the Settlement of Disputes" contained in Annex 2 to the WTO Agreement (hereinafter "Dispute Settlement Understanding" or "DSU").

The DSU is applicable to disputes brought under the so-called "covered agreements", by which are meant the agreements listed in Appendix 1 to the DSU.[350] As far as the "covered" plurilateral agreements are concerned, the appli-

---

[348] UNCITRAL's Model Law on Procurement of Goods, Construction and Services, art. 54.3(d) and (e) in conjunction with art. 53, suggests that this remedy should be available to the head of the procuring unit, but not to any review body external to the procurement unit. *Ibid.*

[349] *See* to the following the WTO Secretariat publication, *A Handbook on the WTO Dispute Settlement System* (2004). An overview of the review initiated in 1997 by WTO Member States of the DSU is presented by R. Rajesh Babu, "Review of the WTO Dispute Settlement Understanding: Progress and Prospects", 2 *AALCO Quarterly Bulletin* 50-74 (2005).

[350] DSU App. 1 lists as covered:
A: the WTO Agreement,
B: Multilateral Trade Agreements:
1) Multilateral Agreements on Trade in Goods, 2) General Agreement on Trade in Services, 3) Agreement on Trade Related Aspects of Intellectual Property Rights, 4) Understanding on Rules and Procedures Governing the Settlement of Disputes
C: Plurilateral Trade Agreements:
1) Agreement on Trade in Civil Aircraft, 2) Agreement on Government Procurement, 3) International Dairy Agreement, 4) International Bovine Meat Agreement.

cability of the DSU is subject to a "triggering" decision of the Parties to each plurilateral agreement setting out the terms for applicability, including any special or additional rules or procedures.[351] The Committee on Government Procurement has taken such a decision regarding the GPA[352] and the Chairman of the Committee has notified the Chairman of the DSB thereof in a letter dated 8 July 1996, listing Article XXII, paragraphs 2 through 7, as special or additional rules or procedures. The Committee's Annual Report for 1996[353] also confirms this step.

By virtue of the notification and pursuant to Article 1.2 of the DSU, to the extent the provisions of Article XXII.2-7 of the GPA differ from the corresponding rules in the DSU, the former provisions prevail over the DSU.

According to Article 2.1 of the DSU, where the DSB administers a dispute arising under the dispute settlement provisions of a plurilateral trade agreement, only those Members who are also Parties to the plurilateral trade agreement concerned may participate in the decisions and actions taken by the DSB with respect to that dispute.

### b.) Dispute Settlement Body

The Dispute Settlement Body (hereinafter the "DSB")[354] administers the rules and procedures of the DSU. This organ is referred to in Article IV.2 and 3 of the WTO Agreement, which establishes a Ministerial Conference, composed of representatives of all Members and mandated to carry out the functions of the WTO and to take actions necessary to this effect. The Ministerial Conference shall meet at least biennially and in intervals between its meetings the General

---

351 According to App. 1 to the DSU, the applicability of the DSU to the Plurilateral Trade Agreements "shall be subject to the adoption of a decision by the parties to each agreement setting out the terms for the application of the Understanding to the individual agreement, including any special or additional rules or procedures for inclusion in App. 2, as notified to the DSB."

352 WTO Secretariat publication, *supra* note 349, at 10. WTO document WT/DSB/7 (1996).

353 WTO document GPA/5. *See under* "Other Matters" on p. 4: "In accordance with the provisions of the Understanding on Rules and Procedures Governing the Settlement of Disputes (Ann. 2 of the WTO Agreement), the Committee notified the Dispute Settlement Body (DSB) of special or additional rules or procedures on dispute settlement in the Agreement on Government Procurement, namely art. XXII, paragraphs 2 through 7".

354 J. Klabbers has recalled that in the GATT/WTO system, "dispute settlement procedures developed largely in practice, and while they started out as exercises in trade diplomacy, they have gone through a distinct process of juridification". J. Klabbers, supra note 140, at 267.

Conference of representatives of all Members shall conduct its functions. The General Conference, *inter alia*, "shall convene as appropriate to discharge the responsibilities of the Dispute Settlement Body provided for in the Dispute Settlement Understanding" and thus effectively acts as the DSB. Consonant with this briefly stated mandate, the DSB has been formally established pursuant to Article 2 of the DSU.

### c.) nature and purpose

According to Article 3.2 of the DSU, the dispute settlement system is intended as "a central element in providing security and predictability to the multilateral trading system." It serves the purposes of preserving the balance between the rights and obligations of Members, which is a task of obvious importance for a multilateral trade agreement, and of clarifying the provisions of the covered agreements "in accordance with customary rules of interpretation of public international law." From these provisions alone, one clearly notices the intention of the Member States to establish an effective system ensuring the observance of the rule of law in their commercial trade activities. In this connexion, it is considered that the DSU "aims to provide a fast, efficient, dependable and rule-oriented system to resolve disputes about the application" of the WTO Agreement as well as the covered agreements.[355] According to Article 23.1 of the DSU, it is mandatory for Member States "to have recourse to, and abide by, the rules and procedures" of the DSU when seeking redress for violations of the covered agreements.

The fact that DSU's rule-bound and structured procedures are clearly distinguishable from the comparatively formless methods available to Member States wishing to pursue complaints or grievances within the United Nations system is recognizable already from the above mentioned provisions of Articles 3.2 and 23.1 of the DSU. An examination of the detailed rules and procedures further reveals that the DSU relies on a multilateral problem-solving approach rather than on the unilateral practices prevailing within the United Nations.

---

[355] WTO Secretariat publication, *supra* note 349, at 2.

### d.) subject matter and establishment of panels

If a Party considers that a benefit accruing to it under the GPA "is being nullified or impaired, or that the attainment of any objective of this Agreement is being impeded as the result of the failure of another Party or Parties to carry out its obligations" under the Agreement, or by any measure applied by another Party, "whether or not it conflicts with the provisions of" the GPA, it may make written representations or proposals to the other Party or Parties concerned with a view to reaching a mutually satisfactory solution. Sympathetic consideration shall be given to representations or proposals by any Party thus approached.[356]

Most complaints raised under the DSU concern an alleged violation of a covered agreement. From the formulation of GPA Article XXII.2, it follows that in addition to the existence of a violation which must have nullified or impaired an accrued benefit or impeded the attainment of an intended objective of the GPA, it is also possible to raise a so-called "non-violation" complaint, i.e. when the nullification, impairment or impediment is caused by the application by a Party of a measure "whether or not it conflicts with" the GPA.[357] Non-violation complaints under the GPA could be based on measures that impeded access of the suppliers from the complaining Party to markets included in the offending Party's annexes to the GPA.[358]

The DSU provides that if[359] consultations are requested, the Party to which the request has been made shall reply within 10 days and enter into consultations within 30 days of receiving the request.[360] If this is not done,[361] or if the consultations fail to settle the dispute within 60 days,[362] the complaining Party may

---

356 GPA art. XXII.2.

357 J. Klabbers, *supra* note 140, at 269 (2002).

358 S. Arrowsmith, *supra* note 284, at 360-364, discussing *inter alia* the panel report, adopted by WTO's Government Procurement Committee 19 June 2000 – not 15 June as in *id.*, – , in the case *Korea – Measures Affecting Government Procurement*, (WT/DS/163/R – not WT/DS/193/R as cited by Arrowsmith).

359 Since GPA art. XXII.2 – which modifies the DSU for GPA disputes – employs the verb "may", the institution of consultations seems to be voluntary. It has been pointed out, however, that under the WTO agreements, including GATT art. XXIII.2, consultations generally must precede the establishment of panels (*i.e.* referral to the CONTRACTING PARTIES). S. Arrowsmith, *supra* note 284, at 366.

360 DSU art. 4.3.

361 *Ibid.*

362 DSU art. 4.7.

request the establishment of a panel and if the consulting Parties jointly agree that consultations have failed in achieving a settlement, the complaining Party may request the establishment of a panel already within the 60-day period.[363] In case of urgency, the 30 day period is reduced to 10 days and the 60 day period to 20 days.[364] A request for consultations must be in writing, addressed to the Party concerned and copied to the DSB and relevant WTO bodies.[365] Any Party approached regarding consultations shall "give sympathetic consideration to the representations or proposals made to it."[366] The request for establishment of a panel also shall be made in writing and shall indicate whether consultations were held, identify the specific measures at issue and provide a brief summary of the legal basis of the complaint.[367]

In accordance with the decision of the Committee on Government Procurement referred to above,[368] certain provisions of GPA Article XXII modify the DSU. Thus, the GPA requires that the Panel must include "persons qualified in the area of government procurement"[369] and that the terms of reference[370] of a panel shall be to examine the dispute in the light of the relevant provisions of the GPA (and of any other covered agreement cited by the Parties) and to make findings that will assist the DSB in making the recommendations or giving the rulings provided for in the GPA. In addition, pursuant to Article XXII.3 of the GPA, the DSB may "establish panels, adopt panel and Appellate Body reports" to deal with the matter referred to it by the complaining Party.

#### e.) amicable settlement

The DSU gives preference to direct and amicable settlement between the Parties involved. As formulated by DSU Article 3.7: ".... A solution mutually acceptable to the parties to a dispute and consistent with the covered agreements is clearly to be preferred. ..."

---

363 *Ibid.*

364 DSU art. 4.8.

365 DSU art. 4.4 and GPA art. XXII.2.

366 GPA art. XXII.2.

367 DSU art. 6.2.

368 *See* section B.2(a).

369 GPA art. XXII.5.

370 GPA art. XXII.4.

According to Article 5 of the DSU, good offices, conciliation and mediation[371] may be undertaken, if the Parties so agree. These voluntary procedures may be requested by any Party to a dispute at any time and they may begin and be terminated at any time. A request for establishment of a panel should await termination of the voluntary procedures and if they have been entered into within the first 60 days after the receipt of a request for consultations, the complaining Party must wait 60 days before requesting a panel to be established, unless the Parties jointly consider that the voluntary procedures have failed to settle the dispute. The proceedings of the voluntary procedures are confidential and without prejudice to the rights of any Party in other proceedings under the DSU. Subject to agreement by the Parties, the voluntary procedures may continue while the panel process proceeds. The Director-General may, *ex officio*, offer good offices, conciliation or mediation to assist the Parties in settling a dispute.

While Article 4.4 of the DSU provides that the DSB shall be notified of a request for consultations, the consultations as such are confidential and without prejudice to the rights of any Member in possible further proceedings. In the course of consultations and before resorting to further action under the DSU, Members should attempt to obtain satisfactory adjustment of the matter under consultation.

#### f.) panel proceedings

Modifying the longer timelines in the DSU, Article XXII.6 of the GPA provides that "the panel shall attempt to provide its final report to the parties to the dispute not later than four months, and in the case of delay not later than seven months, after the date on which the composition and terms of reference of the panel are agreed" and that every effort shall be made to reduce by two months the timelines foreseen by the DSU for consideration and provision to the Parties of panel or appellate body reports by the DSB. Moreover in case of consideration by a panel of a disagreement whether measures taken to comply with previous panel recommendations or rulings are consistent with a covered agreement, the panel shall attempt to issue a decision within 60 instead of 90 days.

Notwithstanding the significant reduction of the timelines, it is obvious that the dispute settlement system under the DSU, as modified by the GPA, is not designed to correct procedural or other mistakes during a pending procurement

---

[371] For the standard definition of these procedures, which are said to be little used, *see* S. Arrowsmith, *supra* note 284, at 367.

action. The DSU procedures and measures are intergovernmental and post-facto in nature. Accordingly, they do not offer immediate relief to private sector suppliers that have participated as bidders, or may have had an interest in the opportunity to participate, in a competitive procurement.[372]

The panel will receive written submissions[373] from the Parties and consult with them to give them "adequate opportunity to develop a mutually satisfactory solution".[374] When no such solution is found, the panel shall submit its findings in a written report to the DSB, setting out "the findings of fact, the applicability of relevant provisions and the basic rationale behind any findings and recommendations that it makes".[375] Panel deliberations shall be confidential, any opinion expressed by individual panellists shall be anonymous and the report shall be drafted without the presence of the Parties.[376]

### g.) composition and decision-making procedure of the DSB

In cases arising under the GPA, only representatives of all Parties to the GPA, including those parties to the dispute, may participate in actions or decisions taken by the DSB.[377] The decision-making rule for the adoption of the panel's report is unique[378] and greatly favors adoption: within 60 days of the circulation of the panel report, the report "shall be adopted at a DSB meeting unless a party to the dispute formally notifies the DSB of its decision to appeal or the DSB decides by consensus not to adopt the report".[379] It naturally will be quite unlikely that a consensus against adoption is formed as this would amount to

---

[372] The same conclusion has been reached by I. Dendauw, *supra* note 343, at 254, including, in particular, an analysis of the provision in GPA art. XXII.3 empowering the DSB to authorize suspension of concessions and other obligations under the GPA or consultations regarding remedies when withdrawal of measures found to be in contravention of the GPA is not possible. However, as all measures by the DSB must be agreed by consensus, also authorization of any suspension is subject to acceptance by the Parties. A similar position has been taken by S. Arrowsmith, *supra* note 284, at 374-375.

[373] DSU art. 12.6.

[374] DSU art. 11.

[375] DSU art. 12.7.

[376] DSU art. 14.

[377] DSU art. 2.1.

[378] J. Klabbers, *supra* note 140, at 268-269 (2002).

[379] DSU art. 16.4.

unanimity. Moreover, effective consultations with the parties to the dispute can remove incentives to appeal. Should other Parties wish to dissent, they may express their views on the panel report, provided that this shall be without prejudice to the adoption procedure.[380]

### h.) the appellate review body[381]

The standing Appellate Body is composed of seven persons appointed by the DSB for staggered four-year terms, subject to re-appointment once. The members shall be unaffiliated with any government, avoid participation in disputes that would create conflicts of interest and be of "recognized authority, with demonstrated expertise in law, international trade and the subject matter of the covered agreements generally".[382]

Only parties to the dispute may appeal a panel report, but third parties with a substantial interest may make written submissions to and be heard by the Appellate Body.[383] An appeal shall be limited to issues of law already covered in the panel report and legal interpretations developed by the panel.[384] The proceedings normally shall not exceed 60 days, and in no case 90 days, from the date the Appellate Body is notified of the decision to appeal.[385] The Appellate Body shall address each of the legal issues[386] raised in the appeal and may uphold, modify or reverse the legal findings and conclusions of the panel.[387]

The report of the Appellate Body shall be adopted by the DSB and unconditionally accepted by the parties to the dispute, unless the DSB decides by consensus not to adopt the report.[388] Thus, as is the case for adoption of panel

---

380 *Ibid.*

381 J. Lockhardt/T. Voon "Reviewing Appellate Review in the WTO Dispute Settlement System", 6 *MJIL* 474 (2005).

382 DSU art. 17.1-3.

383 DSU art. 17.4.

384 DSU art. 17.6.

385 DSU art. 17.5.

386 T. S. Voon/A. Yanovich, "The Facts Aside: The Limitation of WTO Appeals to Issues of Law", 40 *J. World Trade* 239 (2006).

387 DSU art. 17.12 and 13.

388 DSU art. 17.14.

reports, to prevent adoption, there must be a consensus against adoption, not merely for adoption. Under this "reverse consensus" procedure, the probability of the report not being adopted therefore is low.

### i.) remedies

In general, the DSB has authority to:

- make recommendations or give rulings on the matter in dispute
- maintain surveillance of implementation of recommendations and rulings
- authorize consultations regarding remedies when withdrawal of measures found to be in contravention of the GPA is not possible.

Where a panel or an Appellate Body concludes that a measure of a Party is inconsistent with a covered agreement, it shall recommend that the Party bring the non-compliant measure into conformity with the covered agreement.[389] The steps taken by the Party to comply with the recommendations will be monitored by the DSB. In the event the recommendations of the Appellate Body are not implemented within a reasonable time or the Party concerned otherwise fails to comply with the recommendations and rulings, the Party shall, upon request, enter into negotiations with the complaining Party "with a view to developing mutually acceptable compensation".[390]

The available remedies distinguish the general DSU dispute settlement system for disputes arising under any of the covered agreements, other than the GPA, from the dispute settlement system for disputes involving the GPA. On one hand, the GPA in its Article XXII.7[391] excludes both suspension of a Party's concessions or other obligations under a covered agreement, other than the GPA, from the remedies available for the settlement of disputes arising under the GPA, and suspension of a Party's concessions or other obligations under the GPA in a

---

389 DSU art. 19.

390 DSU art. 22.2.

391 GPA art. XXII.7 excludes the suspension of concessions or other obligations under the GPA, in case of a dispute arising under a covered agreement other than the GPA, and, in the event of a dispute arising under the GPA, of concessions or other obligations under such other covered agreement.

dispute arising under one of the other covered agreements. On the other hand, only the GPA, but not the DSU, offers the challenge procedure for suppliers to address procurement infringements.[392] These differences are fully justified by the fact that, due to the difference in subject matter of the instruments, the urgency of remedying an infringement of the GPA in the case of a concrete, pending procurement is incomparably greater than the need to remedy infringements of the general conditions for trade laid down in the other covered agreements. While the GPA does lay down general rules for the conduct of procurement actions, a dispute arising under the GPA normally will concern the conduct of a concrete procurement, rather than the actual observance of general conditions for international trade as set out in the other covered trade agreements, whether multilateral or plurilateral.

In evaluating the role of the DSU for the settlement of GPA disputes it is noticeable that the number of cases since 1 January 1995, i.e. under the new GPA, is quite modest. Even when considering both complaints that have led to a panel report[393] and those that have been settled by mutual agreement and thus obviating a panel report, the DSU, in fact, appears to be considered as more appropriate for traditional trade disputes than for procurement grievances.

---

392 The question of the extent to which such "cross-retaliation" should be allowed was considered in the Uruguay Round of the multilateral trade negotiations during the preparation of the DSU. It was rejected with respect to the GPA *inter alia* due to requests by the developing countries and because procurement was considered an easy area to retaliate in and therefore bore the risk of being often selected for retaliation. A. Blank/G. Marceau, *supra* note 274, at 115.

393 *Korea – Measures Affecting Government Procurement* (WT/DS163/R) is the only known case resulting in a panel report, in which provisions of the new GPA were invoked, namely arts. I(1) and XXII:2. The dispute was brought by the United States and related to its claim that the GPA was applicable to the procuring entity for the construction of Inchon International Airport. The panel, in its report of 15 June 2000, found that the procuring entity was not covered and that the Korean authorities had not acted in bad faith. The actual conduct of procurement therefore was not a principal issue. The panel report was not appealed. S. Arrowsmith, *supra* note 284, at 363-364 (2003). A succinct summary of the case can be found in a Note by A. W. H. Gourly/J. Heilman Grier/F. F. Shaheen, "International Procurement", 35 *Int'l L.* 400-404 (2001).

Moreover, it can appear to be optional whether to characterize a dispute as a trade[394] or as a procurement[395] dispute.

## C. Distinctions Between the GPA and the United Nations Procurement Rules

The foregoing description reveals that although the GPA in large measure pursues the same or similar objectives as the United Nations procurement rules, there are significant procedural and structural differences.

While the GPA's procurement procedures are comprehensive and detailed, the United Nations rules address procedure selectively since they mainly reflect concern with financial and legal control. The transparency of procurement actions conducted in accordance with GPA's procedure rise to a level not reached by procurement done in accordance with the United Nations Financial Regulations and Rules, and the GPA additionally strengthens transparency by provi-

---

394 In the case of *Korea – Laws, Regulations and Practices in the Telecommunications Procurement Sector* (WT/DS40/1) the European Community alleged the Korean Government had infringed GATT by regulating procurement by government agencies in a manner that excluded European suppliers from 90% of the market and favoured products from the United States. No violation of the GPA was alleged, however. – On 29 October 1997, the DSB received notification from the Parties that they had reached a mutually satisfactory solution to the dispute. (WT/DS40/2).

395 In two cases violations of the GPA were alleged: In its complaint of 26 March 1997, the European Community in the case of *Japan – Procurement of a Navigation Satellite* (WT/DS73/1) contended that the specifications in a tender for a satellite for air traffic management were not neutral but referred explicitly to specifications of the United States and, accordingly, alleged violation of several provisions of the GPA. – On 31 July 1997, the European Community notified the DSB that an agreed solution had been reached with Japan (WT/DS73/4/Rev.1) and on 19 February 1998 the Parties communicated the text of their agreement to the DSB (WT/DS73/5). In the second case: *United States – Measures Affecting Government Procurement* (WT/DS/88) the European Community referred to an Act of the Commonwealth of Massachusetts prohibiting public authorities of that federal State from procuring goods and services from any person doing business with Burma (now Myanmar) and alleged this to violate provisions of the GPA. As Japan had raised a complaint on the same subject in case WT/DS95, the DSB established a single panel to consider both complaints. – On 11 February 2000 the authority for the panel lapsed, pursuant to DSU art. 12.12, since it had not been requested to resume its work. (WT/DS88/1, 4 and 6; WT/DS95/4 and 6). The Massachusetts case has been summarized in the Note by A. W. H. Gourley/J. Heilman Grier/F. F. Shaheen, *supra* note 393, at 404-405, which informs that the request for suspension of the panel followed upon a permanent injunction by the United States District Court holding the Massachusetts Act unconstitutional, whereupon the US Supreme Court on 19 June, 2000, also held the Act to be unconstitutional as being preempted by Federal Law and therefore invalid under the supremacy clause of the US Constitution.

sions on mandatory disclosure of information on procurement, which have no counterpart in the United Nations regime.

Regarding dispute settlement, there are significant, indeed structural, differences.

Firstly, with respect to post-facto intervention at the intergovernmental level, the United Nations has no pre-established system or procedure for resolving procurement disputes between or with its Member States. This does not exclude recourse to well-known methods such as negotiation, consultation, mediation or arbitration, but any method is subject to prior acceptance by the parties. In contrast, the GPA in conjunction with the DSU possesses pre-established, mandatory, comprehensive procedures for dispute settlement through consultations, amicable settlement and review by panels and appellate bodies. Moreover, the effectiveness of recommendations and rulings of panels and appellate bodies are not qualified by the need to obtain the agreement of the parties, or of reaching a consensus on the measure in question, but are automatically binding, unless a contrary consensus should emerge.

Secondly, the GPA entitles a bidder to challenge decisions of the procuring entity both during and after the award. A challenge may result in interim measures to correct procurement decisions inconsistent with the GPA and to preserve commercial opportunities, which is imaginable for pre-award challenges seeking either correction of a procedural breach or award of compensation. By leaving the initiative to actual or potential bidders, and by its promptness, the challenge procedure provides an effective means of policing procurement entities for the purpose of ensuring compliance with the applicable procedures and award criteria.

Finally, the content and structure of United Nations Financial Regulations and Rules show that they are intended to serve as instructions and delegations of authority to staff members of the Organization, but not as a statement informing external parties, including suppliers participating in procurement actions of procedures to be followed by the Secretariat's Procurement Service or offering grounds for a cause of action or claim by an external party in case they are infringed. The GPA clearly differs in that its provisions are addressed to both external suppliers and Member States, as well as to procuring entities, and that violations constitute grounds for legal redress under established dispute settlement schemes.

# V. FINDINGS OF THE INDEPENDENT INQUIRY COMMITTEE

## A. The Independent Inquiry Committee

### *1. Establishment*

In response to insistent allegations of serious abuse, the Secretary-General on 21 April 2004 announced that he had established an independent panel to conduct an inquiry into the "allegations of impropriety in the administration and management of the Iraq Oil-for-Food Programme".[396] The Panel was named "Independent Inquiry Committee Into The United Nations Oil-for-Food Programme" (hereinafter the "IIC"). The establishment was reported without delay to the United Nations Security Council, which immediately adopted resolution 1538 (2004),[397] in which the Security Council, inter alia, in the resolution's preambular part, *expressed* its concern at public criticism levelled at the administration and management of the Oil-for-Food Programme, *affirmed* that any illicit activity by United Nations officials, personnel or agents, as well as contractors, is unacceptable, *emphasized* the importance of full cooperation with the IIC inquiry by all United Nations officials and personnel, the Coalition Provisional Authority, Iraq and Member States and, thereupon, in the resolution's operational part, *welcomed* the appointment of the independent high-level inquiry and *called upon* the Coalition Provisional Authority, Iraq and all other Member States including their national regulatory authorities, to cooperate fully by all appropriate means with the inquiry.

The panel comprised three distinguished members: Paul Volcker, the former Governor of the United States Federal Reserve System, as chairman, and as members, Richard Goldstone, formerly a Justice of the Constitutional Court of South Africa and Chief Prosecutor of the United Nations International Criminal Tribunals for the former Yugoslavia and Rwanda, and Mark Pieth, Professor of Criminal Law and Criminology at the University of Basel, Switzerland.

The IIC has been assisted by its own staff of about 75 investigators, lawyers, forensic accountants and support personnel. Although the Secretary-General

---

396 United Nations Press Statement of 21 April 2004, available at http://www.un.org/News (last visited 22 March 2005).

397 S/RES/1538(2004).

appointed the members of the IIC, the IIC was established as an independent body and not as a part the Secretariat. Nevertheless, the Secretary-General gave it the right of access to all relevant records and documents of the United Nations and, to ensure that effective use could be made of the right of access, instructed[398] all United Nations staff members "to cooperate fully with the inquiry" and "to give the inquiry unrestricted access, without prior approval, to all documents and information" and further "not to destroy or remove any documents related to the oil-for-food programme that are in their possession or under their control, and not to instruct or allow any one else to destroy or remove such documents". In addition, the Committee was permitted to interview all relevant United Nations officials and personnel and to seek cooperation from Member States to conduct its inquiry.[399]

## 2. *Mandate*

The Terms of Reference of the IIC[400] were extensive and comprehensive. They included the investigation of possible violations of the established procurement procedures, of whether any United Nations officials, personnel, agents or contractors had engaged in illicit or corrupt activities under the Oil-for-Food programme and of whether the transactions had been correctly accounted for. A closer examination of the Terms of Reference shows that the scope of the investigation was not limited to violations of an administrative or civil law nature, but extended to possible criminal infractions.[401] The IIC did not possess any law

---

398 Secretary-General's bulletin of 1 June 2004, ST/SGB/2004/9. The instruction also applied to "all electronic files, including e-mail and information on hard drives, shared drives, floppy disks and CD-ROM, as well as to all paper copies of documents, including hand-written notes, calendars and any other materials relating to the programme."

399 United Nations Press Statement of 21 April 2004, available at http://www.un.org/News (last visited 22 March 2005).

400 *See* http://www.iic-offp.org.

401 *See* http://www.iic-offp.org on the IIC's Terms of Reference: "The independent inquiry shall collect and examine information relating to the administration and management of the Oil-for-Food Programme, including allegations of fraud and corruption on the part of United Nations officials, personnel and agents, as well as contractors, including entities that have entered into contracts with the United Nations or with Iraq under the Programme:

> to determine whether the procedures established by the Organization, including the Security Council and the Security Council Committee Established by Res. 661 (1990) Concerning the Situation between Iraq and Kuwait (hereinafter referred to as the "661 Committee") for the processing and approval of contracts under the Programme, and the monitoring of sale and de-

enforcement powers, however, and therefore any evidence uncovered could only be prosecuted by the already existing authorities at the national and international levels.

In view of its mandate and the foregoing arrangements, it must be concluded that the IIC was equipped with fully adequate formal powers and practical facilities to enable it to discharge its mandate in an effective, impartial and objective manner. Not only the competence and integrity of the IIC members, but also the grant of access to information and the corresponding obligations imposed on United Nations staff, as well as on its agents and contractors and on Member States, to cooperate, do confirm, in conjunction with the resources made available, the sincerity of the intent behind the launching of the inquiry as well as the authoritative nature of the IIC's factual findings.

Regarding the obligation to cooperate, it is, for the sake of precision, necessary to distinguish according to the categories of the addressees of this obligation, since the nature of the respective obligations differs. United Nations staff members are directly bound by the Staff Regulations and were notified by the Secretary-General's above-mentioned bulletin[402] of the applicability to the inquiry of Staff Regulation 1.2(r), according to which they "must respond fully to requests for information from staff members and other officials of the Organization authorized to investigate misuse of funds, waste or abuse". United Nations personnel other than staff members, i.e. its agents or contractors, were not addressed by the bulletin but may have had similar obligations under their respective contracts or agreements with the United Nations. Accordingly, these categories were mentioned only in the preamble[403] of Security Council resolution

---

livery of petroleum and petroleum products and purchase and delivery of humanitarian goods, were violated, bearing in mind the respective roles of United Nations officials, personnel and agents, as well as entities that have entered into contracts with the United Nations or with Iraq under the Programme;
to determine whether any United Nations officials, personnel agents, or contractors engaged in any illicit or corrupt activities in the carrying out of their respective roles in relation to the Programme, including, for example, bribery in relation to oil sales, abuses in regard to surcharges on oil sales and illicit payments in regard to purchases of humanitarian goods;
to determine whether the accounts of the Programme were in order and were maintained in accordance with the Financial Regulations and Rules of the United Nations."

402 ST/SGB/2004/9.

403 S/RES/1538 (2004) 4th recital: *Emphasizing* the importance of full cooperation with the independent high-level inquiry by all United Nations officials and personnel, the Coalition Provisional Authority, Iraq, and all other Member States."

1538 (2004), which is considered not to be directly operational.[404] In contrast, Member States, including those belonging to the Coalition Provisional Authority and Iraq, and agencies of Member States were addressed by the operational part of the same Security Council resolution, namely its operative paragraph 2,[405] which *calls upon* them to "cooperate fully by all appropriate means with the inquiry." As the resolution does not employ the term "decision", it does not derive binding force from Article 25 of the Charter of the United Nations.[406] In the event, however, that a Member State should decline to cooperate in a situation where appropriate means are considered to be available to it, the Member State arguably will have defaulted on an implied duty arising under Articles 2.2 and 2.5 of the Charter in good faith to comply with a legitimate request of the Security Council and thus be exposed to disapproval and suspicion by other Member States.[407] In a serious case, the Security Council could qualify such disregard as "likely to endanger the maintenance of international peace and security" pursuant to Article 34 or as "a threat to the peace" under Article 39 of the Charter.[408]

## B. The Iraq Oil-for-Food Programme

### *1. Mandate from the Security Council*

In response to Iraq's invasion of Kuwait in 1990, the United Nations Security Council, acting under Chapter VII of the Charter, had adopted resolution 661 (1990) prohibiting imports from and exports to Iraq. On 14 April 1995, due to increasing concern at the deteriorating nutritional and health situation of the Iraqi

---

404 The term "operational" is used to denote a provision that gives rise to a legal duty, obligation or right.

405 S/RES/1538 (2004) operative para. 2: "*Calls upon* the Coalition Provisional Authority, Iraq, and all other Member States, including their national regulatory authorities, to cooperate fully by all appropriate means with the inquiry."

406 It is a commonly accepted view that only decisions taken by the Security Council are binding on Member States and that decisions are distinguishable from mere recommendations. *See* P. Sands/P. Klein, *supra* note 191, at 46, referring to the majority view in the International Court of Justice's *Corfu Channel case* (Judgment of 9 April 1949, *ICJ Reports* 4 (1949)) that the Security Council's recommendation to the Parties (United Kingdom and Albania) to refer their dispute to the ICJ did not create a legal obligation to do so.

407 *See also* M. Hilaire, *United Nations Law and the Security Council* 1-24 (2005).

408 *See further* J. Klabbers, *supra* note 140, at 222-223.

population, the Security Council, again acting under Chapter VII of the Charter, by resolution 986 (1995)[409] established the Iraq Oil-for-Food Programme (hereinafter the "Programme"), permitting Member States to import a limited quantity of petroleum and petroleum products from Iraq and providing that the proceeds from the sales should be used primarily to finance essential supplies of a humanitarian nature for the civilian population of Iraq.[410] [411] The Programme was made subject to certain control measures and to the following conditions for its implementation:

a.) Each purchase required prior application to and approval by a committee of the Security Council (known as the "661 Committee").

b.) The State wishing to import had to submit an application, endorsed by the Government of Iraq, for each proposed purchase.

c.) Payment of the full amount of each purchase should be made into an escrow account to be established by the Secretary-General for the purpose of implementing the resolution. The Secretary-General also was requested to "appoint independent and certified public accountants to audit" the escrow account and to keep the Government of Iraq fully informed.

d.) With the assistance of independent inspection agents to be appointed by the Secretary-General, the 661 Committee[412] was to monitor the sale of

---

409 S/RES/986 (1995).

410 Additionally, lesser shares of the proceeds were used to meet compensation claims arising from Iraq's invasion of Kuwait and to defray the administrative cost of the Programme.

411 Security Council Res. 661 (1990) and 986 (1995) did not specify under which Article of Chapter VII they had been adopted. The initial resolution (Res. 660 (1990)), condemning the invasion by Iraq and calling for withdrawal, had been adopted under art. 39 on the determination of the existence of any threat to the peace, breach of the peace, or act of aggression and art. 40 on provisional measures. The imposition of the oil embargo by Res. 661 (1990) and establishment of the oil-for-food programme by Res. 986 (1995) would seem to fit better under art. 41, however. On peacekeeping measures *generally*, *see* J. Abr. Frowein, "Arts. 39-43", in B. Simma (ed.), *The Charter of the United Nations* Vol. I, 648 (2002).

412 The committee had been established previously under Security Council Res. 661 (1990) of 6 August 1990. The committee consisted of all members of the Council and, according to operative para. 6 of that resolution was mandated to undertake the following tasks and to report on its work to the Council:

"(a) to examine the reports on the progress of the implementation of the present resolution which will be submitted by the Secretary-General;

petroleum and petroleum products to be exported through two designated points in Iraq.

e.) The funds in the escrow accounts were to be used by the Secretary-General to finance the export to Iraq of medicine, health supplies, foodstuffs, and materials and supplies for essential civilian needs, provided that (i) each shipment of goods was at the request of the Government of Iraq and that (ii) Iraq guaranteed their equitable distribution on the basis of a United Nations plan and that (iii) the Secretary-General received authenticated confirmation that the goods had arrived in Iraq.

The resolution further requested the Secretary-General to take the actions necessary to ensure its effective implementation, authorized him to enter into any necessary arrangements or agreements and to report thereon to the Security Council.

## 2. *Memorandum of Understanding with the Government of Iraq*

The Iraqi Government held up the negotiations on arrangements for implementation until early in 1996.[413] Pursuant to Security Council resolution 986 (1995), the Legal Counsel as authorized by the Secretary-General negotiated and, on 20 May 1996, concluded a "Memorandum of Understanding between the Secretariat of the United Nations and the Government of Iraq on the implementation of Security-Council resolution 986 (1995)" which included two Annexes constituting integral parts of the Memorandum.[414]

The Memorandum of Understanding set out agreed modalities for implementation of the Iraq Oil-for-Food Programme in accordance with Security Council

---

(b) To seek from all States further information regarding the action taken by them concerning the effective implementation of the provisions laid down in the present resolution."

413 In a letter of 1 June 1995 to the Security Council, the Secretary-General reported on objections by the Government of Iraq to implementation of Security Council Res. 986 (1995) and by the reply letter of 23 June 1995, the President of the Council conveyed that the members of the Council accepted "that cooperation from the Government of Iraq is an essential prerequisite for the implementation of the resolution" and hoped the Secretary-General would "take the opportunity of your contacts with the Government of Iraq to obtain its agreement to the implementation of the resolution." United Nations documents S/1995/495 and S/1995/507, respectively.

414 United Nations document S/1996/356 (1996). The text of the Memorandum of Understanding, including its two Annexes, and of a side letter from the head of the delegation of Iraq addressed to the Legal Counsel, were reported to the Security Council on 20 May 1996.

resolution 986 (1995). It is pertinent for the procurement actions subsequently investigated by the IIC to recall the following provisions on modalities agreed in the Memorandum:

a.) Paragraph 12 provided that "the Secretary-General, after consultations with the Government of Iraq, will select a major international bank and establish there the escrow account described in paragraph 7 of the Resolution, to be known as 'the United Nations Iraq Account' (hereinafter the 'Iraq Account'). The Secretary-General will negotiate the terms of this account with the bank and will keep the Government of Iraq fully informed of his actions in choosing the bank and opening the account. All transactions and deductions mandated by the Security Council under paragraph 8 of the Resolution shall be made from the 'Iraq Account', which will be administered in accordance with the relevant Financial Regulations and Rules of the United Nations." According to paragraph 14, the Iraq Account "in accordance with the Financial Regulations of the United Nations" would be "audited by the Board of Auditors who are external independent public auditors".[415]

b.) Regarding the sale of petroleum and petroleum products, paragraph 17 provided that each export should be approved by the 661 Committee. In this respect, Annex II to the Memorandum provided that a State wishing to purchase should submit an application to the 661 Committee, containing the contractual documents and the endorsement of the Government of Iraq, for the proposed purchase.[416] The purchaser's bank would open irrevocable confirmed letters of credit payable directly to

---

[415] According to United Nations Financial Regulation 12.1 (ST/SGB/Financial Rules/1/Rev.3 (1985): "The General Assembly shall appoint a board of auditors to perform the audit of the accounts of the United Nations. This board shall consist of three members, each of whom shall be the Auditor-General (or officer holding the equivalent title) of a Member State." While Regulation 12.6 provided that "The Board of Auditors shall be completely independent and solely responsible for the conduct of the audit", other provisions, such as Regulations 12.4, 7 and 11 empowered the General Assembly – but not individual Member States – to give directions on specific matters. The revised Financial Regulations contained in ST/SGB/2003/7 have not introduced any substantive change in this regard.

[416] The requirement of endorsement by the Government of Iraq reiterated the provision of operative paragraph 1(a) of Security Council resolution 986 (1995) requiring that approval by the 661 Committee of oil purchases be based on "an application by the State concerned, endorsed by the Government of Iraq, for each proposed purchase of Iraqi petroleum and petroleum products."

the Iraq Account and directed to the bank holding the Iraq Account, which, in turn would add its own confirmation and forward the letter of credit to the Central Bank of Iraq.[417] The sale of petroleum and petroleum products from Iraq would be monitored by independent oil experts appointed by the Secretary-General and the actual oil exports would be monitored at the loading facilities at the designated export points by independent inspection agents reporting to the United Nations.

c.) Regarding the purchase of the humanitarian supplies permitted by Security Council resolution 986 (1995), paragraphs 19-22 provided that, the purchases would, except for supplies for the three northern (Kurdish) Governorates, "follow normal commercial practices", "be carried out by the Government of Iraq" and that "the Government of Iraq will... contract directly with suppliers to arrange the purchase of suplies, and will conclude the appropriate contractual arrangements". Paragraph 22 of the Memorandum referred to the requirement, stated in operative paragraph 8(a)(i) of Security Council resolution 986 (1995), that "each export of goods shall be at the request of Iraq" and in accordance with the procedures established by the resolution. Exporting States accordingly were required to submit all relevant documentation, including contracts, for all goods to be exported to the 661 Committee for its action.

d.) Purchases of humanitarian supplies required further approvals from the Government of Iraq. According to paragraphs 24-25 of the Memorandum, after appropriate action by the 661 Committee, the Central Bank of Iraq would request the bank holding the "Iraq Account" to open irrevocable letters of credit in favour of the beneficiaries of the approved contracts for humanitarian supplies. These requests would be referred to the United Nations Secretariat for its approval of the opening of a letter of credit permitting payment against presentation of credit-conform documents. The arrival of goods in Iraq further would be confirmed by independent inspectors to be appointed by the Secretary-General and it was expressly provided that "no payment can be made until the independent inspection agents provide the Secretary-General with authenticated confirmation that the exported goods have arrived in Iraq."

---

417 That the bank holding the escrow account merely confirmed the letter of credit and then forwarded it to the Central Bank of Iraq was not foreseen in Security Council resolution 986 (1995) and gave a basis for the claim that the owner of the escrow account was Iraq, rather than the United Nations.

e.) Paragraph 45 referred to the provisions on privileges and immunities in the CPIUN[418] and in the CPISA[419] and made them applicable, as follows, to persons performing functions in connection with the implementation of Security Council resolution 986 (1995):

- Officials[420] of the United Nations or of any of the Specialized Agencies would enjoy the privileges and immunities under Articles V and VII of the CPIUN or Articles VI and VIII of CPISA, respectively.
- Independent inspection agents, technical experts and other specialists appointed by the Secretary-General or by heads of the specialized agencies, whose names were communicated to the Government of Iraq, would enjoy the privileges and immunities provided under the Conventions for experts on mission.
- Persons performing contractual services for the United Nations, whose names were communicated to the Government of Iraq, also would enjoy the privileges and immunities foreseen under the Conventions for experts on mission.

f.) Finally, concerning freedom of movement, paragraph 46 provided that the "officials, experts and other personnel referred to in paragraph 45 shall enjoy the right of unimpeded entry into and exit from Iraq and

---

418 1 *UNTS* 15 and 90 *UNTS* 327. Adopted by the General Assembly of the United Nations on 13 February 1946. Entered into force on 17 September 1946.

419 33 *UNTS* 261 and 290, and subsequent volumes. Approved by the General Assembly of the United Nations on 21 November 1947. Enters into force separately in respect of each specialized agency and for each State in accordance with its instrument of accession. For each specialized agency an Annex details the status of experts on mission. The Convention has entered into force in respect of seventeen specialized agencies, first in respect of the International Labour Organization on 14 September 1948 and last in respect of UNIDO on 15 September 1987. On 9 July 1964, Iraq acceded without reservation to the convention in respect of ILO, FAO, ICAO, UNESCO, IMF, IBRD, WHO, UPU, ITU and WMO.

420 In the case of the United Nations, "officials" include all members of the staff "except those who are recruited locally and assigned to hourly rates", *see* UN General Assembly Res. 76 (I) of 7 December 1946. For the specialized agencies, analogous definitions apply.

shall be issued visas[421] by the Iraqi authorities promptly and free of charge." The grant in paragraph 44 to United Nations personnel of "unrestricted freedom of movement" within Iraq was modified by the qualifying phrase "in connection with the performance of their functions" and their "access to documentary material which they find relevant" was limited by the phrase "having discussed the matter with the Iraqi authorities concerned."

## C. Legal Framework for Implementation of the Oil-for-Food Programme

### 1. *The Security Council Resolution, the Memorandum of Understanding and Procurement*

#### a.) scope of the resolution and of the memorandum

As can be seen from the foregoing, the conditions set out in the mandate from the Security Council established the cornerstones of the legal framework for implementing the programme while more detailed arrangements were laid down in the Memorandum of Understanding with the Government of Iraq concluded in accordance with the mandate from the Security Council. The Memorandum amplified the conditions laid down in resolution 986 (1995) of the Security

---

[421] The statement on p. 48 of Vol. III of IIC's Report on the Management of the Oil-for-Food Programme, dated 7 September 2005, that no visa had been required for the inspectors of the United Nations Special Commission (UNSCOM), established to implement Security Council Res. 687 (1991) of 3 April 1991 on Iraq, is at variance with the formulation of the agreement between the United Nations and Iraq that entered into force on 14 May 1991. The rights of access and of inspection within Iraq were less conditional in the earlier agreement, however. That agreement provided *inter alia:*

> "Unrestricted freedom of entry and exit, without delay or hindrance of personnel, property, supplies, equipment, spare parts and other items as well as means of transport, including expeditious issuance of entry and exit visas;"
> "Unrestricted freedom of movement without advance notice within Iraq of the personnel of the Special Commission and its equipment and means of transport;"
> "The right to request, receive, examine and copy any record, data or information or examine, retain, move or photograph, including videotape, any item relevant to the Special Commission's activities and to conduct interviews;"

*See* Report of the Secretary-General to the Security Council of 25 January 1992, United Nations document S/23514, and further available at http://www.un.org/Depts/unscom/General/basicfacts.

Council, in particular by providing procedural and operational details. Consequently, in order for the Secretary-General to proceed with implementation of key operational tasks, the Memorandum foresaw the need for the Secretariat to undertake three procurement actions to select and retain suppliers to provide:

- Banking services for the establishment and operation of the escrow account, i.e. the "Iraq Account"
- On-site-inspection in Iraq of the quantity and quality of oil to be exported from Iraq under the Programme
- On-shore-inspection of Programme-financed humanitarian goods and supplies entering Iraq.

The engagement of external suppliers of these activities was necessary due to the unavailability of the necessary capacity and capabilities within the Secretariat of the United Nations. It would not only have been prohibitively costly and managerially questionable to attempt discharging the mandate by Secretariat staff alone, but the attendant delay in implementation would have undermined the purpose of the Programme. Moreover, procuring from external sources had long been a well-established modality employed by the United Nations Secretariat to implement numerous, major and minor programmes ranging from the provision of technical assistance or health services to developing countries, over delivery of emergency relief to the construction of headquarters complexes. In the case of the Oil-for-Food Programme, extensive privileges and immunities[422] were granted for individual experts and the personnel of contractors. In particular, they enjoyed immunity from the jurisdiction of national authorities, including immunity from personal arrest and legal process of any kind, with respect to the performance of their functions.[423] Since the immunity was granted under the CPIUN, only the Secretary-General had the right and the duty to waive such immunity where, in his opinion, "the immunity would impede the course of justice and it can be waived without prejudice to the interests of the United Nations".[424] Similarly, immunities provided under an Annex to the CPISA could be waived only by the specialized agency concerned.

As further discussed in the following, the Memorandum of Understanding in important respects gave the Government of Iraq a decisive, indeed a controlling,

---

[422] Memorandum of Understanding, para. 45 (b) and (c). United Nations document S/1996/356.

[423] Art. VI, Section 25, of the CPIUN.

[424] Art. VI, Section 26, of the CPIUN.

influence on the operation of the Oil-for-Food Programme and in this respect went further than legally required by Security Council resolution 986 (1995).

### b.) the escrow account and the bank account

Security Council resolution 986 (1995), in operative paragraph 7, requested "the Secretary-General to establish an escrow account for the purposes of this resolution, to appoint independent and certified public accountants to audit it, and to keep the Government of Iraq fully informed" and, in operative paragraph 8, decided "that the funds in the escrow account shall be used to meet the humanitarian needs of the Iraqi population and for the following other purposes,..." The resolution thus specified the purposes for which the Secretary-General was requested to use the funds in the escrow account, but did not give any further instructions about banking or accounting details. Although the term "escrow account" is not expressly mentioned in the Financial Regulations and Rules of the United Nations, the notion is fully compatible with the well-known instruments of trust fund or special accounts as referred to in Financial Regulations 6.6 and 6.7.[425] These are internal "book-keeping" accounts used to account for funds that are earmarked for specified purposes so as to ensure that the assets of each such fund or account are kept separately from other funds in other internal accounts. In practice, the internal "book-keeping" accounts outnumber by far the few external bank accounts established with commercial or public banks, as necessary, for the purpose of investing and safekeeping deposits and carrying out financial transactions, e.g. payment of staff and contractors. Accordingly, and considering that the Security Council resolution did not explicitly lay down any instruction on whether or not to open one or more external accounts with a bank for the purpose of the Oil-for-Food Programme, the Security Council presumably intended the escrow account to be an internal account of the United Nations,

---

425 ST/SGB/Financial Rules/1/Rev.3 (1985):
Financial Regulation 6.6: "Trust funds, reserve and special accounts may be established by the Secretary-General and shall be reported to the Advisory Committee."
Financial Regulation 6.7: "The purpose and limits of each trust fund, reserve and special account shall be clearly defined by the appropriate authority. Unless otherwise provided by the General Assembly, such funds and accounts shall be administered in accordance with the present Regulations."
ST/SGB/2003/7:
Financial Regulation 6.2: "Appropriate separate accounts shall be maintained for all trust funds and reserve and special accounts."

similar to the numerous trust fund accounts used to earmark funds for multiyear expenditure purposes outside the biennial Regular Budget[426] accounts.

That the escrow account, including the funds to be deposited therein, was intended as an account of the United Nations is clear and is emphasized by the fact that the Security Council in paragraph 15 of its resolution 986 (1995) affirmed "that the escrow account established for the purposes of this resolution enjoys the privileges and immunities of the United Nations". In as much as the privileges and immunities of the United Nations are governed by the Charter and the CPIUN, the Security Council could not legally have conferred such status on an account of a Member Government, nor on an account held jointly by the United Nations and a Member Government.

### c.) consultations with the Government of Iraq

The Memorandum of Understanding in its paragraph 12 referred to the Secretary-General's intent to "select a major international bank and establish there the escrow account described in paragraph 7 of the Resolution...." In the same provision the commitment was made that the Secretary-General would take such action "after consultations with the Government of Iraq." In this manner, the United Nations assumed legal obligations towards the Government of Iraq regarding both the internal escrow account and the external bank account without there being any obligation deriving from Security Council resolution 986 (1995) to do so: the resolution merely had requested the Secretary-General "to keep the Government of Iraq fully informed" and, as will be detailed below, the commitment to act "after consultations with the Government of Iraq" on the selection of the bank to handle the escrow account did not imply a joint decision by the United Nations and Iraq, nor the Government making the final selection.

### d.) approval by the Government of Iraq

It was fully in accordance with requirements laid down in Security Council resolution 986 (1995) that the Memorandum of Understanding made each purchase of Iraqi petroleum or petroleum products for export from Iraq or each sale of humanitarian supplies for shipment to Iraq, subject to prior approval by the Government of Iraq. Nevertheless, the need to obtain governmental approval

---

426 The Regular Budget is biannual and financed by the mandatory contributions assessed on Member States by the General Assembly.

lessened the degree of control that could be (and should have been) maintained by the United Nations and became a vehicle for corrupt practices involving Iraqi authorities and many of the firms seeking business opportunities as purchasers of oil or sellers of goods and supplies under the Programme.[427]

### 2. *Establishment of the Iraq Steering Committee in the Secretariat*[428]

On 28 May 1996,[429] the Secretary-General established the Iraq Steering Committee to "ensure the timely and effective implementation" of the Oil-for-Food Programme and to report to him "on a regular basis." An Under-Secretary-General and Senior Advisor to the Secretary-General chaired the Steering Committee and also its five other members were senior officials that were heads of the departments responsible for the central services charged with implementing the Programme.[430]

The Steering Committee worked by consensus and had no formal rules, terms of reference or written records. Possibly due to such a high degree of informality, the Interim Report had the opportunity to note the consideration by the Steering Committee of the questions "whether the selection of the Programme's inspection contractors should conform to the standard competitive bidding rules" and "whether to use the normal Headquarters Contracts Committee or whether to establish itself as a special contracts committee".[431] On the first issue, the Steering Committee received and adhered, in part,[432] to written advice from the Office of Legal Affairs that "[p]rocurement of goods and services by the United Nations

---

427 The IIC has addressed these aspects in its reports of 7 September 2005 on the Management of the Oil-for-Food Programme and on the Impact of the Programme on the Iraqi People, as well as its report of 27 October 2005 on the Manipulation of the Oil-for-Food Programme. These aspects and the related procurement actions fall outside the scope of the present thesis.

428 (First) Interim Report, Independent Inquiry Committee into the United Nations Oil-for-Food Programme, 3 February 2005, 69-71, available at http://www.iic-offp.org/documents/Interim Report Feb2005.pdf (last visited 15 February 2008).

429 *Ibid.*, at 69 and fn. 66.

430 The five members were the Under-Secretary-General for Humanitarian Affairs, the Under-Secretary-General for Administration and Management, the Under-Secretary-General for Legal Affairs, the Undersecretary-General for Political Affairs and the Assistant Secretary-General and Controller. Interim Report, *supra* note 428, at 69.

431 Interim Report, *supra* note 428, at 70-71.

432 The contract with the bank administering the escrow account, however, was let outside the established procedures and without review by the Contracts Committee.

should be done in accordance with the United Nations Financial Regulations and Rules".[433] That no express decision was taken on the second issue presumably implied that the normal Headquarters Contracts Committee was to be used as required by the Financial Regulations and Rules, while also the Steering Committee should play a role in the selection process.

## D. Procurement of Banking Services

### *1. The Nature of the Escrow Account and of Consultations with the Government of Iraq*

Security Council resolution 986 (1995) in its operative paragraph 7 had requested the Secretary-General "to establish an escrow account for the purposes of this resolution". While there was no explicit mention of an account in a bank, the common practice of the Secretariat was to open accounts in banks to safeguard the Organisation's funds and to carry out its financial transactions. It therefore was consistent with this practice that the Memorandum of Understanding with the Government of Iraq, in its operative paragraph 12, provided that "The Secretary-General will...select a major international bank and establish there the escrow account". The Memorandum, however, added a condition that had not been stated in the Security Council resolution, namely that the Secretary-General would act "after consultations with the Government of Iraq". This additional consultation obligation did not necessarily prevent the Secretary-General from acting independently of directions from the Government of Iraq, provided that it was understood correctly, namely in accordance with the well established legal opinion of the Secretariat that it expresses a commitment to undertake consultations and to give due consideration to the views expressed, but not an obligation to reach or to act in agreement.[434]

---

[433] Interim Report, *supra* note 428, at 70.

[434] A Note of 10 May 1962 to the Legal Counsel of the FAO reviewed the practice of the United Nations regarding the use of the expressions "in consultation with" and "after consultation with" in the Charter, in international agreements concluded under the auspices of the Organization or to which the Organization is a party, and in various resolutions of the principal organs. The Note in para. 1 stated "It appears clearly from the examination of these texts that the obligation "to consult with" was consistently construed as requiring the "consulting party" to seek the views of the party which was to be consulted and to give due consideration to the views expressed in reaching the decision as to the specific action to be taken. The consulting party was considered as having the sole responsibility for taking such final decisions as it considered appropriate in the

Considering that the capability of the Secretary-General to act independently of the Government of Iraq in selecting and contracting with a qualified bank constituted a crucial precondition for correct implementation of the procurement action in accordance with the Financial Regulations and Rules, the interpretation to be given to the expression "after consultations with the Government of Iraq" in the Memorandum of Understanding was of decisive importance.

### 2. *Choice of a Selection Procedure and Preparation of a List of Invitees*

According to the Interim Report of the IIC,[435] during the negotiations on the Memorandum of Understanding, Iraq had sought the right to "propose" the escrow bank to the United Nations, which, however, refused such an arrangement, and ultimately the parties agreed on the expression "after consultations with the Government". In this connexion, immediately after the signing of the Memorandum on 20 May 1996, the Permanent Representative of France to the United Nations received an inquiry from the Secretary-General who wished to know whether France could propose a suitable French Bank. On 22 May 1996, the Permanent Representative of France was informed by the Secretary-General of three French banks proposed by Iraq and asked for an indication of which French banks were possible candidates for handling the escrow account. Also, an Iraqi official stationed in Paris forwarded the name of a Swiss bank. Eventually, on 29 May 1996, a list of five French banks was forwarded to the United Nations by the Permanent Mission of France.

When one considers it was the normal practice of the United Nations to draw up lists of potential contractors to be invited to participate in competitive bidding, it does not appear these preliminary consultations involving Iraq, France and the Secretary-General necessarily constituted a deviation from, or caused prejudice to, the established procurement procedure. Nor does the IIC comment critically on this initial stage of the procurement action.

---

light of the consultations it previously held." Regarding the use in General Assembly resolutions, the Note in para. 33 indicated "that consultation is a process by which the views of the parties consulted are merely sought or ascertained and that the distinction is carefully made between the use of the expressions "in consultation with" or "after consultation with" and such expressions as "with the concurrence of". *UNJYB* 268-279 (1962). United Nations document ST/LEG/8. Legal Opinions of the Secretariat issued by the Office of Legal Affairs.

[435] Interim Report, *supra* note 428, at 73.

A member of the Steering Committee, the Controller, was requested by the Secretary-General to oversee the bank selection process and then proceeded together with the Director of Accounts and the Deputy Treasurer to prepare a list of potential escrow banks to be invited to submit competitive bids. According to objective criteria such as creditworthiness rating, amount of equity and operational capacity, an initial list of 17 banks was drawn up, which was reduced to 16 by the omission of the French bank BNP, apparently due to its low IBCA rating for creditworthiness of "B/C". There was only one other bank retained on the list with a B/C rating, but this bank, Tokyo-Mitsubishi, had a significantly higher equity of 33.2 billion US$ against BNP's equity of only 12.1 billion US$. On 28 May 1996, the slightly reduced list was reported by the Controller to the Secretary-General together with the proposal to forward the list to Iraq for its comments, whereupon a short list of 4-5 banks would be prepared for the purpose of soliciting further information on the services each bank could offer. This information also would be shared with Iraq and then, it was further proposed, the bank would be selected by the Secretary-General who would take into account the advice of the Steering Committee which would in the meantime have reviewed the short list.

In its "Findings and Conclusions",[436] the IIC merely offers the comment on the manner of selecting the escrow bank that "a competitive bid process was initiated but then not completed".[437] It is evident, however, from the IIC's account of the steps taken by the Secretariat's Iraq Steering Committee that the procedure proposed by the Controller amounted to by-passing the Procurement Services and the Headquarters Contracts Committee. It therefore constituted an infringement of the Financial Regulations and Rules, especially of Financial Rule 110.16(a),[438] providing that only authorized officials may invite proposals, negotiate and enter into contracts on behalf of the United Nations, and of Financial Rule 110.17(a),[439] requiring that written advice be given by the Headquarters Contracts Committee on proposed contracts. The circumstance that the contract

---

436 Interim Report, *supra* note 428, at 109-111. The "Findings and Conclusions" addressed the three questions posed by the IIC:

1) was the selection of the major contractors in 1996 conducted in accordance with the United Nations financial regulations and competitive bidding rules?

2) was the selection conducted in a fair and transparent manner?

3) were these selection processes free from improper or illicit influence?

437 Interim Report, *supra* note 428, at 110.

438 ST/SGB/Financial Rules/1/Rev.3 (1985).

439 *Ibid.*

to be concluded with the escrow bank was of a special kind, for which no ready precedent existed, cannot justify why the case was not reviewed by the Headquarters Contracts Committee. It may well have been the practice of Treasury to decide on the opening of bank accounts without recourse to the established competitive procurement procedure for the reasons that no management fee would be charged and that the service charges levied on accounts by the banks in Manhattan were identical or similar. The contemplated escrow account operation nevertheless should have been distinguished since it involved a very high value and volume of similar transactions and thus offered unusual profitability.[440] Consequently, the possibility of requesting interested banks to compete with regard to the level of their service charges, as well as in respect of their creditworthiness, equity and operational capacity, should have been pursued. The United Nations Financial Regulations and Rules, especially the reference in Financial Rule 110.16(a) to "contracts for the purchase, rental or sale of services, supplies, equipment or other requirements...", did not exclude such contracts from the procurement procedures they established. The very intention to select in a competitive process, is an argument in favour of applying the procedures established for this purpose. Finally, the fact that negotiation of the contractual terms eventually must be undertaken by the Secretariat's legal officers and on the basis of the bank's standard contract version, does not speak against following the established procurement procedures, including review by the interdepartmental Contracts Committee, nor against using the services of the authorized procurement officers.

### 3. *Consultations with the Government of Iraq on the Invitee List*

On 30 May 1996, the Controller provided the list of 16 banks to the Permanent Representative of Iraq to the United Nations, inviting his views while cautioning that responsibility for selection of the bank resided with the Secretary-General. On 1 June 1996, the Permanent Representative met with the Controller and stated the wish that the Secretary-General should select one of four banks, two French and two Swiss, which included BNP that had not been among the 16 banks on the Controller's list from the previous day. Having reported on the meeting to the Secretary-General, the Controller on 2 June 1996 issued a "Note

440 The service charges for certification of letters of credit that BNP would receive from the escrow account were estimated at four million US$. (Presumably, this is an annual amount). *See* Note on Steering Committee Meeting on 12 August 1996, prepared by Ms L. Buttenheim. Interim Report, 115-116.

to the Secretary-General",[441] stating in para.1 "In the light of comments received from the Government of Iraq yesterday, I suggest that the following banks be included in the short-list of the Secretary-General" and noting that "although BNP has a B/C rating, it has been included because of the preference of the Iraq Government." On 3 June 1996, the six banks short-listed by the Controller were invited to submit a proposal for provision of services by 10 June 1996. Further interventions followed by Iraqi diplomats to advise the Controller of their desire that either a French bank (BNP), a Swiss bank (Credit Suisse or UBS) or a German bank (Deutsche Bank) be selected.

The IIC concludes that in this as in the two other procurement cases investigated "preferred contractors emerged at an early stage of the selection process" and that accommodating the concerns of Iraq, reflected in the Memorandum of Understanding, that it be consulted with respect to the escrow bank was a "pervasive, but not exclusive, broadly 'political' influence".[442] This conclusion seems to be inescapable and it further appears the intensity of the above mentioned consultations must raise serious questions as to whether the Secretariat in fact acted in accordance with its own legal interpretation of "after consultations with",[443] i.e. without a sense of being bound to comply with the wishes of the representatives of the Iraqi Government on the short-listing of banks for further consideration.

### *4. Evaluation of the Proposals and Intervention by the United States*

Only four banks submitted proposals: BNP, Chase, Credit Suisse and UBS.[444] On 12 and 13 June 1996, Treasury prepared a comparative evaluation[445] of the proposals according to the criteria of investment income and of banking services for, respectively, oil sale, purchases and account support. Credit Suisse received the highest rating in all categories while the other three were rated significantly lower with BNP having the lowest cumulative rating.[446]

---

441 Interim Report, *supra* note 428, at 76.

442 Interim Report, *supra* note 428, at 110.

443 Memorandum of Understanding para. 12 and *supra* note 235 above. United Nations document S/1996/356.

444 Interim Report, *supra* note 428, at 77.

445 Interim Report, *supra* note 428, at 78.

446 Not the second lowest as mistakenly stated in the Interim Report, *supra* note 428, at 77.

On 14 June 1996, the Permanent Representative of the United States to the United Nations called on the Chairman of the Steering Committee to convey the view of the United States that it would be a mistake to select a Swiss bank for the reasons that Swiss banking laws lacked the transparency necessary to maintain the required oversight, that Switzerland was not a Member State of the United Nations, which would make it more difficult to enforce a resolution of the United Nations, and that Saddam Hussein, the President of Iraq, and members of his family maintained bank accounts in Switzerland.[447]

In its conclusions, the IIC has ranked the accommodation of the United States concerns about selection of a Swiss bank with the accommodation of Iraq's wish to be consulted as further examples of a need for decision-makers "to reconcile political concerns of some members" while, at the same time, "Objective criteria, such as the financial and procurement rules are designed to protect the integrity and effectiveness of the organization".[448]

From a legal viewpoint, the IIC's conclusion is too uncritical of the Secretariat's readiness to accommodate the political concerns. In particular, the conclusion overlooks the importance of the timing of the interventions. If only the ambassador of the United States had conveyed the concerns of her country earlier, they could legitimately have been taken into account when drawing up the initial list of invitees. By intervening after the banks had been invited and had submitted their proposals, however, she effectively requested the Secretariat to make an arbitrary and discriminatory decision to exclude proposals from consideration due to factors not stated in the solicitation documents and therefore, alone for this reason, extraneous to a fair and transparent selection process.

### 5. *The Final Selection by the Secretary-General*

On 18 June 1996, the Controller advised BNP that it had been selected to manage the escrow account. In his Interim Report[449] to the Security Council on the implementation of the Council's resolution 986 (1995), the Secretary-General reported that "a working list was prepared of major banks in all parts of the world" and that "after consultations with the Government of Iraq, a small num-

---

447 Interim Report, *supra* note 428, at 79-80, especially the Note to the File of 14 June 1986, prepared by Ms L. Buttenheim.

448 Interim Report, *supra* note 428, at 111.

449 Interim Report, dated 25 November 1996, of the Secretary-General on the Implementation of Security Council Res. 986 (1995), S/1996/978.

ber of those banks were asked to submit written proposals…". The reason for selecting BNP and not the bank with the best-rated proposal was not disclosed in the Secretary-General's report. In this connexion, the Controller has indicated to the IIC that the final selection was considered in the Steering Committee.[450] It appears, however, that the decision to select BNP was taken by the Secretary-General himself as he has informed the IIC that he contacted Iraq to inquire about the Government's choice among the short-listed banks and then concurred with the Government's preference.[451] Moreover, in a faxed statement to the IIC, the Secretary-General has explained that the selection "was done in agreement with the American delegation and the Iraqi delegation. It was a political decision to be able to implement the Memorandum of Understanding which was approved by the Security Council".[452]

Consistent with the foregoing view, the IIC has found that "the former Secretary-General chose a bank that was not the lowest acceptable bidder, and he did so for reasons that were not appropriately disclosed at the time".[453] The IIC also notes that no record was made of any justification of the Secretary-General's decision "in the interests of the Organization" as would have been required by Financial Rule 110.21 of the United Nations.[454] – These findings are convincingly supported by the IIC's account.

As noted above, the concern of the United States about selecting a Swiss bank, as well as the opposition of Iraq to using a bank domiciled in the United States, legitimately could have been taken into account by not inviting any bank from these countries to submit a proposal. It would have required the political consultations to have been finalised before issuing invitations, rather than being performed in parallel with the "bidding process". The resulting mismanagement of the selection process has created the appearance that the Secretary-General failed to honour the fundamental requirement of independence, stated in Article 100 of the Charter, to the effect that "In the performance of their duties, the Secretary-General and the staff shall not seek or receive instructions from any government or any authority external to the Organization". The same injunction is found in the formulation of the oath of office requiring members of the Secretariat – which includes the Secretary-General – "to discharge these functions and

---

[450] Interim Report, *supra* note 428, at 80-81.

[451] Interim Report, *supra* note 428, at 81-82.

[452] Interim Report, *supra* note 428, at 83.

[453] Interim Report, *supra* note 428, at 109-110.

[454] Interim Report p. 109; ST/SGB/Financial Rules/1/Rev.3 (1985).

regulate my conduct with the interests of the United Nations only in view, and not to seek or accept instructions in regard to the performance of my duties from any Government or other authority external to the Organization".[455] To overcome any appearance of a dichotomy between the duty to perform official duties only in the interests of the United Nations and the obligation to avoid to follow instructions from any government or any authority external to the Organization, it is necessary to distinguish between, on the one hand, mandates given by Member State Governments acting as members of an organ of the United Nations, such as the Security Council and the 661 Committee which are internal organs or authorities of the Organization, and, on the other hand, unilateral requests by Member State Governments acting e.g. through their Ministries of Foreign Affairs or Permanent Missions to the United Nations. In the latter case, Members State Governments qualify as authorities external to the Organisation.

## 6. *Preponderance of Political Considerations*

The haste in retaining a bank – only 29 days passed between the conclusion of the Memorandum of Understanding and the notification to BNP of its selection – and the by-passing of the Headquarters Contracts Committee and the Procurement Services prevented a more structured approach and prejudiced any possibility of acting in conformity with the established procurement procedures. It appears the fundamental reason for the approach taken and for the selection was the overall priority given to political considerations[456] that were conveyed through a chain of political authority running from individual Member State Governments over their diplomatic missions to the United Nations, via the Secretary-General, and through members of the Steering Committee and of the Department of Administration and Management to the Legal and then the Procurement Services. In this environment, the Secretariat evidently did not muster sufficient capacity to steer the procurement action and to withstand the pressures coming from the political actors.

[455] ST/SGB/Staff Regulations/Rev.23.

[456] By "political considerations" are in the present context meant considerations of a political nature that are extraneous and unrelated to the observance of the formally established procurement procedure.

## E. Procurement of Oil Export Inspection Services

### *1. Analysis of the Mandate*

The Secretary-General received the mandate to appoint independent inspection agents to monitor the sale of petroleum and petroleum products to be exported by Iraq under the Programme, under operative paragraph 6 of Security Council resolution 986 of 14 April (1995).[457] The mandate was amplified and modalities for its implementation agreed in paragraphs 16 to 18 of the Memorandum of Understanding with the Government of Iraq of 20 May 1996 and in its Annex II.[458] The independent inspection agents were to monitor the movement of oil out of Iraq, including verification of quantity and quality, and to authorize the loading after receiving confirmation from the "United Nations Oil experts" that the relevant contract had been approved. The term "United Nations Oil experts" referred to a few individual expert oil overseers who worked at United Nations Headquarters, were selected by and reported to the 661 Committee and, in particular, reviewed the price level of proposed contracts,[459] while the reference to "independent inspection agents appointed by the Secretary-General" eventually

---

457 Security Council Res. 986 (1995), operative para. 6: "*Directs* the Committee established by resolution 661 (1990) to monitor the sale of petroleum and petroleum products to be exported by Iraq via the Kirkuk-Yumurtalik pipeline from Iraq to Turkey and from the Mina al-Bakr oil terminal, with the assistance of independent inspection agents appointed by the Secretary-General, who will keep the Committee informed of the amount of petroleum and petroleum products exported from Iraq after the date of entry into force of paragraph 1 of this resolution, and will verify that the purchase price of the petroleum and petroleum products is reasonable in the light of prevailing market conditions, and that, for the purposes of the arrangements set out in this resolution, the larger share of the petroleum and petroleum products is shipped via the Kirkuk-Yumurtalik pipeline and the remainder is exported from the Mina al-Bakr oil terminal."

458 In particular, Ann. II, para. 4, to the Memorandum of Understanding provided: "The sale of petroleum and petroleum products originating in Iraq will be monitored by United Nations independent oil experts appointed by the Secretary-General of the United Nations to assist the 661 Committee. The monitoring of oil exports will be carried out by independent inspection agents at the loading facilities at Ceyhan and Mina al-Bakr and, if the 661 Committee so decides, at the pipeline metering station at the Iraq-Turkey border, and would include quality and quantity verification. They would authorize the loading, after they receive the information from the United Nations oil experts that the relevant contract has been approved, and report to the United Nations." United Nations document S/1996/356.

459 Interim Report, *supra* note 428, at 53. Para. 1 of the Procedures of the 661 Committee provided "The Committee will select, upon recommendation of the Secretariat of the Committee, at least four independent experts in international oil trade, to be appointed by the Secretary-General as 'overseers' at the United Nations Headquarters". S/1996/636 (1996).

did not refer to the appointment of individuals as such, but to the acquisition through procurement of the services of the personnel of an inspection company. In this respect, the formulation in Security Council resolution 986 (1995) is ambiguous: although "appointed" is a term more commonly used in the United Nations for retaining the services of individuals than of companies, "agents" is more commonly used to refer to companies or to organs than to appointed individuals. In principle, the modality of individual appointments would offer better control by the United Nations over the work than could be secured through a contract with a company, but only at the price of the presumably prohibitive efforts and cost of directing, administering and managing a large number of such individually appointed persons.

## 2. *Preliminary Steps Taken by the Substantive Officer*

The Secretariat's Department of Political Affairs was responsible for implementation of the Oil-for-Food Programme and assigned substantive responsibility for the contracting of inspection services to one of its officers.[460] Already before the Memorandum of Understanding had been concluded and prior to the advice from the Office of Legal Affairs of 29 May 1996[461] concerning competitive bidding, the substantively responsible officer in the Department of Political Affairs contacted the Ministry of Foreign Affairs of the Netherlands requesting technical advice on implementing oil inspections under Security Council resolution 986 (1995). The political officer had legal training as well as working experience from the diplomatic service of his country and from the Secretariat, but apparently not fully adequate knowledge relevant to the technical aspects of carrying out oil inspections. Among the functions of the officer was to serve as liaison between the 661 Committee and the Steering Committee, a member of the latter being the officer's supervisor, the Under-Secretary-General heading the Department of Political Affairs.

As noted by the IIC, also in the present case preferred contractors emerged at an early stage, even predating the organized (i.e. formal) competitive bidding process[462] and "there was a clear early preference for Saybolt",[463] i.e. Saybolt Eastern Hemisphere B.V. from the Netherlands (hereinafter "Saybolt"). While

---

460 Interim Report, *supra* note 428, at 85-87.

461 Interim Report, *supra* note 428, at 70 and 86. *See also* section 3 below.

462 Interim Report, *supra* note 428, at 110.

463 Interim Report, *supra* note 428, at 110.

these findings are well established, it also is pertinent to point out that although the applicable procurement procedures in no way discouraged substantively responsible officers from seeking information on technical aspects of work to be contracted out, including the capacity of potential contractors to undertake the implementation of the tasks, it would have been advisable for reasons of transparency for such investigations to be conducted in coordination with the Procurement Services and to make use of the data on potential contractors registered in the electronic data banks maintained by the Procurement Services. It appears, however, that in the Saybolt case the political officer acted alone and even that the formal procurement rules may have been breached when his request for information caused the Dutch Foreign Ministry to contact interested companies, one of which submitted a written proposal to the officer already on 22 April 1996, i.e. more than seven weeks prior to the issuance by Procurement Services on 11 June 1966 of the Request for Proposals. Such a development may have infringed, if not the letter, at least the intent of Financial Rule 110.16(a),[464] according to which only "officials duly authorized for the purpose" may invite proposals or tenders and negotiate with potential suppliers or purchasers. Procurement officers were so authorized, but not the political officer.

### *3. Choice of the Established Competitive Bidding Procedure for the Selection*

The company that submitted a proposal on 22 April 1996 was Saybolt. The company initially may have anticipated a possibility of obtaining the contract without a competitive procedure, but on advice of the Office of Legal Affairs from 29 May 1996, the Steering Committee decided "the selection of the oil and goods inspection companies would be through a competitive bid process".[465] The same position, i.e. that the case did not fit the criteria for allowing an exception to the competitive bidding rules, was taken by the procurement officers assigned to the procurement action during a meeting in June 1996 with the substantively responsible political officer.[466] The officer and the Department of Political Af-

---

464 ST/SGB/Financial Rules/1/Rev.3 (1985).

465 Interim Report, *supra* note 428, at 70 and 86.

466 Interim Report, *supra* note 428, at 87. It is unclear whether the political officer indicated that a decision had been made to select Saybolt for the oil inspections contract (and Lloyd's for the goods inspection contract, for which the Official was also substantively responsible) and attributed the decision to the "powers to be". That expression (or "the powers that be") is commonly used by United Nations Staff to refer to influential Member States.

fairs then agreed to follow the normal bidding procedures and, being substantively responsible, enumerated the technical requirements to be incorporated in the Terms of Reference section of the Request for Proposals.

### 4. *Distribution of the Request for Proposals and the Deadline for Submission of Proposals*

The Request for Proposals was distributed by the Procurement Services to eight invitees, including Saybolt, on 11 June 1996 with a deadline for submitting proposals on 18 June 1996.

That only seven days were allowed for the preparation and submission of a proposal for a major contract of a non-standard nature is an unusually short period of time.[467] As a consequence, the invitees other than Saybolt, who did not have the advantage of having been briefed at least two months earlier on the requirements of the forthcoming business opportunity,[468] were unfairly handicapped. In this connexion, the IIC merely noted that "an expedited competitive bidding process for the oil inspection contract was put in place",[469] but failed to point out that the short deadline had the effect of unfairly favouring Saybolt.

### 5. *Evaluation of the Original Proposals and Request for Pricing Updates*

The very short time permitted for submission of proposals may explain in part why only six of the eight invitees did submit a proposal and why three of the proposals were evaluated by the Procurement Services as not acceptable having regard to costs, financial acceptability, compliance with the requirements of the Request for Proposals and an overall assessment. Only the proposal submitted by the Swiss company Société Générale de Surveillance S.A. (hereinafter "SGS") was evaluated as fully acceptable, while the proposals by Saybolt and Petrak were evaluated as acceptable only with limitations.[470]

---

[467] The practice followed by the procurement services in the United Nations, UNIDO and CTBTO would be to allow for four to six weeks between issuing the invitations and the deadline for receiving proposals.

[468] The information was ample enough to have enabled Saybolt to submit a proposal already on 22 April 1996.

[469] Interim Report, *supra* note 428, at 109.

[470] Interim Report, *supra* note 428, at 87-88.

The comparison of costs of the three remaining, technically acceptable proposals showed that the proposed cost was 3.3 million US$ in case of Petrak, 2.9 million US$ for Saybolt, including oil testing but without oil overseers, and 2.1 million US$, including 684.000 US$ for oil overseers but without oil testing, in case of SGS.[471] The Procurement Services concluded that SGS should be awarded the contract, as it was the lowest bidder and its proposal was fully acceptable. This position, however, was opposed by the substantive officer who advanced arguments in favour of selecting Saybolt, such as the need to provide oil testing. The ensuing conflict of views also was due to the importance attributed by the substantive officer to the nationalities of the inspection personnel offered in the two proposals, in spite of the fact that the Request for Proposals had not laid down any criteria or requirements in this respect. In addition, the cost comparison was hampered by the omission from Saybolt's proposal of the services of the oil overseers.[472] Consequently, on 25 June 1996, the Procurement Services informed Saybolt and SGS that they had been short-listed and requested them to submit updated pricing proposals, which should be based on a revised "Statement of Requirement". The revision clarified, *inter alia*, that the requirement of providing oil overseers now had been eliminated and that the updated proposals should include verification of both quantity and quality of oil.[473]

The established procurement rules of the United Nations do allow such requests for updated pricing proposals, even when the requests are made on the basis of a minor clarification or revision of the technical requirements or specifications. It is a condition, however, that all actual bidders, i.e. the invitees having submitted proposals, must be treated equally. It therefore is permissible during the additional round to disregard those bidders whose proposals have been evaluated as not being technically acceptable or, if the selection criteria are lowest cost and technically acceptable, those whose proposals are the most expensive. In practice, use is being made regularly of this legitimate approach under the Request for Proposals procedure, but not under the formal bidding procedure. – Presumably Petrak was eliminated due to the high cost of its proposal.

---

[471] Interim Report, *supra* note 428, at 88 and fn. 143.

[472] Referred to as "United Nations independent oil experts" in para. 4 in Ann. II to the Memorandum of Understanding (United Nations document S/1996/356).

[473] Interim Report, *supra* note 428, at 89.

## 6. *Passing of Information to a Bidder through a Foreign Ministry*

On the basis of written notes made available to it and from interviews conducted with the individuals involved, the IIC has found that already on 22 June 1996, i.e. three days before the request for updated pricing proposals, a Saybolt executive received quite sensitive information from a member of the Dutch Ministry of Foreign Affairs, including the information that SGS's initial proposal was 1.5 million US$ lower than that of Saybolt.[474] The IIC commented that it is "not known from whom at the United Nations the Dutch official received this information".[475]

The findings of the IIC did not refer expressly to this serious breach of the confidentiality with which all information contained in bidding documents must be treated. Passing of such information by a staff member constitutes a violation of the duties of discretion and confidentiality laid down in Staff Regulation 1.5. To ensure confidentiality, it is clear that only those staff members, whether in the Procurement Services or in the substantively responsible units, who directly handle a procurement action should have access to the documents concerned and to the information contained therein.[476] Under no circumstance must such confidential information be released to others, whether they are employed in the Secretariat or the diplomatic representations of Member States.[477] Unless such strict confidentiality is observed, it will not be possible to warrant to the invitees that their proprietary business information presented in their bids or proposals will not be divulged to their competitors or for other purposes that also will undermine the effectiveness, fairness and integrity[478] of the competitive process.

---

474 Interim Report, *supra* note 428, at 89 and fn. 143.

475 Interim Report, *supra* note 428, at 89.

476 Staff Regulation 1.5: "Staff members shall exercise the utmost discretion in regard to all matters of official business. They shall not communicate to any person any information known to them by reason of their official position that has not been made public, except in the course of their duties or by authorization of the Secretary-General. Nor shall they at any time use such information to private advantage. These obligations do not cease upon separation from the Secretariat". ST/SGB/Staff Regulations/Rev. 23 (1995).

477 The appropriate manner in which Member States may ensure oversight with respect to the procurement activities of the Organisation is through the annual audits performed by the Board of Auditors appointed by the General Assembly pursuant to United Nations Financial Regulation 12. All documents and files are available to the auditors.

478 Due consideration to the general principles of fairness, integrity and effective international competition is a requirement of Financial Regulation 5.12 of ST/SGB/2003/7.

## 7. *Passing of Information to a Bidder through a Middleman*

In it's Third Interim Report of 8 August 2005, the IIC concluded that the procurement officer assigned to deal with the procurement action to acquire oil inspection services had passed confidential information through a middleman to SGS concerning the initial proposals received and on how SGS could best respond to the request for updated pricing information relating to the quality testing, namely in a lump sum not exceeding a specified amount. The information on the proposals was in the form of a copy of the procurement officer's draft of the evaluation by Procurement Services, to which was attached two tables summarizing and assessing the competing proposals.[479]

As pointed out by the IIC in its Third Interim Report, these acts constitute clear violations of the duty of staff under Article 100 of the Charter to "refrain from any action which might reflect on their position as international officials responsible only to the Organization" as well as of the prohibition in Staff Regulation 1.5[480] that staff members "communicate to any person any information known to them by reason of their official position that has not been made public" or "use such information to private advantage." The IIC also found the acts to clearly violate the duty not to pass any "information with respect to the probable acceptance or rejection of an offer" to any person external to the Organization.[481]

The IIC further set forth information and allegations that the procurement officer and the middleman attempted to solicit a bribe from SGS for assistance in obtaining the award, but were unsuccessful.[482] Regarding the procurement officer, the allegations further included the suspicion that a series of payments, amounting to almost 1.3 million US$, which he received from various companies that were awarded contracts by the United Nations, may have been bribes.[483] On 21 June 2005, after the IIC had requested information from the procurement officer, he resigned from his post and the United Nations accepted the resignation the following day. An internal investigation by the Secretariat's Office of Internal Oversight Services also uncovered incriminating information, which was turned over to the competent United States prosecutor in July 1996. Finally,

---

479 Third Interim Report, *supra* note 116, at 57-59.

480 ST/SGB/Staff Regulations/Rev. 23.

481 United Nations Procurement Manual, as cited by Third Interim Report, *supra* note 116, at 55.

482 Third Interim Report, *supra* note 116, at 60-64.

483 Third Interim Report, *supra* note 116, at 65.

upon receiving a request from the United States attorney for the Southern District of New York on 8 August 1996 to waive the procurement officer's immunity, the Secretary-General immediately agreed to do so. Thereafter, the procurement officer was taken into custody by United States law enforcement authorities,[484] and subsequently pleaded guilty to United States federal charges of conspiracy, wire fraud and money laundering.[485]

Notwithstanding that the procurement officer upon acceptance of his resignation no longer had the status of an official of the United Nations under Article V of the CPIUN, he continued, according to Article V, Section 18(a), of the CPIUN, to "be immune from legal process in respect of words spoken or written and all acts performed by...[him in his]...official capacity." As the acts in question had been performed before the resignation became effective, waiving of the officer's functional immunity was a necessary prerequisite for his prosecution by United States authorities. The Secretary-General's decision to waive reflected the United Nations position that only the Secretary-General has competence to determine whether an act is carried out in an official capacity[486] and the decision thus discharged his duty to waive "where, in his opinion, the immunity would impede the course of justice and can be waived without prejudice to the interests of the United Nations".[487] Also with respect to the former director of the Oil-for-Food Programme did the Secretary-General indicate willingness to waive the director's immunity should criminal charges be brought against him.[488]

## 8. *The Updated Proposals*

On 28 June 1996, both Saybolt and SGS responded with updated proposals. The cost of SGS's proposal now was 1.9 million US$ while Saybolt asked 2.4 million US$. During the following two weeks, memoranda again were exchanged between the Procurement Services and the substantive officer, in which the

---

484 Opening statement by United Nations Chief of Staff at a press conference held on 8 August, 2005. Available at http://www.un.org/News.

485 As reported in the section on "Contemporary Practice of the United States", 99 *AJIL* 904-906 (2005).

486 *See* pp. 65-66 and fns. 208-212 above.

487 CPIUN art. V, Section 20.

488 Section on "Contemporary Practice of the United States", 99 *AJIL* 905 (2005). On 17 February 2007, United States prosecutors announced the indictment in the Manhattan federal district court of the former director on charges of corruption in connexion with the Oil-for-Food programme. New York Times of 17 February 2007.

Chief, Procurement Services, maintained that SGS should be selected as the lowest bidder and the substantive officer insisted on Saybolt for various reasons such as the method of calculating the cost of SGS's proposal – which was the responsibility of the Procurement Services -, the fact that SGS had offered a crude assay – although this had not been requested – and concerns attributed to members of the Steering Committee regarding "the effective implementation of the sanctions regime." As these arguments did not cause any change in the position of Procurement Services,[489] the substantive officer reverted to the question of the nationalities of the oil inspectors and raised this issue with the Steering Committee. As a result, the Steering Committee, through the substantive officer, asked the Procurement Services to request SGS to provide "additional names of qualified on-site inspectors with no links to the region". The Procurement Services complied but, in line with the maxim of equal treatment, on 15 July 1996 requested additional names and CVs of candidates with no links to the region from both SGS and Saybolt.

The action of the Procurement Services to address its request to both remaining contenders would appear to be justified by the need to ensure equal opportunities at this crucial stage of the selection process, especially when it is considered that neither the original, nor the revised requirements had provided any criteria to be met in connection with the nationality of proposed oil inspectors, including that they should not have any links to the region where the inspections would take place. In as much as the nationality of the oil inspectors eventually was seen to be an important question, it can only be termed an oversight in the preparation of the Terms of Reference, attributable to the substantive officer, that this issue had not been addressed at the outset. A further shortcoming was the absence of coordination between the procurement officers and the substantive officer regarding the evaluation. Such differences should have been clarified and settled in direct talks rather than being recorded in subsequent written exchanges.

Both SGS and Saybolt responded to the request for additional names and CVs, but Saybolt also took the opportunity to reduce its overall price so that it

---

[489] In a memorandum, dated 11 July 1996, to the substantive officer, the Chief, Procurement Services, correctly emphasized that "the guidelines of the Financial Regulation and Rules of the United Nations and other applicable procedures" provide "that proposals can be assessed/evaluated only against the scope of the requirements stipulated in the RFP document, for sake of fairness, transparency and objectivity of the process." Cited after the Interim Report, *supra* note 428, at 90.

became ca. 38.000 US$ lower than that of SGS.[490] The major part of the reduction was due to the substitution of less costly inspectors and a minor part involved the cost of oil quality testing. Therefore, only the reduction relating to the inspectors was legitimate, since it merely was a consequence of the substitution of inspectors. The other reduction related to an item, oil quality testing, that had not been mentioned in the request for updated price proposals and therefore was not permitted under the established procedures; in fact, it was expressly prohibited by a provision in the procurement manual.[491] It was only the cumulative effect of the two reductions, however, that brought the total cost of Saybolt's proposal below that of SGS's proposal.

### *9. Request for Confirmation and Explanation of Pricing*

In order to remove the ambiguity that had been created by Saybolt's two price reductions, the Procurement Services, on 22 and 23 July 1996, by faxed messages to both SGS and Saybolt requested confirmation of pricing information with respect to the inspectors as well as to oil quality testing. The fax to Saybolt also emphasized that oil quality testing had nothing to do with the additional inspectors and therefore insisted on an explanation of the reduction of the cost of oil quality testing in Saybolt's updated price proposal.[492]

### *10. Final Evaluation and Award*

On 24 July 1996, SGS and Saybolt confirmed their updated price proposals. But while SGS had not changed its proposal, Saybolt had done so.[493] Firstly, as mentioned above, Saybolt had reduced its cost for the oil inspectors. Secondly, Saybolt explained that the reduction in the cost it would charge for oil quality testing was made possible because Saybolt planned to sell its assays of the oil quality testing to interested third parties. The explanation implicitly was accepted by the Procurement Services as its Chief now recommended selection of Saybolt as the lowest bidder to the Headquarters Contracts Committee. The basis for

---

490 A reduction by 360.000 US$ was due to the substitution of cheaper labour cost for the inspectors and another reduction by 132.000 was in the cost for oil quality testing. Interim Report, *supra* note 428, at 92, fn. 154.

491 Interim Report, *supra* note 428, at 92, fn. 155.

492 Interim Report, *supra* note 428, at 92-93.

493 Interim Report, *supra* note 428, at 93-94.

Saybolt's reduction, i.e. the planned sale to third parties of the assays, was contrary to the General Terms and Conditions of contract that formed part of the solicitation documents and this circumstance was discovered by and objected to by the Contracts Committee, although it had not been clearly stated in the recommendation of Saybolt by the Chief, Procurement Services. Subject to this point, on 30 July 1996, the Contracts Committee nevertheless recommended to award the contract to Saybolt. Accordingly, on 31 July 1996 Saybolt was informed by Procurement Services that the sale of the oil testing results to third parties was unacceptable, since it contradicted a provision of the General Terms and Conditions of contract that "all conditions of crude oil testing....shall remain the property of the UN" and "shall not be disclosed, sold, shared or made known to any third party." Saybolt replied on the same day confirming it would comply with this provision, whereupon the United Nations proceeded to finalise and sign the contract with Saybolt on 16 August 1996.

The IIC found that Saybolt's bid had been invalidly amended to lower the price and that Saybolt nevertheless prevailed because the Procurement Services accepted its amended bid with the acquiescence of the Steering Committee.[494] The finding focuses on the essence and is convincing. But also the Contracts Committee erred in agreeing to recommend Saybolt for the award.

The Procurement Services had observed the maxim of equal treatment by requesting confirmation of the prices from both remaining contenders and a clarification from Saybolt of its reduction of cost for oil quality testing. It would have been more correct, however, to disallow this reduction on the ground that it was not within the ambit of the request for updated price proposals. In that event the cost comparison would have established SGS' proposal as the lowest. Subsequently, upon receipt of the explanation by Saybolt of the basis for its reduction, i.e. the impermissible sale of data to third parties, an additional and sufficient ground for disallowing this reduction came about. Nevertheless, Saybolt was given a further chance, enabling it to maintain its reduction and thus to stand as the lowest bidder while a similar opportunity to reduce its price was not offered to the competitor SGS. In the end, the Procurement Services failed to offer a level playing ground. Although political considerations and pressures are less evident than in the case of the selection of a bank for the escrow account, the position taken by the substantive officer favoured Saybolt at all stages of the process. In particular, his advance and extensive consultations with Saybolt gave that supplier an unfair advantage, while the support he obtained from the Steering Committee for requesting pricing updates was an important factor during the

---

494 Interim Report, *supra* note 428, at 109.

evaluation stages. In spite of its attempts, the Procurement Services proved to be incapable of guiding the process and of resisting the pressures by ensuring strictly equal treatment, especially during the final evaluation stage.

## F. Procurement of Inspection Services for the Importation of Goods

### *1. The Mandate*

The final major initial procurement action for the Programme was for the inspection services to monitor the entry of humanitarian goods and supplies into Iraq. The need for such inspection services arose from operative paragraph 8(a) of Security Council resolution 986 (1995) which made the use of funds from the escrow account by the Secretary-General for the approved purposes, including meeting the humanitarian needs of the Iraqi population, subject to the condition that "the Secretary-General receives authenticated confirmation that the exported goods concerned have arrived in Iraq". The Security Council also had required each purchase to be approved both by the Government of Iraq and by the 661 Committee. These conditions and additional modalities were reiterated and amplified in the Memorandum of Understanding with the Government of Iraq of 20 May 1996.

### *2. Preliminary Steps Taken by the Permanent Mission of the United Kingdom and by the Substantive Officer*

A United Kingdom company, Lloyd's Register Inspection Ltd. (hereinafter "Lloyd's"), had been conducting on-shore inspections at the seaport of Aqaba of arriving goods for the purpose of enforcing the economic sanctions imposed by the Security Council as a consequence of Iraq's invasion of Kuwait. For this task Lloyd's had not been retained by the United Nations but by shipping companies interested in on-shore inspection as an alternative to ship-board inspection by the naval contingents of the so-called Multinational Interception Force.[495]

---

[495] Interim Report, *supra* note 428, at 97. While the Multinational Interception Force had not been established by the Security Council, it included significant naval contingents from Member States committed to active enforcement of the sanctions laid down by the Security Council.

In the view of the authorities of the United Kingdom, Lloyd's performance at Aqaba had been effective and as early as two months before the signing on 20 May 1996 of the Memorandum of Understanding, the Permanent Mission of the United Kingdom to the United Nations was assisting Lloyd's in its efforts to be awarded the goods inspection contract anticipated under the Oil-for-Food Programme.[496]

The substantively responsible Department of Political Affairs assigned the same political officer to deal with the goods inspection contract as it had for the oil inspection contract. On 4 April 1996, the substantive officer met with an official at the United Kingdom Mission and discussed the potential participation of Lloyd's and around that time the substantive officer also met with an executive of Lloyd's to discuss that question. Further contacts and exchanges followed, some of which involved a proposal and a revised proposal prepared by Lloyd's.

IIC found that there was "a clear and early preference for Lloyd's" and that "the regular competitive bidding process was tainted" by the political officer's contacts with the Permanent Mission of the United Kingdom to the United Nations.[497] As observed above regarding the substantive officer's preliminary steps to prepare for the oil inspection contract, while explorative soundings are permitted by the established procurement procedure, no advantage should be given to any one company. Moreover, only authorized procurement officers may invite proposals or make commitments on behalf of the Organisation. Taking into account that only one potential contractor was taken under consideration, although others showed interest, and that Lloyd's presented a proposal already at this preliminary stage, it seems the substantive officer disregarded these restraints.[498]

### *3. The Request for Proposals and Submission of Proposals*

On 22 July 1996, the Procurement Services issued a Request for Proposals to seventeen companies in nine countries for six months of inspection services by

---

496 Interim Report, *supra* note 428, at 97.

497 Interim Report, *supra* note 428, at 110.

498 According to the Interim Report, *supra* note 428, at 97-98, Lloyd's record includes a letter of 15 May 1996 from the Permanent Mission of the United Kingdom to the Lloyd executive, commenting on a revised proposal received from Lloyd's on 9 May 1996 and cautioning that "you should avoid a suggestion in the preface that the UN has officially approached you since other companies might complain that they were not similarly approached."

thirty-two inspection agents to be deployed at three points of entry into Iraq. Proposals had to be received within only eight days, which was unusually short and deviated from the normal practice of allowing four to six weeks for invitees to prepare and submit their proposals.[499]

While the IIC noted that "an expedited competitive bidding process" was initiated, it did not make a negative finding in this connexion.[500] There can be no doubt, however, that the very short time lessened the effectiveness of the competitive procedure, since for many companies it is a practically complex task to respond with a well-prepared and competitive proposal for such a major undertaking. This observation is supported by the fact that only five of the seventeen companies submitted a proposal within the deadline. Moreover, as was the case for Saybolt in the procurement of oil inspection services, also in the present case, the short deadline enhanced the unfair advantage enjoyed by Lloyd's due to the information this supplier had gained during the advance discussions about the anticipated requirements.

### *4. The Evaluation*[501]

The lowest cost proposal was from a French company, Bureau Veritas, (hereinafter "Veritas"). The cost was approximately 4.3 million US$ or 1.1 million US$ lower than the second lowest proposal which cost 5.4 million US$ and was submitted by Lloyd's.[502] As the proposal from Veritas was found to be technically acceptable, the Procurement Services recommended to the substantive officer that it be selected. The substantive officer, however, recommended Lloyd's on the basis of its record in providing inspection services for the sanctions' enforcement, its experience gained in the region and because some of its inspectors had customs background and commercial investigatory expertise. Further substantive grounds were cited against Veritas whose readiness and reliability was questioned by the substantive officer, *inter alia* because more than half of the proposed inspectors were believed to have links to the region. The substantive officer also felt that Veritas' proposal did not comply with the requirements in the Request for Proposals because it proposed risk analysis inspection instead of inspection of each particular consignment of goods.

---

[499] Interim Report, *supra* note 428, at 98.

[500] Interim Report, *supra* note 428, at 109.

[501] Interim Report, *supra* note 428, at 98-99.

[502] Interim Report, *supra* note 428, at 98.

Concerning the cost comparison – which was within the province of Procurement Services -, the substantive officer acknowledged that the proposal of Veritas had the lowest cost and, consequently, all the objections he raised to selecting Veritas were of a substantive nature. The response by the Chief, Procurement Services, however, took issue with and rejected these substantive points. The quantity and quality inspection services offered by Veritas were found by the Chief, Procurement Services, to be compliant with the Request for Proposals and the comparison of the nationalities of the inspectors in the two proposals, which had been prepared by Procurement Services, showed that the differences were minimal and it was noted that candidates from Pakistan and Turkey could be replaced by additional qualified candidates offered by Veritas. Accordingly, the proposal of Veritas was seen by Procurement Services to be compliant also with regard to the composition of the nationalities of the candidates presented and Procurement Services thereby entered into evaluation of technical aspects, for which the substantive officer was primarily responsible.

Concerning these differing views on evaluation, which were summarized but not evaluated by IIC, it would appear to constitute a deviation from the organisational division of responsibilities between the Procurement Services and the substantive unit that the Chief, Procurement Services, on key substantive points chose to rely on the evaluation by Procurement Services, rather than on that of the substantive officer. Moreover, both officers failed to reconcile their views and merely committed their differences to written communications.

### 5. *Passing of Information to a Bidder through a Permanent Mission*

In view of the above mentioned deadlock, the substantive officer informed the Permanent Mission of the United Kingdom to the United Nations of the situation and, in particular, of the use of local inspectors foreseen in Veritas' proposal and of how much the cost of Lloyd's proposal would have to be reduced in order to be lower than the proposal from Veritas. This information was conveyed to Lloyd's by an official of the Permanent Mission of the United Kingdom and on 9 August 1996, the Permanent Representative of the United Kingdom addressed a letter to the Chairman of the Steering Committee to inform the Steering Committee of Lloyd's agreement to lower its cost to 4.5 million US$ – a reduction by 900.000 US$.[503]

[503] Interim Report, *supra* note 428, at 99-100 and 107-108.

The IIC's finding that "the regular competitive bidding process was tainted by [the substantive officer's] contacts with a member state mission"[504] is not incorrect but anodyne in understating the seriousness of the transgressions. Clearly, the initiative to contact the Permanent Mission of the United Kingdom and to pass on highly sensitive, confidential information was a violation of the duty arising out of the procurement action to treat all business data confidentially. It also was a clear breach of the obligation stated in Article 100 of the Charter of the United Nations and in the oath of office of members of the Secretariat not to seek or to accept instructions from any Government regarding the performance of official duties and to refrain from actions that might reflect on their position as international officials responsible only to the Organization. Finally, it was a violation of the duties of discretion and confidentiality stated in Staff Regulation 1.5 and of the established procurement procedures. As far as the letter of 9 August 1996 from the Permanent Representative of the United Kingdom is concerned, it must be characterized as an attempt to manipulate the procurement action in favour of a national company that constituted an infringement of the duty of a Member State under Article 100 of the Charter "to respect the exclusively international character and of the responsibilities of the Secretary-General and the staff and not to seek to influence them in the discharge of their responsibilities".[505]

### 6. *Intervention by the Steering Committee*

The Steering Committee convened on 9 August 1996 to "review the dilemma caused by the bid by Veritas, a French company,..." .[506] The dilemma was that while Veritas, which had submitted the lowest offer, stood to receive the award according to the criteria of lowest cost and technically acceptable, Veritas was a French company and it was perceived to present a political problem again to award a major contract under the Programme to a French company, when taking into account that recently, on 18 June 1996, the French bank, BNP, had been selected for servicing the escrow account and that a French oil overseer also had been appointed. Accordingly, the Steering Committee was of the view that it

---

[504] Interim Report, *supra* note 428, at 110.

[505] The last sentence of the letter reads: "I hope this will enable the Steering Committee to come to the right decision."

[506] Note on the Steering Committee Meeting held on 9 August 1996, by Ms. L. Buttenheim. Interim Report, at 101 and 113-114.

would be unacceptable to award also the goods inspection contract to a French company.[507] The Steering Committee considered this question at three meetings, held on 9, 12 and 13 August, 1996, and on the advice of the Legal Counsel who attended the meetings, decided to invoke Financial Rule 110.21 which permitted the rejection of all bids "where the interests of the Organization so require". Thereafter, according to the legal advice, negotiations could be opened with Lloyd's only. According to Financial Rule 110.21, when all bids are rejected, the Assistant Secretary-General for General Services[508], or other authorized procurement official, shall record the reasons in writing and determine whether to call for new bids or proposals or whether to proceed directly to negotiation of a contract.[509] The rule does not state expressly who should take the decision to reject all bids, but implies that such a decision can be taken by the Assistant Secretary-General or an authorized procurement officer and also by a senior official or group of senior officials such as the Steering Committee. Nevertheless, the Steering Committee was reluctant to disclose the real reason for its decision, which it felt would not be welcomed by France. Therefore, the Steering Committee decided that France should be informed *post facto*, that its chairman should inform the Assistant Secretary-General for General Services and that Procurement Services should seek authorization from the Headquarters Contracts Committee to enter into negotiations with Lloyd's.[510]

Strictly speaking, the Steering Committee's position that Procurement Services should seek the authorization of the Headquarters Contracts Committee to enter into negotiations with Lloyd's is an erroneous application of the Financial Rules. While review and advice by the Contracts Committee was mandatory,

---

[507] *Ibid.*

[508] The Procurement Services formed part of General Services, headed by the Assistant Secretary-General for General Services.

[509] Financial Rule 110.21 read in full: "Contracts shall be awarded to the lowest acceptable bidder, due consideration being given to the utilization of currencies available to the Organization and which require special management, provided that where the interests of the Organization so require, all bids may be rejected. In the latter instance, the Assistant Secretary-General for General Services or such other official authorized under rule 110.16 shall record in writing the reasons for rejection of the bids and determine whether to invite new competitive tenders or to enter into a negotiated contract." ST/SGB/Financial Rules/1/Rev.3 (1985).

[510] Interim Report, *supra* note 428, at 103. According to the Note by Ms. L. Buttenheim on the Meeting of the Steering Committee, held on 13 August 1996, "the Committee was unanimously of the view that PTD should seek authorization from the Headquarters Committee on Contracts to enter into negotiations with Lloyds." *Id.*, at 119.

according to Financial Rule 110.17,[511] the Committee's mandate was merely advisory. Moreover, Financial Rule 110.21[512] expressly charged the Assistant Secretary-General for General Services or "such other official authorized under rule 110.16" with the responsibility to "record in writing the reasons for rejection of the bids" and to "determine whether to invite new competitive tenders or enter into a negotiated contract." Therefore, either the Assistant Secretary-General or the Steering Committee – which included among its members the supervisor of the Assistant Secretary-General[513] – should have definitively discharged the duty to make the determination to reject all proposals in the interests of the United Nations and to define the nature of those interests in writing; the Contracts Committee merely should have been informed of the determination to open negotiations with Lloyd's and taken the determination and the reasons therefore into account.

## 7. *Implementation of the Steering Committee's Decision*

On 14 August 1996, the Assistant Secretary-General for General Services addressed a "strictly confidential" memorandum to the Officer-in-Charge of Procurement Services,[514] advising of the decision by the Steering Committee "to recommend the rejection of all proposals made in response to the RFP on the above subject, in the interest of the United Nations, as permitted by Financial Rule 110.21. Accordingly you are directed to reject all proposals concerned". The memorandum further conveyed the recommendation of the Steering Committee to pursue negotiations with Lloyd's, but the language here became quite obscure: "....also recommended that the Procurement and Transportation Division (PTD)[515] seek the authorization from the Committee on Contracts, pursuant to the above mentioned Rule, to enter into a negotiated contract with the contractor that PTD considers is the best for the discharge of the duties. In the light of the considerations of, and the recommendations made by the Steering Committee, the obvious conclusion is that PTD should enter into negotiations with Lloyd's Register, and seek the best terms of a contract."

---

511 ST/SGB/Financial Rules/1/Rev.3 (1985).

512 *Ibid.*

513 The Under-Secretary-General for Administration and Management.

514 Interim Report, *supra* note 428, at 103-104.

515 Official designation in 1996 of the unit referred to in this thesis as the "Procurement Services".

As can be seen, neither the Steering Committee, its chairman, nor the Assistant Secretary-General recorded any real reason for rejecting all the proposals, the only ground cited being the circular logic of referring to Financial Rule 110.21 as both enabling clause and substantive ground. Moreover, the reasons given for negotiating with Lloyd's were contradictory, since the Procurement Services, had it been allowed to choose, is likely to have opted for negotiating with Veritas, rather than with Lloyd's, due to the large difference in cost. Had the true nature of the "interests of the Organization", namely to avoid a further award to a French company, been recorded and communicated, the rationale for negotiating with Lloyd's would have become obvious.

The lack of transparency presented a difficulty for the Procurement Services and, in particular, for the procurement officer assigned to prepare the submission to the Headquarters Contracts Committee to request its authorization. Eventually, he did so under protest after having recorded his objections and stating he had no option but to comply with the instructions from the Assistant Secretary-General for General Services,[516] who had employed the circular reasoning of merely referring to Financial Rule 110.21.[517] The Headquarters Contracts Committee initially considered the request in a conference call[518] and obliged after also having received confirmation from Lloyd's of its 900.000 US$ price reduction. The Procurement Services then proceeded to inform all bidders that their proposals had been rejected and the contract was awarded to and concluded with Lloyd's at the reduced price of 4.5 million US$.[519]

The IIC's findings correctly did not take issue with the Steering Committee relying on political reasons for the purpose of rejecting all proposals.[520] In fact, the policy objective of avoiding to the extent possible an accumulation of contract awards to companies in one or a few Member States is legitimate, notwithstanding that the Financial Regulations and Rules did not broach the issue. The policy had been endorsed by the General Assembly in the field of the

---

516 Note to the File of 15 August 1996 by the procurement officer. Interim Report, *supra* note 428, at 106.

517 Interim Report, *supra* note 428, at 104.

518 The minutes from this conference call record that "The committee was informed that, in a strictly confidential memo from the [C]hairman of the Iraq Steering Committee, dated August 14, 1996, a unanimous decision had been taken by the Steering Committee to recommend the rejection of all proposals made in response to the RFP, in the interest of the UN, as permitted by FR 110.21." Interim Report, *supra* note 428, at 105.

519 Interim Report, *supra* note 428, at 107.

520 Interim Report, *supra* note 428, at 109.

Organisation's operational activities for development[521] and is implicitly justified by the need neither to favour nor to discriminate against any Member State. Given that the policy is self-evident, it should have informed the planning for the initial, fundamental and major procurement actions for the Programme, in particular the composition of the invitee lists. That the policy does not seem to have played a role at the planning stage detracts, when taken together with the documented interventions and preference of the substantive officer and the United Kingdom authorities for Lloyd's, from the acceptability and credibility of using this concern as the decisive reason for excluding the lowest proposal from consideration. Formalistically, an acceptable ground may have been adduced, but the spirit of the rules was disregarded.

The IIC did criticize that no written record was made of the ground justifying the decision "in the interests of the United Nations" and qualified the non-disclosure of the political reason as contrary to fairness and transparency. This finding is unobjectionable in the light of the circumstances described by the IIC. In general, there emerges a picture of considerable reluctance at all levels – the Steering Committee, the Assistant Secretary-General, the Headquarters Contracts Committee and the Procurement Services – to go on record and take responsibility for the exclusion of Veritas through the procedure of rejecting all proposals.

## G. Causes of the Infringements found by the IIC

The foregoing analysis of the three major procurement actions for the Iraq Programme has identified several instances of serious infringements of the formal norms of the regulatory framework and of the established procurement practices that are described, respectively, in chapters II and III above. In order to consider possible remedial measures to the United Nations procurement regime that can prevent future violations in the field of procurement of the Charter or of the Financial or Staff Regulations and Rules, it is appropriate first to analyse the nature of the identified infringements. The following analysis therefore will investigate whether the infringements exhibit common features and/or share probable causes and a further analysis in chapter VI will address the question at which level of norms of the legal framework the infringements have occurred and attempt to characterize the legal nature of the infringed norms. While the analysis in the present chapter may suggest remedial measures, a fuller treatment of recommended changes is reserved for chapters VII and VIII.

---

[521] *See* Chapter I, Section B, above.

The following analysis is presented in the typical sequence of procurement actions.

## *1. Inadequate Planning and Preparation*

Serious shortcomings have been revealed to exist already at the early stage of planning and preparing for procurement actions.

Planning comprises the formulation and preparation of appropriate rules and regulations that are clear, comprehensive, effective and transparent. In these respects, the United Nations regulatory framework must be deemed to be inadequate in the area of procurement. Rather than a publicly available, single body of rules, covering all essential aspects of direct importance to substantive and procurement officers, as well as to companies and institutions interested in competing for contracts, there are several levels of regulations, rules, instructions and manuals. The levels are hierarchically organized corresponding to the hierarchical status of the issuing organ. The hierarchy of norms serves well to reflect juridical principles of interpretation, but is an ambiguous, cumbersome and thus ineffective instrument for substantive as well as procurement officers who normally are not legally trained and in any event without competence within the organization to interpret the rules authoritatively and thus definitively. In addition, the rules are not comprehensive, considering that the Financial Regulations and Rules on procurement are dedicated primarily to the purposes of financial management and control and, thus, address procurement procedures merely incidentally rather than comprehensively. The lower level instructions and manuals may aim at a comprehensive coverage, but typically provide an excessive amount of detailed and frequently changing provisions that often fail to fully integrate the regulations and rules. Moreover, there is no effective policy of making a comprehensive collection of the applicable provisions publicly available, an undertaking that would be demanding if coverage were to be limited to the Procurement Services at United Nations headquarters alone and most cumbersome if it were extended to all the procurement services of the United Nations, not to speak of the specialized agencies. The combined effect of the foregoing is a pervasive lack of clarity, comprehensiveness, effectiveness and transparency.

The issues surrounding the criteria for selecting the winner in a competitive bidding procedure offer an illustrative example. In this respect, the Financial

Regulations and Rules in their version from 1985[522] were not unambiguous in their references to such essential terms as "tenders", "bids", "calling for proposals", "competitive bidding", "formal invitations to bid" and "lowest acceptable bidder". Consequently, practice has developed distinctions that are not beyond questioning. In a memorandum of 19 June 1991, the Chief, Procurement Services[523] pleaded against public opening of competitive *proposals* on the ground that representatives of the bidders attending the opening were likely not to have understood the selection criteria and therefore, erroneously, would anticipate the award to be given to the company having presented the least costly proposal while, in fact, the practice followed in the evaluation of proposals was that "the quality of competing products and services may be compared and tradeoffs made regarding the price, quality, extent, and nature of the products and services offered. Consequently, the award is made to the responsible proposer whose proposal is considered most advantageous to the Organization." The memorandum contrasts this practice with the method for evaluating competitive (and sealed) *bids* where "judgemental factors may be used only to determine if the supply, service or construction item bid meets the description" (in the invitation of competitive bids). The adoption and endorsement in practice of so different evaluation criteria and methods clearly constitute an amplification of the rules that would not be understandable for interested suppliers, even if they had gained access on their own initiative to the Financial Regulations and Rules. In addition, the memorandum reveals that it was not the practice to ensure the selection criteria and method were clearly stated in the Solicitation Documents. Accordingly, the suppliers would have been unaware of the real criteria and could neither tailor their proposals exactly to the criteria, nor form an informed opinion of whether the evaluation had been performed correctly.

The more flexible procedure of requesting proposals is considered appropriate where it is not feasible to definitively state the Technical Terms of Reference or Specifications in the Solicitation Documents, while the more formal procedure of inviting bids is considered suitable where all the requirements are known and can be stated in a definitive manner. Such flexibility in the Request for Proposal procedure should not serve to lessen the expectation that every effort must be made by the substantive officer to state the technical requirements as clearly and as comprehensively as possible, however. Specifically, the possibility of Pro-

---

[522] ST/SGB/Financial Rules/1/Rev.3 (1985).

[523] Memorandum dated 19 June 1991 from the Chief, Commercial, Purchase and Transportation Service, Office of General Services, to a Senior Legal Officer, General Legal Division, Office of Legal Affairs. Third Interim Report, *supra* note 116, App. B, 12-13.

curement Services asking for clarification of already submitted proposals should be permitted only within the scope of the original Request for Proposal and in no way be allowed to alter the nature of the original requirements. Should the facts of the case and/or the limited know-how of the substantive officer for some reason prevent the drawing up of sufficiently definitive requirements and specifications, e.g. where the final choice of the preferred technology has not yet been made, then consideration should be given to following the alternative procedure of first inviting expressions of interest and descriptions of the suppliers' preferred approach, including choice of technology, and only inviting proposals or bids subsequent to a decision on the choice of technology made on the basis of the expressions of interest. Rather than such preparations, which would have treated all potential contractors even-handedly, the substantive officer for the two inspection contracts engaged in so intensive preliminary consultations regarding each contract with a single supplier that the supplier in each case was able to present a proposal even before Procurement Services had issued a Request for Proposals. These suppliers therefore had an unfair advantage – an advantage that was exacerbated when Procurement Services stipulated an unusually short period for submitting proposals.

In the case of the two inspection contracts, it would have been preferable to have added an initial stage of inviting expressions of interest and then used the information from the responses to prepare not only the final list of invitees but also the definitive Terms of Reference and a comprehensive statement of the selection criteria for inclusion in the solicitation documents. Such additional information also could have assisted the Secretariat in composing the lists of invitees for the two contracts in a manner that would have avoided the need to subsequently resort to rejecting proposals on political grounds, as referred to in section 5 below.

The reasons for acting precipitously were unrelated to the procurement process as such. Presumably, the cause was the wish of the substantive officer to accommodate the political objective of avoiding any further delay in commencing implementation of the Oil-for-Food Programme, beyond the delay of fourteen months already incurred since the adoption of Security Council resolution 986 on 14 April 1995, a delay that had been caused by the need to first secure Iraq's cooperation.

The Financial Regulations and Rules in the version from 2003[524] have taken a step to address the shortcomings discussed above. Financial Rule 105.15 now more clearly defines the two formal methods of solicitation i.e. "formal invita-

---

[524] ST/SGB/2003/7.

tion to bid" and "formal request for proposals", to which Financial Rule 105.14 adds "informal methods of solicitation such as requests for quotations". Unfortunately, the respective evaluation and selection criteria to be used in connexion with each of these solicitation methods are not defined in a clear, comprehensive and transparent manner by the Financial Rules, in particular since they neither state the weights to be assigned to the relevant criteria nor require the solicitation documents to include a comprehensive statement of the criteria applicable to each procurement action. This lack of transparency also can reduce efficiency by making it necessary for Procurement Services to ask for clarification of proposals.[525]

## 2. *Procurement Outside the Established Procedure*

With respect to the two inspection services contracts it initially was considered whether to follow an – undefined – *ad hoc* approach or the established procurement procedure. In accordance with an opinion by the Office of Legal Affairs, it was accepted by the Steering Committee that the established procedures were mandatory. Concerning the contract for banking services, however, the Treasury Section disregarded the established procedures and proposed to the Secretary-General that a list of major banks be prepared, which would be shortened in the light of consultations with Iraq and then considered by the Steering Committee. The proposal further was that the final selection would be by the Secretary-General "taking into account the advice of the Steering Committee".[526] Although the proposal meant that the Steering Committee would usurp the role of the Contracts Committee and Treasury the role of Procurement Services, the Steering Committee apparently acquiesced in the Treasury in this manner acting outside the established procurement procedure, thereby eliminating a professionally competent contribution by the Procurement Services and oversight by the Headquarters Committee on Contracts. As there does not appear to be any grounds or justification in the Financial Regulation and Rules, nor in the man-

---

[525] *See* memorandum dated 4 August 2005 from the former Chief, Procurement Services, to the Chairman of the IIC, which refers to the differences between Invitation of Bids and Requests for Proposals and "why RFPs sometimes require vendors to clarify their proposals". The memorandum continues: "I am aware that subsequent to my retirement, the U.N. has gone one higher by using BAFO – Best and Final Officer [sic], which can be achieved only after vendors have clarified their offers." No doubt "Officer" should have been "Offer". Third Interim Report, *supra* note 116, App. B, 9-10.

[526] Interim Report, *supra* note 428, at 75.

date from the Security Council or the commitments to the Government of Iraq,[527] for such *ad hoc* approach to procurement of a major contract, the cause appears to lie in an executive and managerial failure, which manifested itself in a violation of the procurement procedure laid down in the Financial Regulations and Rules.

The use of the unregulated *ad hoc* approach also facilitated the selection on political grounds, referred to in section 6 below, i.e. anticipation of political considerations of Member States and preparedness to accommodate such extraneous factors may have been the decisive motive.

### 3. *Infringement of Confidentiality*

In the course of the procurement of oil inspection services, information was passed to a prospective supplier by an official of the Ministry of Foreign Affairs of the country (the Netherlands) of the supplier. The information was confidential and most likely originated from within the Secretariat of the United Nations. Thus, the confidentiality of essential bid information was respected neither by members of the Foreign Ministry concerned, nor by members of the Secretariat with access to the information.

Also in the case of the contract for goods inspection services did a breach of the confidentiality of bidding information occur. Having failed to persuade the Procurement Services to recommend a supplier that had not submitted the lowest proposal, the substantive officer contacted the Permanent Mission of the country (the United Kingdom) of his preferred supplier and provided information on the amount by which the cost of its proposal would have to be reduced in order to become the lowest. This information was passed on to the supplier, enabling it to propose a reduced price.

In both of the above mentioned instances, the cause of the infringements appears to have been the intent of the substantive officer and of the members of the permanent missions concerned to secure the award for the preferred supplier in question. Considering that no ulterior motives have been revealed, the motivation seems to have been of a political nature and to have prevailed over the

---

[527] The Memorandum of Understanding between the United Nations and Iraq provided for the applicability of the Financial Regulations and Rules of the United Nations in two provisions: para. 12 regarding the administration of the Iraq Account and para. 14 concerning audit of the account. United Nations document S/1996/356. The establishment of an external bank account can well be subsumed under the administration of the internal escrow account. *See further* Chapter V, Sections C.1(b) and D.1, above.

faithful observance of the established, objective procurement procedure, i.e. the requirements of confidentiality, independence and non-intervention.

The norms infringed were, in particular, Article 100.1 of the Charter as well as of Staff Regulation 1.5[528] in case of the staff members concerned. To the extent the initiative was not exclusively with the staff member, the members of the permanent missions concerned appear to have violated Article 100.2 of the Charter. There clearly was an infringement of the independence of the Organization from external authorities, in particular from governments of Member States, which Article 100 of the Charter seeks to preserve.[529]

In a further instance involving the contract for oil inspection services, the responsible procurement officer through an outside middleman passed information to a supplier participating in the competition. The cause of this infringement appears to have been the individual seeking of personal gain in the form of a bribe.

The passing of information for the purpose of soliciting a bribe is a violation of Staff Regulation 1.5. It also is a criminal act under applicable municipal law of the country of the offeror of the bribe, for which competent law enforcement authorities of a Member State appropriately may prosecute a staff member after the official's immunity has been waived.

### 4. *Clarification of Proposals versus Revision of a Request for Proposals*

While it is permissible, if necessary, for the Procurement Services to communicate with suppliers to obtain a clarification of their already submitted proposals, including the requesting of additional information, these established procurement procedures were infringed in the course of procuring oil inspection services by the circumstance that the cumulative effect of the repeated rounds of requests for additional information from SGS and Saybolt went materially beyond the scope of the original Request for Proposals. The permissibility of revising the requirements to include the nationalities of the proposed inspectors as a material factor already was questionable and that a price reduction offered by Saybolt at its own initiative was accepted as the basis for giving Saybolt the award as the lowest

528 ST/SGB/Staff Regulations/Rev. 23.

529 C. Ebner, "Article 100", in B. Simma (ed.), *The Charter of the United Nations* Vol. II, 1230 (2002).

bidder amounted to a clear infringement of the established procedures as well as of the principle of fairness.

The nationality factor was introduced due to intervention by the Steering Committee at the behest of the substantive officer. The Procurement Services failed to resist the pressure to add a consideration not contained in the original Request for Proposals as well as to disallow the uninvited price reduction by Saybolt. While the *prima facie* cause of the infringement therefore consisted in professional failures by the Procurement Services, the underlying causes were the pressures of a political nature applied by the Steering Committee and the substantive officer as well as the inadequate guidance provided by the applicable Financial Regulations and Rules, and by the Procurement Manual, on the degree of flexibility permitted in the evaluation of "informal" proposals.

### *5. Rejection of All Proposals on Political Grounds*

Notwithstanding the price reduction proposed by the preferred bidder for the contract for goods inspection services, the lowest proposal remained that of a French supplier. The Steering Committee felt it would cause political problems to award also this contract to a French supplier and therefore seized on the Legal Counsel's advice to reject all proposals and open negotiations with the preferred supplier from the United Kingdom. Although the Financial Rules permitted such rejection "where the interests of the United Nations so require" provided the reasons were recorded in writing, the Financial Rules nevertheless were infringed since no reasons were recorded.

Moreover, while the formulation of the exemption "where the interests of the United Nations so require" generally does not exclude giving weight to political considerations at the evaluation stage, it was an oversight of the Secretariat not to have taken the particular political concern of avoiding an additional award to a French company into account when determining the list of suppliers to be invited to submit competitive proposals. French suppliers in this way unnecessarily were burdened by pointless efforts and costs for reasons not intended by the Financial Rules on competitive bidding. An indirect cause of the infringement thus appears to be a managerial failure, in a timely way to integrate the appropriate political considerations, which were later dealt with by the Steering Committee, into the execution of the procurement action carried out by the Procurement Services.

## 6. *Selection on Political Grounds*

The *ad hoc* approach to selecting the escrow bank involved the selection from a short list by the Secretary-General. The preparation of the short list was done "in agreement with" rather than "after consultations with" the Governments of Iraq and the United States, which approach the Secretary-General deemed necessary in order to implement the Memorandum of Understanding with the Government of Iraq.[530] This accommodation of Iraq, however, went beyond the wording in the Memorandum of Understanding which, in turn, went beyond the requirements stated in the Security Council's mandate in this respect. Already the short list took into account the opposition to selection of a Swiss bank expressed by the Permanent Representative of the United States in her personal intervention with the Chairman of the Steering Committee. The final selection by the Secretary-General from the short list was preceded by consultations with Iraq on the short-listed banks and coincided with the preference of the Government of Iraq stated during this final round of consultations. Fundamentally, the established procurement procedures were infringed by their non-application, however. The cause appears to have been awareness of the political sensitivity of the choice of the bank that would *de facto* become privy to all the key financial data from the crucially important Oil-for-Food Programme. Nevertheless, the choice of an *ad hoc* approach and the way it was implemented gave overriding priority to extraneous political considerations that went beyond those legitimated by the Security Council mandate and the commitments made to Iraq and did not pursue the mandated objectives of fairness, integrity and transparency, nor was it an effective international competition resulting in the best value for money.

## 7. *Common Causes*

The causes of the infringements identified in the foregoing have in common that they relate to the procurement rules of the United Nations set out in the Financial Regulations and Rules and internal directives and other issuances derived from these norms, which all satisfy the well known definition of "rules of the organi-

---

530 Statement of 27 January 2005 faxed by the Secretary-General to the IIC: "The choice of the bank, BNP, for the programme for the escrow account was done in agreement with the American delegation and the Iraqi delegation. It was a political decision to be able to implement the Memorandum of Understanding which was approved by the Security-Council." Interim Report, *supra* note 428, at 83.

zation" found in article 4.4[531] of the ILC's draft text on the topic of Responsibility of International Organizations – as well as in the ILC's Articles on Responsibility of States for Internationally Wrongful Acts[532] – as meaning, in particular: "the constituent instruments; decisions, resolutions and other acts taken by the organization in accordance with those instruments; and established practice of the organization". This has been shown to be the case whether the problem originated in the inadequate formulation of the rules or in their erroneous application, whether by violation or outright disregard. The provision of the constituent instrument of the United Nations repeatedly challenged by transgressions was article 100 of the Charter demanding from the Secretariat (i.e. the Secretary-General and the staff[533]) not to seek or receive instructions from any external authority and requiring Member States to respect the exclusively international character of the Secretariat's responsibilities and not to seek to influence the Secretariat in the discharge of its responsibilities. Thus, while various causal factors for the infringements can be identified, the most pervasive fundamental reason has been shown to be the imposition by interested Member States of political considerations on a Secretariat unable, or at least indisposed, to resist such pressures, although this would have been necessary in order to ensure a correct implementation of the established internal procurement procedures.

---

531 Draft Art. 4.4 reads: "For the purpose of the present draft article, "rules of the organization" means, in particular: the constituent instruments; decisions, resolutions and other acts taken by the organization in accordance with those instruments; and the established practice of the organization". Report of the ILC on its 56th session (2004).United Nations document A/59/10.

532 Report of the ILC on its 53rd session (2001). United Nations document A/56/10 and Corr. 1. The articles are also annexed to General Assembly Res. A/RES/56/83 (2002).

533 Art. 97 of the Charter: "The Secretariat shall comprise a Secretary-General and such staff as the Organization may require. ..."

# VI. ACCOUNTABILITY FOR UNITED NATIONS PROCUREMENT ACTIONS

## A. Sources of International Law on Accountability of International Organisations

The most authoritative statement of the nature and ranking order of sources of international law has been laid down in Article 38.1 of the Statute of the International Court of Justice,[534] which is annexed to and forms an integral part of the Charter. While couched in terms of stating the rules to be applied by the ICJ in contentious proceedings, the provision has acquired general acceptance as an authoritative statement of the classic sources of international law, although it does not mention such generally recognized sources as decisions by international organizations and unilateral acts.[535] It thus offers a suitable, basic framework for analysing and searching the recognized sources for rules on the pertinent aspects of accountability.

### *1. International Conventions*

At the level of international conventions, the ILC[536] has completed its codification work on the topic of International Responsibility of States for Internationally Wrongful Acts with the adoption of a set of draft articles in the form of a convention.[537] As recommended by the ILC, the United Nations Gen-

---

[534] ICJ Statute, art. 38.1: "The Court, whose function it is to decide in accordance with international law such disputes as are submitted to it, shall apply:

> international conventions, whether general or particular, establishing rules expressly recognized by the contesting states;
> international custom, as evidence of a general practice accepted as law;
> the general principles of law recognized by civilized nations;
> subject to the provisions of Article 59, judicial decisions and the teachings of the most highly qualified publicists of the various nations, as subsidiary means for the determination of rules of law."

[535] On these additional sources, *see* H. Neuhold/W. Hummer/C. Schreuer (eds.), *Österreichisches Handbuch des Völkerrechts*, Vol. 1, 86–109 (2004).

[536] On the work of the International Law Commission, *see* C.-A. Fleischhauer, *supra* note 56, at 298-305.

[537] Report of the ILC on its 53rd session (2001). A/56/10 and Corr. 1.

eral Assembly has annexed the draft articles to its resolution 56/83, by which it also took note of the articles and commended them to the attention of Member States "without prejudice to the question of their future adoption or other appropriate action".[538] As already indicated by the title, the draft articles expressly address the responsibility only of States. At the same time, since draft article 57 provides that the articles shall be "without prejudice to any question of the responsibility under international law of an international organization, or of any State for the conduct of an international organization", the ILC in principle has recognized the possibility of their analogous application to international organizations.

Directly relevant for the accountability of international organizations is the ongoing work of the ILC on codification of the topic of Responsibility of International Organizations. In the three reports[539] so far forwarded to the General Assembly, the ILC has presented certain provisionally adopted draft articles that closely follow the structure of the above mentioned draft articles on the Responsibility of States.

Notwithstanding that these codification efforts have not yet resulted in the adoption and entry into force of international conventions on the international responsibility of States or of international organizations, the adopted articles represent both authoritative statements of general principles of law and, to a certain extent progressive development of international law rules.[540] To draw the line between the two components would be a complex undertaking that may well prove practically fruitless as a comprehensive exercise, while still relevant for the evaluation of specific issues and especially pertinent for the pleadings in concrete disputes. With the passing of time and accumulation of evidence of general acceptance, potentially all the draft articles may develop into generally accepted principles or customary rules of international law. Conversely, the codification of the articles will be a factor operating against the emergence of different general principles or customary rules of international law that are incompatible with the draft articles.

---

[538] A/RES/56/83 (2002).

[539] First report of 26 March 2003, A/CN.4/532. Second report of 2 April 2004, A/CN.4/541 and third report of 13 May 2005, A/CN.4/553.

[540] C.-A. Fleischhauer, *supra* note 56, at 302.

## 2. *International Custom*

The circumstance that evidence of recognition of pertinent customary rules on the international responsibility of international organizations has not been found may well be due to the fact that such important activities of international organizations as might potentially give rise to a need to address accountability and responsibility issues belong to relatively recent developments.

## 3. *General Principles of Law*

A determination of "general principles of law recognized by civilized nations" can be made by the subsidiary means, referred to in Article 38.1.d of the Charter, i.e. judicial decisions and teachings of the most highly qualified publicists.

On the topic of Responsibility of International Organizations, the ILC's Special Rapporteur,[541] as an example of a pertinent general principle, has pointed to the advisory opinion of the ICJ in the matter of *Difference Relating to Immunity from Legal Process of a Special Rapporteur of the Commission on Human Rights,* in which the Court stated that the United Nations can be required to bear responsibility for damage caused by acts performed by it or by its agents acting in their official capacity[542] and that the issue of damages is distinct from the question of immunity from legal process.[543] In the same vein, the Final Report (2004) of the ILA on the question of Accountability of International Organizations[544] takes the view that "There is no reason in principle why primary rules of

---

[541] Mr. G. Gaja, *Third Report on Responsibility of International Organizations*, United Nations document A/CN.4/553 (2005), at 19.

[542] On the issue of responsibility of international organizations, *see also* J. Klabbers, *supra* note 140, at 300-319.

[543] *ICJ Reports* (1999), Advisory Opinion of 29 April 1999, para. 66: "Finally, the Court wishes to point out that the question of immunity from legal process is distinct from the issue of compensation for any damages incurred as a result of acts performed by the United Nations or by its agents acting in their official capacity. The United Nations may be required to bear responsibility for the damage arising from such acts. However, as is clear from Article VIII, Section 29, of the General Convention, any such claims against the United Nations shall not be dealt with by national courts but shall be settled in accordance with the appropriate modes of settlement that "[t]he United Nations shall make provisions for " pursuant to Section 29. Furthermore, it need hardly be said that all agents of the United Nations, in whatever official capacity they act, must take care not to exceed the scope of their functions, and should so comport themselves as to avoid claims against the United Nations."

[544] International Law Association, *supra* note 172, at 18.

international law should not apply to collective enterprises undertaken by States in the framework of [international organisations]" and in support of this view invokes the finding in the ICJ's advisory opinion on *Interpretation of the Agreement of 25 March 1951 between the WHO and Egypt* that "international organisations are subjects of international law and, as such, are bound by any obligation incumbent upon them under general rules of international law".[545]

The ICJ in the above mentioned advisory opinion in the matter of the *Difference Relating to Immunity from Legal Process of a Special Rapporteur of the Commission on Human Rights* further found that claims for damages based on the international responsibility of the United Nations should not be heard by national courts but dealt with in accordance with the appropriate modes of settlement which the United Nations must provide for pursuant to Article VIII, Section 29, of the CPIUN. This finding appears to neither follow from a general principle of law – but rather from the applicability of the CPIUN -, nor has it been so characterized by the ILC or the ILA. However, when considering that Article 105.3 of the Charter conveys a mandate to the General Assembly to propose conventions to the Members of the United Nations on "the details of the application" of the privileges and immunities, referred to in Article 105.1 of the Charter, it is arguable that the CPIUN sets out "obligations of the Members of the United Nations under the present Charter" in the sense of Article 103 of the Charter, and that such obligations therefore shall prevail over "their obligations under any other international agreement". In this regard, it has been stated that "To the extent that the Charter provides for the competence of UN organs to adopt binding decisions, measures taken in accordance with such provisions can lead to obligations of the members that prevail under Art. 103, notwithstanding any other commitment of the members concerned"[546] and further that "if, for example, under Article 101(1) the GA establishes staff regulations, obligations resulting from such obligations would seem to fall under Article 103".[547] The same reasoning would appear to be applicable to obligations of Member States under the CPIUN as for obligations arising for Member States under Staff Regulations, both instruments having been adopted by the General Assembly pursuant

---

545 *ICJ Reports* (1980), Advisory Opinion of 20 December 1980, para. 73. Cited after the above mentioned Final Report (2004) of the International Law Association.

546 R. Bernhardt, "Article 103", in B. Simma (ed.), *The Charter of the United Nations* Vol. II, 1295 (2002).

547 *Ibid.*, Vol. II, 1296.

to Charter mandates.[548] Should this view be relied on, it would afford a ground for distinguishing the United Nations (but not necessarily its specialized agencies as well) from other international organizations with regard to the supervisory obligations of States to ensure the observance also by international organizations, which they establish or of which they are members, of obligations, such as due process obligations, arising under general human rights instruments including, in particular, the obligation to ensure that also claims against international organizations can be heard by independent courts.[549] [550]

## B. Level and Nature of United Nations Procurement Rules and Actions

The legal status of the United Nations procurement rules is not an entirely settled question. Internal rules of an international organisation does in the view of some authors not necessarily entail that they form part of international law.[551] A different view has been expressed by the United Nations Office of Legal Affairs in its reply to the Rapporteur of the *Institut de droit international* on the question of the law applicable to contracts concluded by international organisations with private parties.[552] The reply initially affirmed that neither the United Nations Charter, the CPIUN nor any of the (internal) regulations granting legal capacity to contract to subsidiary organs of the Organization have specified the law appli-

548 On the question of hierarchy of norms in international law, *see* J. Klabbers, *supra* note 140, at 247-250.

549 The International Law Association Report, *loc. cit.* fns. 65-70, embraces the non-delegable nature of the human rights obligations of States and refers to literature and cases decided by the European Court of Human Rights, in particular the ECHR decision of 18 February 1999, para. 67, in the case of *Richard Waite and Terry Kennedy* v. *Germany*.

550 J. Klabbers, *supra* note 140, at 151-152.

551 Among others this view has been taken by P. Cahier, "Le droit interne des organisations internationals", 67 *Revue générale de droit international public* 563 (1963); J. Barberis, "Nouvelles questions concernant la personnalité juridique internationale", 179 *Receuil des cours de l'Académie de droit international de la Haye* 145, at 222-225 (1983-I) and by R. Bernhardt, "Qualifikation und Anwendungsbereich des internen Rechts internationaler Organisationen", 12 *Berichte der Deutschen Gesellschaft für Völkerrecht* 7 (1973).

552 The question was included in a questionnaire presented by the Rapporteur in preparation of his report to the Fourth Committee of the *Institut* and was considered at the *Institut's* Oslo session in 1977. UNJYB 159-176 (1976).

cable to such contracts with private parties.[553] Notwithstanding the provision in the Headquarters Agreement[554] with the United States that "Except as otherwise provided in this agreement or in the General Convention, the federal, state and local law of the United States shall apply within the headquarters district", and the fact that a great number of contracts are executed by the United Nations at its headquarters, the Organization does not consider such contracts to be governed by United States local, state or federal law. In support of this position the Office of Legal Affairs has pointed out that the Headquarters Agreement and the General Convention, the CPIUN, must be interpreted as being complementary[555] and that the Headquarters Agreement must be construed so as to enable the United Nations to discharge its responsibilities and fulfil its purposes.[556] In the latter respect the Office of Legal Affairs further has maintained that it "could result in confusion and in difficulties not consonant with the proper and efficient performance of the functions of the Organization", if contracts signed at headquarters were governed by United States law, whereas contracts signed elsewhere would be governed by general principles of law or by the law specified in the contract. Accordingly, the Organization's position was explained to be to rely on general principles of law in the interpretation of contracts it has concluded with private parties.[557] Generally speaking, such United Nations contracts did not specify the applicable law, whether by reference to a particular municipal law, general principles of law or a combination thereof.[558] Interestingly, the continuation of this policy recently has been confirmed by Karin Rudolph.[559] Moreover, two specialized agencies, the UNIDO and the CTBTO, while adhering to the same principle as the United Nations, have taken the further step of inserting a clause into their model procurement contracts that makes the 1980 United Nations Convention on Contracts for the International Sale of Goods applicable to the settlement of "matters arising under but not settled in this Contract." This exercise of contractual party autonomy has not given rise to any difficulty.

---

553 UNJYB 160 (1976).

554 Art. III, Section 7(b), of the Agreement between the United Nations and the United States of America regarding the Headquarters of the United Nations, signed at Lake Success, on 26 June 1947. 2 *UNTS* 11.

555 Headquarters Agreement, Section 26.

556 Headquarters Agreement, Section 27.

557 *UNJYB* 161 (1976).

558 *Ibid.*, at 164.

559 K. Rudolph, *supra* note 146, at 1312-1313.

Regarding procurement rules, the reply of the Office of Legal Affairs in response to another question from the Rapporteur of the *Institut de droit international* on which rules govern the procedures for "the establishment of contracts (for supplies etc.) preceded by calls for tenders on a competitive basis", merely referred to the responsibility to procure "equipment, supplies and services in accordance with the prescribed Financial Regulations and Rules ....of the United Nations", on which the reply thereafter expounded.[560]

The legal nature of the procurement rules is relevant, indeed an essential determining factor, for the applicability of rules of international law to the Organization's responsibility for breaches of those rules. The ongoing work of the International Law Commission on the topic of Responsibility of International Organizations has not resulted in a clear-cut view on the issue, however.[561] In this regard, while draft article 8[562] does provide that also "the breach of an obligation under international law established by a rule of the international organization" is a breach of an international obligation, this, of course, does not amount to much more than a tautological statement. More pertinent is the retention by draft article 4.4 of the definition known, *inter alia*,[563] from the ILC's Articles on Responsibility of States for Internationally Wrongful Acts[564] of "rules of the organization" as meaning, in particular, "the constituent instruments; decisions, resolutions and other acts taken by the organization in accordance with those instruments; and established practice of the organization". These draft articles, 8 and 4.4, appear to be in conformity with the comments on

560 *UNJYB* 166 (1976).

561 *See* the Commentary on Draft Art. 8 in the ILC's Report on its 57th Session. United Nations document A/60/10, at 89 (2005).

562 Draft art. 8 reads:

"1. There is a breach of an international obligation by an international organization when an act of that international organization is not in conformity with what is required of it by that obligation, regardless of its origin and character.

2. Paragraph 1 also applies to the breach of an obligation under international law established by a rule of the international organization."

United Nations document A/CN.4/568/Add. 1, p. 16.

563 As noted in Chapter II, Section A, above, essentially the identical definition also is found in the Vienna Convention on the Representation of States in their Relations with International Organizations of a Universal Character, of 14 March 1975 and in the Vienna Convention on the Law of Treaties between States and International Organizations or between International Organizations, of 21 March 1986.

564 United Nations document A/56/10. The articles are also annexed to General Assembly Res. A/RES/56/83 (2002).

the topic of Responsibility of International Organizations received by the ILC from the International Criminal Police Organization,[565] where it is maintained that "The obligations resting on international organizations by virtue of their constituent instruments and the secondary law of international organizations are international legal norms in the same way as the obligations from the treaties to which an organization may be a party and other applicable rules of customary international law. Simply there cannot exist an internal legal order of international organizations which is autonomous from the law to which it owes its existence". In the same vein, the comments received from the International Monetary Fund[566] on the concept of "acts wrongful under international law" emphasize in addition to general principles of law "the overriding legal effects of the provisions of the charters of international organizations, which have been expressly agreed upon and are primary sources of international law." These comments also stress that it should be (made) clear in the draft articles that "when an international organization acts pursuant to its charter, it would not be subject to doing so under general international principles" ...."but its liability would be determined under its own charter."

Accordingly, there is adequate authority in the writings of eminent jurists that the United Nations internal procurement rules, as well as any related rules on responsibility and liability for their observance and breach, must be characterized as international law rules.

In this connexion it is recalled that, notwithstanding the extensive legal capacity enjoyed by the United Nations under Article 104 of its Charter, and as contemplated by Karin Rudolph in analysing a finding of the ICJ in the case of *Certain Expenses of the United Nations*,[567] the possibility of an act of the United Nations being *ultra vires* cannot be excluded, e.g. if it was unnecessary for the functions and purposes of the United Nations.[568]

---

[565] United Nations document A/CN.4/556, at 30 (2005).

[566] United Nations document A/CN.4/545, at 9 (2004).

[567] "But when the Organization takes action which warrants the assertion that it was appropriate for the fulfilment of one of the stated purposes of the United Nations, the presumption is that such action is not *ultra vires* the Organization." Advisory Opinion of 20 July 1962 in the matter of *Certain Expenses of the United Nations, ICJ Reports* 168 (1962).

[568] K. Rudolph, *supra* note 146, at 1306.

## C. Accountability and Immunity

### *1. Purpose of Immunity*

In its report[569], the ILA endorsed the view that the "paramount rationale for granting jurisdictional immunity is to secure the independence, and guarantee the functioning, of the respondent IO", a view previously formulated by August Reinisch after a comprehensive and detailed investigation of the practice and rationales of municipal courts when ruling on claims of immunity.[570] That this also is the overriding purpose in case of the United Nations cannot be doubted. It not only follows from the formulations found in the Charter, but is confirmed by the wide extent of immunity granted by the CPIUN and its importance is sustained by the report and findings of the IIC as discussed above.

### *2. Judicial and Arbitral Remedies*

In addressing the topic of accountability, the ILA examines the availability and appropriateness of various remedies. As a starting point, it's report[571] confirms the need to keep a "balance between preserving the necessary autonomy in decision-making of International Organisations and guaranteeing that the International Organisation will not be able to avoid accountability". This proposition is buttressed by the references in the report to legal literature and the *obiter dicta* by the ICJ in its advisory opinion on *Effects of Awards of Compensation made by the UN Administrative Tribunal* that not to afford any judicial or arbitral remedy would "hardly be consistent with the expressed aim of the Charter to promote freedom for individuals and with the constant preoccupation of the UN to promote this".[572]

Notwithstanding the basic soundness of endorsing, as a general proposition, access to judicial or arbitral remedies as essential means of ensuring accountability of international organizations, the application of these remedies normally would not be especially effective in the area of claims alleging infringement of

---

569 International Law Association, *supra* note 172, at 41.

570 "The paramount rationale for granting immunities to international organizations in general and immunity from legal process in particular lies in securing their independence and guaranteeing their functioning." A. Reinisch, *International Organizations Before National Courts* 233 (2000).

571 *Ibid.*, at 33.

572 Advisory Opinion of 13 July 1954, *ICJ Reports* 57 (1954).

procurement procedures. The main reason is that the time required to process a claim and reach a decision is too long to allow an ongoing procurement action to be interrupted in order to take the decision into account and therefore the disputed procurement action is likely to be allowed to proceed and the final stage of award and contract conclusion will be completed before a judicial or arbitral decision is arrived at. The effect of these remedies only is *post facto*.

Already for this reason, the possibility of limiting in various ways the jurisdictional immunity of the Organization would not result in ensuring effective accountability of the United Nations for its procurement actions before municipal courts. This is so, whether one were to follow the route of permitting or expanding the acceptance of implied waivers of immunity or, through reliance on an analogy with State immunity, find it acceptable to exclude activities or transactions of a commercial nature from the scope of immunity of international organisations.[573] [574] Moreover, either form of limiting the immunity would seriously reduce the capacity of an international organisation of acting independently and of functioning properly and without undue burdens. In particular, as far as the United Nations is concerned, the above mentioned view of its Office of Legal Affairs that exposure to proceedings before the national courts of the large number of its Member States "could result in confusion and in difficulties not consonant with the proper and efficient performance of the functions of the Organization" should not be ignored. It is not merely a matter of expanding the professional resources of the Secretariat, but the ability of the Secretariat to develop and implement uniform measures and policies in all Member States would be severely circumscribed. This concern goes beyond procurement claims and relates to activities in all areas that would not be covered by jurisdictional immunity such as contract disputes. In any event, it, of course, also would be incompatible with the CPIUN.

The foregoing reservations about the advisability of limiting the immunity of the United Nations should not be seen as diminished concern for the possibility of private parties to assert their rights against the United Nations, but merely as

---

573 "The main underlying policy reasons that have led to a restrictive immunity standard valid for states, *i.e.* an expression of fairness to the parties dealing with them and to other third parties affected by their activities as well as growing concern over the private parties' rights of access to judicial determination of their rights, are probably equally valid for relations between international organizations and private parties. This suggests that a similar limitation of the immunity of international organizations would be appropriate". A. Reinisch, *supra* note 570, at 261.

574 "With states, it is generally accepted nowadays that immunities are limited to imperial acts; in such a climate, it seems rather implausible to insist that organizations retain their absolute immunities". J. Klabbers, *supra* note 140, at 165.

doubts about the appropriateness of having recourse to national courts, as long as their capacity and sometimes objectivity in a not insignificant number of Member States are subject to debate at the international level.

### *3. Procurement Regime*

Focusing again on the accountability for procurement actions, it has been shown in the foregoing that the legal framework for the United Nations procurement regime suffers from several material shortcomings.

The framework is neither comprehensive, since the Financial Regulations and Rules omit to address such essential aspects of the procurement procedure as the evaluation methodology and the scope for seeking clarifications of Requests for Proposals, nor is it transparent, since the internal administrative instructions amplifying and supplementing the Financial Regulations and Rules are not made generally available to interested suppliers. Moreover, both the multi-layered, hierarchical structure of the legal framework and a lack of clarity of certain formulations prevent the desirable level of transparency from being reached and contribute to the ineffectiveness of the procedures. These problems are located in the Financial Regulations and Rules and the related internal administrative instructions and do not affect the provisions of the Charter or the Staff Regulations Rules that are applicable also with respect to procurement. In principle, the issuance of a single, consolidated, comprehensive set of rules on the procurement procedure and publication of the rules could remedy these shortcomings.

### *4. Political Context*

A more difficult issue is presented by the question whether the political context, in which the Secretariat works, in fact offers the necessary pre-conditions for faithful observance of the prescribed procurement procedure. This question arose in connexion with all three major procurement actions investigated by the IIC. The selection of the escrow bank was, as stated by the Secretary-General, a necessary political choice made to accommodate the concerns of two Member States and the *ad hoc* approach taken greatly facilitated interventions by interested Member States in the selection process. In the case of both inspection contracts, active cooperation was established at the outset between the Secretariat and the respective permanent missions to the United Nations, through which a particular national supplier was identified already at the planning stage of the procurement action and eventually awarded the contract in no small measure due to information illegitimately passed on by the Secretariat to the supplier through the permanent mission of the supplier's country and, in case of the goods inspection contract also due to direct intervention by the Permanent Representative of an interested Member State. As was admitted in the case of the escrow bank contract, the rationale of close cooperation between the Secretariat and important and interested Member States, including the acceptance of direct intervention by Permanent Representatives, must also in respect of the inspection contracts be deemed to be due to the perception of a political necessity to accommodate without being restrained by the legal framework, a perception that was shared by the members of the Secretariat and of the permanent missions.

Since it must be assumed that the political interest of certain Member States in the outcome of the three major procurement actions for the Iraq Programme was significantly greater than in the event of procurement of other requirements, the perceived political need for disregarding the procurement procedures may not be pervasive. Nevertheless, the political context, in which the Secretariat works,[575] makes it dependent on continued support by Member States as represented by the permanent missions. It therefore follows that to the extent of the existence of a general perception of political necessity, the existing legal framework does not ensure observance of the procurement procedures with adequate fairness, integrity and transparency. Thus, since an essential pre-condition for faithful application of the existing legal framework is unmet,[576] a further juridification of the procurement procedure may be considered.

---

[575] J. Klabbers, *supra* note 140, at 173-176.

[576] Regarding improper collaboration between staff members and Member States, the view has been expressed that "The root of the problem is to be found not so much in corrupt individuals, but rather in the legal and political constraints under which the nationals of some member States operate in the Secretariat". C. Ebner, *supra* note 529, at 1247. The view finds considerable support in the present thesis.

# VII. *DE LEGE FERENDA*

## A. Comparison with the GPA

The foregoing chapters have described and analyzed the legal framework and procedural regime for procurement to be undertaken by the United Nations as well as the procedures and rules laid down by the GPA for the procurement of goods and services by procuring entities of the governments of States Parties to that Agreement.

The treatment of the United Nations procurement regime was expanded to include an account of the findings of the IIC concerning the three major procurement actions to implement the Iraq Oil-for-Food programme and, in particular, of the extent to which the procurement actions were carried out in conformity with the applicable rules of the United Nations.

Wherever appropriate, the treatment of the GPA's procedures included comparisons with the corresponding procedures of the United Nations. A comparative account also was given of the remedies available under the procurement regime of the United Nations and under the GPA, whether to Member Governments or to interested private firms or suppliers participating in, or eligible to participate in, a particular procurement action in order to assert their interest in ensuring the correct application of the prescribed procedures. On this comparative basis, the following observations and recommendations regarding United Nations procurement regime appear to be appropriate.

## B. Recommendations

### *1. Structure of Procurement Rules*

The GPA has the advantage of being a single, comprehensive instrument, which ensures greater clarity and readability, while the multi-layered, hierarchical structure of the rules of the United Nations is an obstacle in these respects. Important rules may be found either in the Financial Regulations, the Financial Rules or in administrative instructions or manuals, thus exhibiting a structure that corresponds to the primary levels of formal authority within the Organization of the United Nations, but is unrelated to the procurement process as such. Moreover, the subject matters addressed by the rules demonstrate a concern for constitutional authority, and an emphasis on financial, legal and administrative control, that prevail to the detriment of providing a comprehensive and coherent regulation of the entire procurement process.

Consideration therefore should be given to replacing the present set of rules by a single, comprehensive instrument.

## *2. Purposes*

The comparison of the two procurement regimes has shown substantial similarities between their purposes. The stated purposes generally are identical or similar. The differences among the purposes are mainly attributable to differences inherent in the legal frameworks for the procurement regimes: on the one hand, the procedures for procurement undertaken by a global international organisation such as the United Nations, and on the other hand, the common rules for the procurement entities of a substantial number of governments of Parties to the GPA. In this context, the objective of facilitating and promoting international trade, while reciprocally balancing the rights and obligations of the Parties, is not stated as a purpose of the rules of the United Nations, nor would it be sensible to do so.

## *3. Independence*

With respect to the procurement of the services of a bank, including the opening of an account, for the custody and management of the funds that would be derived from the sale of Iraqi oil, the margin of independence of the Secretariat from Member States was narrowed to a degree that approaches disregard for Article 100 of the Charter. This can be seen both from the negotiation and inclusion of the clause "after consultation with the Government of Iraq" in paragraph 7 of the Memorandum of Understanding between the United Nations and the Government of Iraq, and subsequently from the Secretary-General's role in opening consultations with France on the preliminary acceptance of French banks proposed by Iraq. Moreover, the Secretary-General's final selection of BNP, which he has explained to be "a political decision" and "done in agreement with the American delegation and the Iraqi delegation", is far removed from the procurement rules and raises questions about whether Article 101.1 of the Charter was faithfully observed. Also the United States, however, did not show the respect required of Member States for the independence of the Secretariat by

Article 100.2 of the Charter when their Permanent Representative intervened to oppose possible award to a Swiss bank.[577]

## 4. *Consultations and other Amicable Settlement Procedures*

The Dispute Settlement Understanding set out in the WTO Agreement is applicable to disputes arising under the GPA, in which a Party considers that another Party fails to honour its obligations. The DSU procedures do not have a direct counterpart in the Charter or in the rules established by the Organization.[578] They are elaborate and explicit and, as a matter of preference, encourage direct consultations between the affected Parties with a view to arriving at a mutually acceptable solution. Only if an amicable settlement is not achieved within the given time limits can a complaining Party request consideration by a panel of independent experts and eventually, if it is not prepared to accept the report of the Panel, appeal the legal aspects to an Appellate Body. While there is no direct parallel in the form of standing procedures within the United Nations, *ad hoc* use of consultations, good offices, mediation, and expert panels is well known and also practised. In relation to a concrete infringement of procurement procedures, it is pertinent to point out, however, that the DSU procedures are available only *post facto* and therefore of greater value for traditional trade disputes, for which they are regularly employed,[579] and less useful for disputes arising under the GPA.[580] The same characteristics pertain to the above-mentioned procedures

---

[577] Observing that the Secretary-General "is subject to numerous political influences and pressures," Christian Ebner has taken the balanced position that these "will not normally bring the SG or member States into conflict with art. 100 as long as they do not result in his submission to the wishes of individual States at the cost of fulfilling his international responsibilities towards the Organization as a whole". C. Ebner, *supra* note 529, at 1245.

[578] Art. 22 of the Constitution of UNIDO provides a procedure for settlement of disputes "among two or more Members concerning the interpretation or application" of the Constitution. If not settled by negotiation, the dispute shall be referred to the Industrial Development Board of 53 Member States, unless the parties agree on another mode of settlement. If no solution satisfactory to the parties concerned is found, the parties may agree to refer the matter to either the International Court of Justice or to an arbitral tribunal. If there is no agreement, any party dissatisfied with the suggested solution may refer the matter to a conciliation commission. Rules concerning the arbitral tribunal and the conciliation commission are contained in Ann. III to the Constitution. The procedures in art. 22 have not been used so far and, in any event, are available only to Member States and not to any private sector supplier. 1401 *UNTS* 3.

[579] Extensive documentation is available at http://www.wto.org .

[580] *See* Chapter IV, Section B *in fine* above.

available within the United Nations to Member States for the amicable settlement of disputes, which therefore normally would be ineffective in dealing with questions arising out of ongoing procurement actions.

## *5. Challenge Procedure*

Presuming that a procurement action of the United Nations is required to be carried out by authorized organs and in the established procedure – which would include a case such as the banking services – it would seem to be both more appropriate and more effective for the prevention of infringements to establish a challenge procedure available to the bidders participating in, or interested to participate in, a competitive selection procedure. A challenge procedure similar to that required by Article XX of the GPA would be a useful and effective addition to the existing possibilities of Member States to lodge complaints – *inter alia* because commercial entities are unlikely to be inhibited by political factors and motives to a similar extent as Member States. Commercial entities can be assumed to be strongly motivated by the prospect of preserving the opportunity of being awarded the contract. Moreover, the preventive effect on members of the Secretariat and on representatives of Member States of the possible lodging of a challenge should not be underestimated. The mere possibility of being exposed may well effectively discourage from infringements of or interventions into the prescribed procedures.

It is noteworthy that the United Nations does not offer suppliers any possibility for redress of grievances similar to the challenge procedure offered under the GPA to suppliers participating in procurement as bidders or having an interest to participate. *Prima facie,* it appears to constitute an anomaly that the same States, that have agreed on a rapid challenge procedure for suppliers to complain about procurement actions by their own governmental procuring entities, have not required a similar procedure to be instituted for procurement done by the United Nations. With the gradual establishment in national jurisdictions of systems for challenges by bidders, it is a common feature that protests by bidders play a fundamental role in protecting the integrity of the procurement system since experience confirms that transparency counteracts corruption.[581] A robust and transparent system enhances the accountability of procurement officials and agencies and serves as a deterrent to improper conduct by officials as well as to

---

581 D. I. Gordon, *supra* note 345, at 17.

bid rigging, misrepresentation and other infringements by bidders.[582] The effectiveness of a challenge system derives from its self-policing and self-enforcing character which is due to the fact that it provides avenues for the suppliers participating, or interested in participating, in a given procurement process to intervene with a challenge or protest relating to the conduct of the process. That the initiative lies with the suppliers is a unique feature of the challenge procedure distinguishing it from other review systems such as public audit or inquiry, criminal prosecution[583] or intergovernmental dispute settlement procedures, which all rely on government officials to initiate action.[584] The latter category clearly are further removed from the concrete procurement process than the directly involved suppliers and cannot be presumed to be as keenly motivated as the suppliers who find themselves in a competitive mode.

Accordingly, a challenge procedure modelled on the procedure in GPA Article XX should be established.

## 6. *Transparency*

The two procurement regimes contain a substantial number of substantively similar procedural requirements. Nevertheless, a detailed analysis reveals significant differences as well. The procurement procedures of the GPA are more comprehensive and detailed. Significant differences were noticed with respect to the existence in the GPA of rules in the field of transparency requirements while such provisions are generally absent from the United Nations Financial Regulations and Rules.

The main areas where transparency requirements are imposed by the GPA are the registration of potential suppliers, the contents of solicitation documents, the negotiations with suppliers after the receipt of bids or proposals and the duty

[582] *Ibid.*, at 3-4.

[583] Art. 1.1 and 2 of the Convention on Combating Bribery of Foreign Public Officials in International Business Transactions commits each Party to establish under its law that it is a criminal offence to bribe, to be complicit in an act of bribery of or to attempt or conspire to bribe a foreign public official. Art. 1.3 includes "any official or agent of a public international organisation" under its definition of "foreign public official", 37 *ILM* 1 (1998). On the incorporation into the United States Code, *see* the note by M. McGrath/A. V. Closser/L. M. Norrett, "International Procurement", 33 *Int'l L.* 315 (1999), and regarding Australia *see* M. Wilder/M. Ahrens, "Australia's Implementation of the OECD Convention on Combating Bribery of Foreign Public Officials in International Business Transactions", 2 *MJIL* 568 (2001).

[584] D. I. Gordon, *supra* note 345, at 2.

to provide information on the evaluation and award to all participants. In every instance, such differences exemplify that the GPA is more comprehensive and benefits from a higher standard of legal certainty and transparency than the Financial Regulations and Rules of the United Nations.

Although the United Nations Procurement Services also, but only as a voluntary matter, may provide certain information on registration and evaluation upon request, consideration should be given to include certain provisions on transparency from the GPA, that are now absent from the United Nations rules.

## *7. By-passing Procedures*

In its analysis of the procurement of banking services for the escrow account, the IIC found that data on the capacity of commercial banks had been collected by the office of the United Nations controller, thus by-passing the exclusively authorized procurement officers in violation of Financial Rule 110.16(a). As further related by the IIC, also the Headquarters Contracts Committee was by-passed in favour of consideration by the *ad hoc* Steering Committee, contrary to Financial Rule 110.17. To the extent essential procedural safeguards are ignored, a resulting decision may be held to be tainted and vitiated under rules of administrative law prevailing in countries respecting the rule of law.

Accordingly, the introduction of a challenge procedure modelled after Article XX of the GPA would enable a competitor to launch an effective challenge under such circumstances.

## *8. Pre-selection of Potential Suppliers*

The IIC does not relate on what basis the Controller decided from which banks to collect data relating to their capacity to handle the escrow account, nor on how the procurement officers composed the lists of suppliers invited to submit proposals for the inspection contracts. The United Nations Financial Regulations and Rules do not address this preparatory stage, although the procuring entities of the United Nations, as well as of the specialized agencies, make widespread use of computerized data banks to identify potential suppliers to be invited to submit competitive proposals.

To enhance transparency and fairness at the preparatory stage, rules should be adopted and published, based on the GPA's[585] detailed requirements concer-

---

585 GPA art. VIII.

ning the listing of qualified suppliers, including eligibility and the duty to provide information on how to become listed and on the reasons for declining to list in individual cases.

## *9. Information to be included in Invitations to Bid*

In all three procurement actions considered, the IIC found that decisive selection criteria had not been included in the Requests for Proposals, namely the Swiss nationality of the banks in case of the banking services, the inspectors' nationalities of the region in both procurements of inspection services and the French nationality of a goods inspection company. The Request for Proposals for oil inspection even contained the superfluous requirement of oil overseers, the removal of which opened the door for Saybolt's uninvited lowering of its price.

While the United Nations Financial Regulations and Rules are silent on the information that must be provided with the invitation to participate in a competitive procedure, the GPA[586] lists the categories of information in a detailed way.

To enhance transparency and limit arbitrary evaluations, rules similar to those of the GPA should be added to the United Nations rules.

## *10. Provision of Official Information*

On an *ad hoc* basis, the United Nations may provide information to suppliers or to governments on the applicable procurement procedures, the reasons why a bid was not accepted and the relative advantages of the bid that was accepted. The Financial Regulations and Rules of the United Nations do not provide any guidance on when and how to provide such information, however. In contrast, the GPA[587] regulates this subject in a detailed manner, thus enhancing transparency, clarity and predictability.

Consideration should be given to regulating these aspects of United Nations procurement.

---

586 GPA arts. VI, IX and XII.

587 GPA arts. XVIII and XIX.

### *11. Unauthorized Official*

In both procurement actions for inspection services, the substantive officer, rather than the procurement officer, initiated consultations that led in each case to the submission of a proposal even before a Request for Proposals had been issued. Since Financial Rule 110.16(a) provides that only authorized officials, i.e. procurement officers, may invite proposals and negotiate with suppliers, this rule was infringed. Internal disciplinary action may, whenever appropriate, be taken but may not be initiated in all cases and, *inter alia* for this reason, not be the most effective remedy to guard against such unfair head-start being given to a potential supplier.

A more effective measure would be to make a challenge procedure available to competing suppliers who would be motivated to keenly monitor any sign of being placed at a disadvantage.

### *12. Short Deadline for Submissions*

Suppliers invited to prepare and submit proposals for inspection services for, respectively, oil exports or goods imports were allowed only seven days between the invitation and the deadline for submission. Even in the absence of any provision in the Financial Regulations and Rules, the normal practice of the United Nations would be to allow five to six weeks in order to give adequate time for thorough preparation by as many of the invited suppliers as possible. Again, the GPA[588] sets out detailed time limits for the minimum periods to be allowed.

Due to the importance of avoiding arbitrary practices and unreasonably short deadlines, it would be advisable to regulate the question of appropriate deadlines in the Financial Regulations and Rules of the United Nations.

### *13. Passing Information to a Supplier*

The duty to treat all submitted proposals confidentially was breached in both procurement actions for inspection services. The bidder for oil inspection services, Saybolt, received information from the Dutch Ministry of Foreign Affairs on the other proposals submitted, which most likely had been leaked by the Secretariat and definitely assisted Saybolt in responding to the subsequent re-

---

588 GPA art. XI.

quests for updated proposals and eventually to reduce its price on its own initiative. In a quite similar manner the bidder for goods inspection services, Lloyd's, received information from the Permanent Mission of the United Kingdom on the amount with which the price of its proposal had to be reduced in order to become the lowest. This enabled Lloyd's to present a corresponding reduction of its price.

In both instances, disciplinary action would be possible under the existing Staff Regulations and Rules, if appropriate. Absent any political pressure, this normally would suffice to dissuade the staff from indiscretions, but would not reach the representatives and officials of Member States with privileged knowledge. Nor could the latter category be effectively influenced through the complaint and intervention possibilities available to Member States.

If a challenge procedure were made available to competing suppliers, a supplier gaining actionable knowledge of such egregious procedural infringements would be likely to take action by lodging a formal challenge. As mentioned above, the mere possibility of an infringement becoming publicly known would act as a strong disincentive for the Secretariat and not less for Member States.

Also the other bidder for oil inspection services, SGS, received information regarding the initial other proposals. The procurement officer assigned to that procurement action provided SGS with a draft of his evaluation of the other proposals and written guidance on how SGS could best respond to the request for updated proposals. As disciplinary action was taken against the procurement officer and the Secretary-General co-operated with United States law enforcement authorities enabling these to bring criminal charges by waiving the official's immunity, the existing rules appear *prima facie* to be adequate for such incidents.

Notwithstanding the existing disciplinary rules and the possibility of waiving an official's immunity for the purpose of criminal prosecution, it seems possible, however, that the infringement – which appears to have been repeated by the same officer in several other cases – could have been revealed sooner, if it had been possible for competing suppliers to present formal complaints in an established challenge procedure.

### *14. Unauthorized Reduction of Price and Acceptance of Reduced Price*

At the last stage of the procurement action for oil inspection services and in response to the request for updated proposals, Saybolt, at its own initiative, reduced its price although the updated Request for Proposals from the United Nations only had concerned the names and nationalities of additional inspectors.

The reduced price therefore should not have been taken into account in the final evaluation but nevertheless was accepted and the award on this basis went to Saybolt. As pointed out by the IIC, the Procurement Services committed an error and infringed a rule in the Procurement Manual. The Financial Regulations and Rules of the United Nations do not address this situation, while detailed rules are contained in the GPA.[589]

Therefore, rules, based on the GPA, on the conduct of negotiations and on the requesting of clarifications and additional information need to be developed and incorporated into the United Nations Financial Regulations and Rules.

### *15. Non-recording and Concealment of Reason for Rejecting All Proposals*

In order to avoid selection of another French company, namely Veritas, for the provision of goods inspection services, the Secretariat's Steering Committee decided to reject all proposals and open negotiations with Lloyd's. The requirement of Financial Rule 110.21 that the reason for the rejection be recorded was not complied with and the reason was concealed, even from the Procurement Services. Such concealment enhances the risk of misusing the right to reject in order to circumvent the established procedure. The possibility of instituting disciplinary action in such a case seems for practical reasons relating to the high rank of the members of the Steering Committee not to be a realistic option. A complaint by France also would seem an unlikely step considering the rejection was motivated by the desire not to appear to favour French suppliers for implementation of the Oil-for-Food programme.

The most effective remedy to discourage disregard of the obligation to record the real reason for rejection would seem to be to permit a challenge by a competing supplier such as the lowest bidder Veritas.

---

589 GPA art. XIV.

# VIII. CONCLUSION

In view of the emergence at the international level[590] of binding obligations for States to establish procedures for bidders to challenge or protest against the conduct of procurements by national procurement entities, the lack of similar, or equivalent, procedures for procurement undertaken by the United Nations can be seen as a failure by the Organization to implement in respect of its suppliers its obligation under Article VIII, Section 29(a) of the CPIUN to make provisions for appropriate settlement of disputes of a private law character, to which it is a party. Therefore, and taking into account the extensive immunity enjoyed by the United Nations, as well as the general principle that the international legal responsibility of international organizations may be engaged by acts or omissions they commit in contravention of international law, such settlement procedures appear to be required and ought to be established, either by Member States acting within the General Assembly or by the Secretary-General in his capacity of chief administrative officer. Challenge procedures similar to those in GPA Article XX would be preferable to extending the consent to arbitrate contractual disputes to include action taken in the course of procurement, because arbitration would not normally be a rapid modality capable of determining an appropriate remedy, such as correction of the procedure, before the end of the procurement action concerned and the award of the contract.

A challenge procedure established by the United Nations could authorize panels of competent persons, with personal integrity and specialized knowledge of procurement, to hear the complaints and decide on appropriate remedies, including compensation or rapid interim measures to correct procedural breaches.

A challenge procedure for claims against the United Nations arising out of procurement actions can and should be established as an internal measure of the Organization so that the procedure would constitute "rules of the organisation" as defined in Article 2.1(j) of the 1986 Vienna Convention on the Law of Trea-

---

590 In addition to the challenge procedures under the GPA, similar systems allowing suppliers to challenge the conduct of procurement processes have been mandated by the European Union (Council directive 89/665/EEC) and art. 10017 of the North American Free Trade Agreement (concluded by the United States, Canada and Mexico on 8, 11, 14 and 17 December 1992, entered into force 1 January 1994) and endorsed by the UNCITRAL Model Law on the Procurement of Goods, Construction and Services of 1994, chapter VI (34 *ILM* 718 (1995)). In 2004 UNCITRAL voted to update the Model Law, *see* the note by C. R. Yukins *et al.*, *International Procurement*, 40 *Int'l L.*, at 337 (2006), available at http://papers.ssrn.com/sol3/papers.cfm?abstract_id =903423 (last visited 15 February 2008).

ties between States and International Organizations or between International Organizations. Actions taken and decisions made in accordance with the challenge procedure thus would be attributable to the United Nations and therefore covered by the Organization's "immunity from every form of legal process" under Article II.2 of the CPIUN and by its related provisions. Precisely because of the immunity, the challenge procedure would be a clear example of the United Nations making provision for an appropriate mode of settlement of disputes of a private law character and thereby discharging its obligation under Article VIII, Section 29, of the CPIUN.

Such a challenge procedure would be an effective means of strengthening the transparency and objectivity of the procurement rules and of the conduct of procurement by the United Nations. Accountability for an important area of activity would become possible by regulating the matter and thereby extracting the subject from the sphere of undue political influence. Ideally, but not unrealistically, the preventive effect would exceed the remedial, since the Procurement Services would be given additional motivation to further develop and strictly apply the prescribed procedures, while un-authorized actors would be discouraged from intervening and applying pressure. Staff members being found to have acted without authorization would be subject to disciplinary and other administrative measures. Even if representatives of Member States or of suppliers were not to be made subject to sanctions under the challenge procedures of the United Nations, the risk of public exposure would have a meaningful deterrent effect on them.

Much procurement by the United Nations is done to meet mundane requirements, but the discharge of the Organization's often complex and sensitive political tasks frequently requires the assistance of the Procurement Services. With the analysis above of the procurement for the Iraq Oil-for-Food Programme in mind, the politically motivated interventions into the conduct of procurement do not appear to have yielded a perceivable benefit. On the contrary, it appears it would have been preferable for managerial, financial, legal and, ultimately, also political reasons to have shielded the procurement process as such from political factors, except for the preliminary planning stages involving the preparation of technical Terms of Reference and Specifications and of the list of invitees.

If the Organization itself were to establish a challenge procedure as part of its internal rules, that provides adequate relief for actual and potential bidders as well as a basis for effective sanctions against transgressing staff, it would not be necessary, nor does it appear to be advisable, to exempt the procurement related claims from the scope of the immunity presently enjoyed by the Organization under the CPIUN. The challenge would be heard and decided based on the applicability of United Nations Charter and internal rules, including in particular the published procurement procedures. Infringements of procurement rules would entail the Organizations international legal responsibility and could constitute *ultra vires* acts that might nevertheless bind the Organization.[591]

Acceptance of exposure to a challenge procedure would considerably facilitate the task of revising the procedures as recommended above.

[591] Certain Expenses, *ICJ Reports* 168 (1962).

# ANNEX I

UNDP/IAPSO

Common Guidelines for Procurement
by Organizations in the UN System

General Business Guide. 20th Edition (June 2006)

# UNITED NATIONS SYSTEM

# GENERAL BUSINESS GUIDE

FOR
POTENTIAL SUPPLIERS OF GOODS AND SERVICES
WITH
COMMON GUIDELINES FOR PROCUREMENT BY
ORGANIZATIONS IN THE UN SYSTEM

**20th Edition (Update June 2006)**

# ANNEX I

## *COMMON GUIDELINES FOR PROCUREMENT BY ORGANIZATIONS IN THE UN SYSTEM*

**THE INTERNATIONAL NATURE OF UN BUSINESS**

**The global extent of the United Nations activities presents opportunities for commercial firms and entities to receive international exposure and resultant recognition may lead to increased business opportunities. Acknowledging this fact, and also taking into consideration the unique humanitarian role of the United Nations system, suppliers of equipment and services to organizations in the United Nations system often grant preferential prices**

## INTRODUCTION

THE PURPOSE OF THE COMMON *GUIDELINES* IS TO:

... COMMUNICATE BASIC PRINCIPLES FOR PROCUREMENT BY THE ORGANIZATIONS WITHIN THE UN SYSTEM;

... GUIDE PROCUREMENT ACTIVITIES AND FACILITATE HARMONIZATION OF PROCUREMENT PROCEDURE AMONG UN ORGANIZATIONS.

## 1. PREAMBLE

The objective of procurement activities within the UN system is the timely acquisition of goods, works and services while addressing the following:

- the objectives of the UN Organizations concerned;
- fairness, integrity and transparency, through competition;
- economy and effectiveness;
- best value for money.

Procurement in the UN system is governed by the established regulations and rules of each UN Organization. While such regulations and rules may differ in matters of detail, all organizations are guided by this document.

These Common *Guidelines* cover procurement stages from sourcing activities that precede a requisition to the execution of a procurement contract. They do not cover either the details of procurement, logistics or contract implementation matters that may be particular to each UN Organization concerned **(Procuring Entity).**

## 2. PARTICIPATION BY SUPPLIERS

**2.1 Suppliers (i.e. providers of goods, works and services)**
participate, as a general rule, in procurement proceedings without regard to country of origin, unless the UN General Assembly or Security Council decides otherwise. The geographical scope of procurement may also be limited in certain cases determined by the Procuring Entity in accordance with the rules of each organization.

**2.2 Eligibility of Suppliers**

2.2.1 To be eligible, Suppliers must satisfy certain objectively justifiable minimum requirements, which include the legal capacity to enter into a contract, the necessary professional and technical competence, financial strength, plant, equipment and other physical facilities and qualified personnel to satisfy the requirements of the Procuring Entity.

2.2.2 Such minimum eligibility requirements should be distinguished from pre-qualification procedures used to determine the suitability of a Supplier for a specific project or contract. Being eligible for contracts with a Procuring Entity does not mean that a Supplier will be solicited to participate in bidding procedures or will pre-qualify for each relevant procurement activity.

2.2.3 Subject to the right of a Supplier to protect its intellectual property or trade secrets, the Procuring Entity may require the Supplier to provide documentary evidence or other information that it may deem useful to verify that the Supplier meets the requirements referred to above.

2.2.4 A Supplier that has been found at any time to have intentionally submitted false, materially inaccurate or materially incomplete information will not be considered eligible.

## 2.3 REGISTRATION

2.3.1 Rosters of eligible Suppliers are maintained by the Procuring Entity to ensure that a list of potential Suppliers is readily available.

2.3.2 Suppliers, wishing to be registered, should communicate directly with the Procuring Entity to request inclusion in its roster. Instructions on how to register will be provided by the Procuring Entity.

2.3.3 The information submitted by the Supplier will be evaluated by the Procuring Entity to establish the eligibility for inclusion in the roster.

2.3.4 Procuring Entities may invite from a Supplier directly or indirectly, e.g. by advertisement or other means, expressions of interest for general purposes, or a particular procurement activity.

# 3. SOLICITATION DOCUMENTS

## 3.1 General

3.1.1 Solicitation Documents are used to request bids, proposals or quotations (offers) from Suppliers for the goods, works or services required. While the details and complexity of Solicitation Documents will vary according to the nature and value of the requirements, they will contain all information necessary to prepare a suitable Offer. Solicitation Documents will include, as appropriate: an invitation to offer, instructions to the offerer, form of the offer requested (bid, proposal or quotation), form of the proposed contract, conditions of contract – both general and special, technical specifications, lists of goods or bills of quantities and drawings, description of work, as well as necessary appendices, evaluation criteria and minimum qualification requirements.

3.1.2 In the Solicitation Documents, descriptions of the required goods, works or services will normally be generic. References to brand names, trademarks, catalogue numbers or similar classifications should be avoided. If it is necessary to quote a brand name or catalogue number of a particular manufacturer to clarify an otherwise incomplete description, the words "or equivalent" will be added after such references.

3.1.3 Solicitation Documents will specify internationally accepted standards, such as those issued by ISO, wherever these are available and appropriate. When particular national or other standards are required, the Solicitation Document will indicate that other standards may be acceptable, provided they ensure an equivalent or higher level of performance than the specified international standard.

3.1.4 Where it becomes necessary to clarify the Solicitation Documents for any reason, all Suppliers who have received the Solicitation Documents will be notified simultaneously in writing of the clarification. At any time before the deadline for submission of Offers, the Procuring Entity may, for any reason, whether on its own initiative or because of a request for clarification by a Supplier, modify the Solicitation Documents by issuing an addendum. The addendum will be communicated promptly to all Suppliers, to which the Procuring Entity has provided the Solicitation Documents and will be binding on those Suppliers.

### 3.2 Types of Solicitation Documents

3.2.1 *Invitation to Bid (ITB)*: A Solicitation Document issued by a Procuring Entity in which the requirements for formal competitive bidding are specified. The ITB describes the Procuring Entity's requirements quantitatively and qualitatively in a manner which permits prospective bidders to submit bids on the same basis so that the award can be made to the lowest priced, technically acceptable bidder or best value bidder as evaluated in accordance with the ITB.

3.2.2 *Request for Proposals(RFP)*: A Solicitation Document issued by a Procuring Entity in order to obtain proposals to satisfy a requirement which cannot be described in a complete or definitive manner. An RFP leads to the selection of the proposal that offers the best value in accordance with the evaluation criteria. Where appropriate, the RFP will indicate that negotiation may be undertaken in respect of one or more proposals.

3.2.3 *Request for Quotation(RFQ)*: An informal Solicitation Document, normally used for low value procurement requirements, in which Procuring Entities request prices and commercial terms from Suppliers, for goods, works or services that meet standard specifications and are readily available on the market.

## 4. SOLICITATION OF OFFERS

### 4.1 Competition

4.1.1 Procuring Entities, as a general rule, use competition to procure goods, works or services. Such competition may be undertaken on an informal or formal basis and be either open or limited. As many Suppliers as is practicable will be given the opportunity to offer the required goods, works or services.

### 4.2 Open International Competition

4.2.1 Open International Competition (OIC) is initiated by an advertisement, which invites interested Suppliers to request the Solicitation Documents from the Procuring Entity. Use of OIC is appropriate for goods, works or services of a relatively high value.

4.2.2 The Procuring Entity, at its discretion, may arrange the publication of a Procurement Notice in the United Nations' "Development Business", UNDP/IAPSO's "Procurement Update" or a publication of wide international circulation. The advertisement will contain information such as the scope of procurement, name and address of the Procuring Entity, and the scheduled date for availability of Solicitation Documents.

4.2.3 For complex or specialized goods, works or services, pre-qualification may be undertaken by advertising. Any Supplier requesting to participate will be provided with pre-qualification documents, which will contain instructions on preparing and submitting applications, the procurement requirements contemplated, and any specific qualifications that may be deemed necessary for pre-qualification. Only suppliers that have been pre-qualified following evaluation are entitled to participate in further procurement proceedings for the specific requirement.

### 4.3 Limited International Competition

4.3.1 Limited International Competition (LIC) is limited to a short-list of qualified Suppliers selected in a non-discriminatory manner by the Procuring Entity from rosters, pre-qualifications, expressions of interest and other sources. LIC is appropriate where OIC is unsuitable for economical and efficient procurement because of the value, urgent demand or limited availability of the required goods, works or services.

### 4.4 Local Competition

4.4.1 For specified reasons the Procuring Entity may restrict the use of the solicitation methods as described in 4.2 and 4.3 to Suppliers located in the country or region where the goods, works or services procured will be used.

### 4.5 Direct Contracting

4.5.1 As an alternative to competition, and in the interest of the Procuring Entity, Direct Contracting through negotiation may be an appropriate method when, for example:

- the contract relates to the procurement of proprietary goods, works or services;
- standardization of equipment or spare parts require compatibility with existing equipment;
- rate contracts or standing offers were established by the Procuring Entity or following joint negotiations by several Organizations of the UN system;
- the urgency of the requirement is such that the delay involved in applying other methods of procurement would be unacceptable;
- offers for identical items have been obtained through competition within a reasonable period and the prices and conditions offered remain competitive;
- the monetary value of the proposed contract is considered insufficient to make competitive procurement economical.

## 5. SUBMISSION, RECEIPT, OPENING AND EVALUATION OF OFFERS

### 5.1 General

5.1.1. All Offers will be received, accepted, opened, recorded and evaluated in accordance with impartial procedures established by the Procuring Entity.

### 5.2 Submission and Receipt of Offers

5.2.1 Suppliers must comply with the procedure for submission of Offers as well as the technical requirements expressed in the Solicitation Documents in order to protect the confidentiality, and allow for fair and non-discriminatory treatment, of their Offers.

5.2.2 An Offer may be modified or withdrawn before the deadline for its receipt. Such modification or withdrawal shall be made in the form indicated in the Solicitation Documents for the Offer.

### 5.3 Opening of Bids and Proposals

5.3.1 The Procuring Entity will fix a date and place for the opening of bids and proposals. Where the opening is public, the date, time and place will be indicated in the Solicitation Documents. The purpose of the opening is to verify that all formalities indicated in the Solicitation Documents are met, including the timeliness of the receipt of each bid or proposal and, where required, their sealed condition.

5.3.2 When the opening is public, Suppliers who have submitted bids are entitled to attend the opening, where each bid is opened and the names and addresses of each bidder, as well as the total value of each bid is announced.

### 5.4 Evaluation of Offers

5.4.1 Once bids, proposals or quotations have been received and opened, they will be evaluated to determine which Offer best responds to the requirements established by the Solicitation Documents.

5.4.2 The Offers will be evaluated in accordance with the evaluation criteria specified in the Solicitation Documents. To the extent appropriate, the evaluation criteria will be given relative weight. Bids, proposals and quotations submitted in different currencies will be converted into a single currency, usually US dollars, using the United Nations operational rate of exchange in effect at the date specified in the Solicitation Document.

5.4.3 Except when negotiations have been authorized by the Procuring Entity, Suppliers will not be allowed to alter any Offer after the deadline for receipt provided for in the Solicitation Documents. The Procuring Entity may, however, request clarification of any offer during the evaluation.

### 5.5 Rejection of Offers

5.5.1 The Procuring Entity may reject any or all Offers at any time before the conclusion of a procurement contract.

## 6. PROCUREMENT CONTRACTS

### 6.1 Formalization of Procurement Contracts

6.1.1. Once the Procuring Entity has decided on the award of contract, that decision is formalized by the establishment of a legally enforceable relationship with the successful offeror. Normally, this is accomplished by a written procurement contract between the parties.

6.1.2 After a procurement contract has been awarded or the procurement proceedings have ended, unsuccessful offerors normally will be sent a formal letter of regret by the Procuring Entity.

6.1.3 The Procuring Entity will not disclose:

- information that may prejudice legitimate commercial interests of the parties or inhibit fair competition;
- information relating to the examination, evaluation and comparison of Offers.

**6.2 Terms and Conditions**

6.2.1 All procurement contracts are subject to the General Conditions of the Procuring Entity. The Solicitation Documents will include a copy of, or incorporate by reference, the General Conditions of the Procuring Entity and Special Conditions, if any.

6.2.2 The General Conditions will include, inter alia, a clause on the settlement of disputes by arbitration and relevant provisions concerning the privileges and immunities of the United Nations that apply to the Procuring Entity.

**6.3 Performance Securities**

6.3.1 The Procuring Entity may require Suppliers to provide a security to guarantee performance in accordance with the procurement contract. This performance security may be requested in the form of a bank guarantee, a standby letter of credit, or other means, in an amount related to the value of the goods, services or works involved and the payment conditions.

## 7. ETHICAL BEHAVIOUR AND RELATIONSHIPS WITH SUPPLIERS

7.1 All procurement officials will maintain an unimpeachable standard of integrity in all their business relationships both inside and outside the Organizations in which they are employed. They will never use their authority or office for personal gain and will seek to uphold and enhance the standing of their Organization.

## 8. STATISTICAL REPORTING

8.1 Each Organization of the UN system will keep appropriate statistics on its procurement activities, including details of geographical distribution of contracts. These statistics will be made available regularly to the Member States through the General Assembly of the United Nations.

# ANNEX II

## FINANCIAL REGULATIONS AND RULES OF THE UNITED NATIONS

Secretary-General's Bulletin
ST/SGB/Financial Rules/1/Rev.3 (1985)

*EXCERPTS*

ST/SGB/Financial Rules/1/Re.3 (1985)

# FINANCIAL REGULATIONS AND RULES OF THE UNITED NATIONS

## (SERIES 100)

## SECRETARY-GENERAL'S BULLETIN

UNITED NATIONS

New York, 1985

*be reimbursed to the Fund as soon as and to the extent that income is available for that purpose.*

Regulation 6.4: *Except when such advances are recoverable from some other source, advances made from the Working Capital Fund for unforeseen and extraordinary expenses or other authorized purposes shall be reimbursed through the submission of supplementary programme budget proposals.*

**Advances from the Working Capital Fund**

*Rule 106.2*

(a) Advances from the Working Capital Fund may be made only for the purposes and within the terms and conditions prescribed by the General Assembly, and only on the basis of a written authorization signed by the Controller.

(b) All advances necessary to finance budgetary appropriations pending the receipt of contributions or to finance obligations under resolutions relating to unforeseen and extraordinary expenses duly approved in accordance with the provisions of rule 103.9 shall be reimbursed to the Working Capital Fund as soon as the cash balance in the General Fund is sufficient for the purpose.

Regulation 6.5: Income derived from investments of the Working Capital Fund shall be credited to miscellaneous income.

Regulation 6.6: Trust funds, reserve and special accounts may be established by the Secretary-General and shall be reported to the Advisory Committee.

Regulation 6.7: The purpose and limits of each trust fund, reserve and special account shall be clearly defined by the appropriate authority. Unless otherwise provided by the General Assembly, such funds and accounts shall be administered in accordance with the present Regulations.

**Establishment of trust funds, reserve and special accounts**

*Rule 106.3*

Trust funds, reserve and special accounts may be established outside the programme budget appropriations in respect of specific activities entrusted to the Organization.

*Rule 106.4*

The purpose and limits of each trust fund, reserve or special account established shall be as defined by the appropriate authority. Such funds and accounts shall be administered in accordance with these Financial Rules unless otherwise provided by the General Assembly. (*See also rules 107.5, 107.6 and 107.7 with respect to acceptance of voluntary contributions, gifts or donations.*)

## ARTICLE VII. OTHER INCOME

Regulation 7.1: *All other income except*:

(a) *Contributions to the programme budget;*
(b) *Direct refunds of expenditures made during the financial period;*
(c) *Advances or deposits to funds; and*
(d) *Revenue derived from the Staff Assessment Plan*
(e) *shall be classed as miscellaneous income, for credit to the General Fund.*

### Miscellaneous income

*Rule 107.1*
Proceeds from rental of property or loan of services

Proceeds from tile rental of property or from the loan of staff members or other services rendered shall be credited as miscellaneous income. (See also rules 114.2 and 114.3 with respect to provision of goods and services to others and accounting for goods and services provided to others, respectively.)

*Rule 107.2*
Refunds of expenditures

*(a)* Refunds of expenditures which had been charged in the same financial period against the budgetary accounts may be credited against the same accounts, but refunds of expenditures of prior financial periods shall be credited to miscellaneous income.
*(b)* Adjustments which arise subsequent to the closing of an extrabudgetary account, i.e. a trust fund, special account, project etc., shall be classed as miscellaneous income and charged or credited to miscellaneous income of the appropriate account. (*See also rules 114.2 and 114.3 with respect to provision of goods and services to others and accounting for goods and services provided to others, respectively.*)

### Revenue-producing activities

*Rule 107.3*
Financial control

Revenue-producing activities (e.g., the United Nations Postal Administration, the Visitors' Service, sale of publications, United Nations garage operations, the United Nations gift centre and catering and related services) which are not directly financed out of the programme budget appropriations, but the net income from which accrues as miscellaneous income to the Organization, shall be subject to the same financial controls as apply to activities financed from the programme budget appropriations and shall be administered in accordance with these Financial Regulations and Rules.

*Rule 107.4*
Programme budget presentation

The proposed programme budget shall include information on the revenue-producing activities referred to in rule 107.3 above, showing the estimates of gross revenue and expenditure for each such activity as well as the credit to the income section of the budget in respect of the net revenue from each such activity.

**Voluntary contributions, gifts or donations**

Regulation 7.2: *Voluntary contributions, whether or not in cash, may be accepted by the Secretary-General provided that the purposes for which the contributions are made are consistent with the policies, aims and activities of the Organization, and provided that the acceptance of such contributions which directly or indirectly involve additional financial liability for the Organization shall require the consent of the appropriate authority.*

Regulation 7.3: *Moneys accepted for purposes specified by the donor shall be treated as trust funds or specific accounts under regulations 6.6 and 6.7.*

Regulation 7.4: *Moneys accepted in respect of which no purpose is specified shall be treated as miscellaneous income and reported as "gifts" in the accounts of the financial period.*

**Acceptance of voluntary contributions, gifts or donations**

*Rule 107.5*

In cases other than those approved by the General Assembly, the establishment of any trust fund or the receipt of any voluntary contribution, gift or donation to be administered by the United Nations requires the approval of the Secretary-General, who may delegate this authority to the USG/AM.

*Rule 107.6*

No voluntary contribution, gift or donation for a specific purpose may be accepted if the purpose is inconsistent with the policies and aims of the United Nations.

*Rule 107.7*

Voluntary contributions, gifts or donations which directly or indirectly involve an immediate or ultimate financial liability for the Organization may be accepted only with the approval of the General Assembly.

## ARTICLE VIII. CUSTODY OF FUNDS

Regulation 8.1: *The Secretary-General shall designate the bank or banks in which the funds of the Organization shall be kept.*

### Receipt, management and disbursement of funds

*Rule 108.1*
Bank accounts

*(a)* The Controller or those United Nations officials authorized by the Controller shall designate the banks in which the funds of the United Nations shall be kept. The designation of a bank shall cover all branches of that bank.
*(b)* The Controller or those authorized by the Controller shall establish such official bank accounts as may be required for the transaction of United Nations business and shall designate signatories to operate those accounts. Officials other than those authorized to establish bank accounts may, with appropriate notification to the bank, be authorized to amend signatory panels.
*(c)* If, at an office away from Headquarters, it is necessary to open a bank account at such short notice that there is not time for the Controller to make the usual arrangements, the head of the office may open the account on the following conditions:

- i.) Wherever possible, the bank shall be a branch of one of the banks designated under rule 108.1 *(a);*
- ii.) The bank shall he instructed that the account is an official account of the United Nations and that the bank is authorized to provide any information that the Controller may request concerning the account;
- iii.) The bank shall also be instructed that monthly bank statements (accompanied by all paid cheques, withdrawal instructions and debit and credit advices) are required and to whom they are to be sent;
- iv.) An immediate report by telegraph shall be made to the Controller, who shall promptly advise the head of office and the bank as to whether the account is, in fact, an official account of the United Nations;
- v.) Wherever possible, two signatures shall be required on all cheques and on all withdrawal instructions. *(See also rule 108.11.)*

*Rule 108.2*
Receipt of moneys

*(a)* An official receipt shall be issued on the date of receipt for all moneys received.
*(b)* Only officials duly designated by the Controller shall be authorized to issue such receipts. In cases where officials other than those authorized to issue official receipts receive moneys intended for the Organization, they shall immediately transmit such moneys in full to the cashier or other official authorized to issue an official receipt.
*(c)* Receipts shall be recorded in the accounts on the date the remittance is received.

*Rule 108.3*
Deposit of receipts

All moneys received shall be deposited intact in an official bank account not later than the business day following the date of receipt.

*Rule 108.4*
Petty cash advances and Cashier's Fund advances

Petty cash advances and Cashier's Fund advances may be made to officials designated by the Controller. The accounts therefore shall normally be maintained on an imprest system. The amount and purposes of each advance shall be defined by the Controller, the amount being held to the minimum compatible with working requirements.

*Rule 108.5*
Responsibility of holders of cash advances

Officials to whom cash advances are issued under rule 108.4 shall make use of such advances only for the purpose for which the advances were authorized and shall be held personally responsible and financially liable for the proper management and safekeeping of the cash so advanced. They shall render accounts as required by the Controller which, unless otherwise provided, shall be not less frequently than once each month. They shall be in a position at all times to account for the advances. Cash or negotiable instruments shall be kept in safe custody.

*Rule 108.6*
Other cash advances

In addition to advances specified in these Rules, the Controller may make such other cash advances as may be permitted by the Staff Rules and administrative instructions or as may be approved by him or her. (*See also rules 108.9 (d) and 110.23 with respect to progress payments and advance payments, respectively.*)

*Rule 108.7*
Remittances to offices away from Headquarters

Offices away from Headquarters shall obtain their funds by remittances from Headquarters. In the absence of a special authorization from the Controller, the remittances shall not exceed the amount required to bring the cash balance of the office concerned to the estimated cash requirements for the next two-and-one-half months.

*Rule 108.8*
Exchange of currencies

Officials responsible for the operation of United Nations bank accounts or for holding United Nations cash or negotiable instruments are not authorized to exchange one currency for another, except to the minimum extent essential for the transaction of official business.

*Rule 108.9*
Approval of obligations and payments

*(a)* Only those officials designated by the Controller as approving officers may approve obligations for recording in the accounts. Any such obligations must have been duly certified by certifying officers designated by the Controller for that purpose. (*See also rule 110.3 with respect to certification and approval of obligations and expenditures.*)
*(b)* Only those officials designated by the Controller as approving officers may approve payments on behalf of the Organization. In addition, all authorizations, whether by telegraph or by letter, to effect payments at another duty station are to be issued and signed by the Controller or on behalf of the Controller by those officials who have been duly designated to do so.
*(c)* Payments shall be made only on the basis of duly certified supporting vouchers and other documents which indicate that the goods or services have been received in accordance with the documents establishing the obligation. An approving officer must also verify that payment has not previously been made and that the supporting documents do not have irregularities on their face which indicate that the payment is not properly due; nor shall an approving officer approve a payment if any other information known to him or her would bar the payment.

vi.) Payments directly related to and not in excess of a recorded obligation which have previously been certified by a certifying officer designated under rule 110.3 shall not require a certification on the invoice;

vii.) For payments under $1,000 for which credits did not need to be reserved in advance by the recording of an obligation under the authority of rule 110.5, the supporting documentation indicating that a payment is due must be certified by a certifying officer designated under rule 110.3 before the payment may be approved.

*(d)* In addition to payments authorized under rule 110.23, and notwithstanding paragraph (c) above, the Controller may, when deeming it in the interest of the United Nations so to do, authorize progress payments. (*See also rules 108.6 and 110.23 with respect to other cash advances and advance payments, respectively.*)

*Rule 108.10*

Disbursements to be made by cheque

*(a)* All disbursements shall be made by cheque, except to the extent that cash disbursements are authorized by the Controller.

*(b)* Disbursements shall be recorded in the accounts as of the date when the disbursement is made, that is, when the cheque is issued or cash is paid out.

## ARTICLE X. INTERNAL CONTROL

Regulation 10.1: *The Secretary-General shall:*

(a) *Establish detailed financial rules and procedures in order to ensure effective financial administration and the exercise of economy;*

(b) *Cause all payments to be made on the basis of supporting vouchers and other documents which ensure that the services or goods have been received and that payments have not previously been made;*

(c) *Designate the officers who may receive moneys, incur obligations and make payments on behalf of the Organization;*

(d) *Maintain an internal financial control which shall provide for an effective current examination and/or review of financial transactions in order to ensure:*

  (i) *The regularity of the receipt, custody and disposal of all funds and other financial resources of the Organization;*

  (ii) *The conformity of obligations and expenditures with the appropriations or other financial provisions voted by the General Assembly, or with the purposes and rules relating to trust funds and special accounts;*

  (iii) *The economic use of the resources of the Organization.*

Regulation 10.2: *Obligation for the current financial period or commitments for current and future financial periods shall be incurred only after allotments or other appropriate authorizations have been made in writing under the authority of the Secretary-General.*

### Administration of budget appropriations

*Rule 110.1*
Appropriations made available by authorization from the USG/AM

*(a)* The USG/AM is responsible to the Secretary-General for ensuring that the expenditures of the Organization remain within the appropriations as voted and are incurred only for the purposes approved by the General Assembly. (*See also rule 106.1 with respect to authority for expenditure.*)

*(b)* Such authorization may take the form of:

  (i) An allotment of funds or other authorization to commit funds covering a specific period and/or a specific purpose; and/or

  (ii) An authorization for the employment of staff or of consultants.

*Rule 110.2*
Review of obligations and expenditures by the Controller

*(a)* Certifying officers are responsible for the submission to the Controller of the appropriate documents in support of proposed obligations and expenditures.

*(b)* The Controller may, on adequate grounds, disallow any proposal for an obligation or expenditure.

*(c)* Certifying officers shall submit such explanations and justifications as the Controller may require.
*(d)* No transfers between allotments may be made, except on the written authorization of the Controller.

*Rule 110.3*
Certification and approval of obligations and expenditures

Every obligation or proposal for the incurring of expenditure shall require:
*(a)* Certification by a certifying officer designated for the purpose by the Controller before the expenditure is actually incurred, provided that the Controller shall have authority to certify obligations and expenditures under all accounts; and
*(b)* Subsequent approval by an approving officer designated for that purpose by the Controller before the obligation is recorded or payment made. (*See also rule 108.9 with respect to approval of obligations and payments.*)

*Rule 110.4*
Certifying officers

*(a)* One or more officials shall be designated by the Controller as certifying officer(s) for each department on the recommendation of the head of the department. Certifying officers shall be responsible for the specific account(s) assigned to them by the Controller. Alternates may be designated by the Controller to act in the absence of the certifying officer(s).
*(b)* The responsibilities of certifying or alternate certifying officers shall be established by the Controller. The authority granted and responsibility assigned to such officers is a personal one and cannot be delegated.

*Rule 110.5*
Reservation of credits to meet expenditures

*(a)* Apart from the employment of staff under an authorized staffing table, and consequential commitments under the Staff Regulations and Rules, no contract, agreement or undertaking of any nature for an amount exceeding $1,000 shall be entered into until credits have been reserved in the accounts, through the recording of an obligation, to meet any expenditures which may accrue in the financial period. Additionally, unless the amount of the change in the credits reserved exceeds $1,000, no change need be made in the amount previously obligated. In cases where the change exceeds $1,000, the payment is to be made in

Writing-off of losses or deficiencies

Regulation 10.4: *The Secretary-General may, after full investigation, authorize the writing-off of losses of cash, stores and other assets, provided that a statement of all such amounts written off shall be submitted to the Auditors with the accounts.*

**Writing-off of losses of cash, receivables and property**

*Rule 110.14*
Writing off of losses of cash and receivables

*(a)* The Controller may, after full investigation, authorize the writing-off of losses of cash and the book value of accounts receivable and notes receivable deemed to be irrecoverable, except that the writing-off of amounts in excess of $10,000 shall require the approval of the Secretary-General.
*(b)* The investigation shall, in each case, fix the responsibility, if any, attaching to any official of the United Nations for the loss. Such official may be required to reimburse the loss either partially or in full. (*See also rule 109.5 with respect to losses of cash or negotiable instruments.*)

*Rule 110.15*
Writing-off of losses of property

*(a)* The Controller may, after full investigation in each case, authorize the writing-off of losses of United Nations property or such other adjustment of the records as will bring the balance shown by the records into conformity with the actual quantities.
*(b)* Final determination as to all surcharges to be made against staff members or others as the result of losses will be made by the Controller.

Contracts and purchases

Regulation 10.5: *Tenders for equipment, supplies and other requirements shall be invited by advertisement, except where the Secretary-General deems that, in the interests of the Organization, a departure from the rule is desirable.*

**Contracts and purchases**

*Rule 110.16*
Authorized official

*(a)* Contracts for the purchase. rental or sale of services, supplies, equipment or other requirements shall be entered into on behalf of the United Nations only by officials duly authorized for the purpose. Purchasing, renting or selling activities include, in addition to entering into contracts, the invitation of proposes or tenders and the negotiation with potential suppliers or purchasers on the basis of detailed specifications.

*(b)* Unless otherwise directed by the Secretary-General, the USG/AM or officials duly authorized by the USG/AM shall be responsible for purchasing, renting or selling activities on behalf of the Organization, provided that:

i.) The Director-General or an official duly authorized by the Director-General shall be responsible for purchasing, renting or selling activities in respect of the United Nations Office at Geneva;

ii.) The Executive Directors or officials duly authorized by them shall be responsible for purchasing, renting or selling activities relating to their respective offices in respect of the United Nations Industrial Development Organization, the United Nations Environment Programme and the United Nations Centre for Human Settlements;

iii.) The Executive Secretaries of the United Nations regional commissions (except the Economic Commission for Europe) or officials duly authorized by them shall be responsible for purchasing, renting or selling activities relating to their respective offices, subject to the limits provided in clauses *(e)* (i) and (ii) of rule 110.17.

*Rule 110.17*
Committee on Contracts

*(a)* There shall be established a committee on contracts at United Nations Headquarters to render written advice to the Assistant Secretary-General for General Services or such other officials authorized under rule 110.16, on:

i.) All contracts to be entered into which involve commitments to a single contractor in respect of a single requisition or a series of related requisitions totalling $40,000 or more;

ii.) All contracts or series of related contracts, including those for television or film activities, which involve income to the Organization of $10,000 or more, and any contracts relating to activities where the estimated annual income therefrom when aggregated with the estimated annual income from any other contract or contracts already made with the same purchaser in the same year amounts to $10,000 or more, except that contractual arrangements resulting from the recommendations of the Property Survey Board shall not be referred to the Committee on Contracts;

iii.) Proposals for modification or renewal of contracts previously reviewed by the Committee;

iv.) Such other matters as may be referred to the Committee by the Assistant Secretary-General for General Services or such other officials authorized under rule 110.16.

*(b)* The composition of the Headquarters Committee and its terms of reference shall be determined by the Secretary-General.
*(c)* There shall be established local Committees on Contracts, similar to the one at United Nations Headquarters, at the United Nations Office at Geneva, the United Nations Industrial Development Organization, the United Nations Environment Programme, the United Nations Centre for Human Settlements and the respective headquarters of the United Nations regional commissions (except the Economic Commission for Europe). The composition of each local Committee shall be determined by the head of office concerned in consultation with the Secretary-General.
*(d)* The local Committees on Contracts at the United Nations Office at Geneva, the United Nations Industrial Development Organization, the United Nations Environment Programme and the United Nations Centre for Human Settlements shall render written advice to the respective heads of office on;

i.) All contracts for the purchase or rental of services, supplies, equipment and other requirements involving commitments in respect of a single requisition or a series of related requisitions totalling $40,000 or more;

ii.) All contracts or series of related contracts, including those for television or film activities, which involve income to the Organization of $10,000 or more, and any contracts relating to activities where the estimated annual income therefrom when aggregated with the estimated annual income from any other contract or contracts already made with the same purchaser ir. the same year amounts to $10,000 or more, except that contractual arrangements resulting from the recommendations of the local Property Survey Board shall not be referred to the Committee on Contracts;

iii.) Proposals for modification or renewal of contracts previously reviewed by the Committee;

iv.) Such other matters as may be referred to the Committee by the head of office concerned.

*(e)* The local Committees on Contracts at the headquarters of the United Nations regional commissions shall render written advice to the respective Executive Secretaries on:

i.) All contracts for the purchase or rental of services, supplies, equipment or other requirements involving commitments in respect of a single requisition or a series of related requisitions exceeding $20,000 but less than $40,000. All contracts above $40,000 shall be referred to the Committee on Contracts at United Nations Headquarters;

ii.) All contracts or series of related contracts, including those for television or film activities, which involve income to the Organization exceeding $5,000 but less than $10,000, and any contracts relating to activities where the estimated annual income therefrom when aggregated with the estimated annual income from any other contract or contracts already made with the same purchaser in the same year is an amount exceeding $5,000 but less than $10,000, except that (a) all contracts involving income to the Organization in excess of $10,000 shall be referred to the Headquarters Committee on Contracts and (b) contractual arrangements resulting from the recommendations of the Property Survey Board shall not be referred to the Committee on Contracts;

iii.) Proposals for modification or renewal of contracts previously reviewed by the Committee;

iv.) Such other matters as may be referred to the Committee by the Executive Secretary concerned.

*(f)* The Assistant Secretary-General for General Services, in consultation with the Controller, may authorize the establishment of a local committee on contracts at a location other than the ones specified in (c) above.

*(g)* Where, under the preceding provisions of this rule, the advice of the Headquarters Committee on Contracts (or of the appropriate local committee) is required to be sought, no commitment may be entered into before such advice is received. In cases where the Assistant Secretary-General for General Services or such other official authorized under rule 110.16 decides not to accept the advice of the Committee, he or she shall record in writing the reasons for that decision.

*Rule 110.18*
Calling for bids or proposals

Except as provided in rule 110.19, contracts for the purchase or rental of services, supplies, equipment and other requirements shall be let after competitive bidding or calling for proposals. Tenders shall be invited by advertising through publication or distribution of formal invitations to bid; provided that in cases where the nature of the work involved precludes invitation of tenders and where proposals are called, a comparative analysis of such proposals shall be kept on record.

*Rule 110.19*
Exceptions to calling for bids or proposals

Contracts may be awarded without calling for proposals, advertising or formal invitations to bid when:

*(a)* The proposed contract involves commitments of less than $10,000 in the case of United Nations Headquarters, the United Nations Office at Geneva, the United Nations Industrial Development Organization, the United Nations Environment Programme and the United Nations Centre for Human Settlements, and $5,000 in the case of the United Nations regional commissions, provided that the award is made after an assessment of competitive quotations, based on conformity with specifications, delivery schedules and prices or comparative prices, where available;

*(b)* The prices or rates are fixed pursuant to national legislation or by regulatory bodies;

*(c)* A standardization of supplies or equipment has been approved on the advice of the Committee on Contracts which renders competition impracticable;

*(d)* The exigency of the service does not permit the delay attendant upon the issue of invitations to bid or the calling for proposals;

*(e)* The contract relates to the purchase of proprietary articles or perishable supplies;

*(f)* The proposed contract relates to professional services other than staff services;

*(g)* The proposed contract relates to medicines, medical supplies, hospital or surgical supplies or prosthetic appliances;

*(h)* The Assistant Secretary-General for General Services or such other official authorized under rule 110.16 determines that competitive bidding or calling for proposals will not give satisfactory results. In such cases, appropriate reasons shall be recorded in writing.

*Rule 110.20*
Opening of bids

All bids shall be publicly opened at the time and place specified in the invitation to bid and an immediate record made thereof.

*Rule 110.21*
Awarding of contracts

Contracts shall be awarded to the lowest acceptable bidder, due consideration being given to the utilization of currencies available to the Organization and which require special management, provided that where the interests of the Organization so require, all bids may be rejected; In the latter instance, the

Assistant Secretary-General for General Services or such other official authorized under rule 110.16 shall record in writing the reasons for rejection of the bids and determine whether to invite new competitive tenders or enter into a negotiated contract.

*Rule 110.22*
Purchases to be made in writing

*(a)* Written contracts or written purchase orders for goods and services shall be established, as appropriate, for every purchase from a single contractor or vendor in the following amounts:

(i) In the case of United Nations Headquarters, the United Nations Office at Geneva, the United Nations Industrial Development Organization, the United Nations Environment Programme, the United Nations Centre for Human Settlements and the United Nations regional commissions (except the Economic Commission for Europe), an aggregate amount of $2,500 or more for one or more items;

(ii) In the case of other offices or groups of offices away from Headquarters, such amounts as may be prescribed by the Assistant Secretary-General for General Services, in consultation with the Controller.

*(b)* Written contracts and purchase orders shall specify in detail:

i.) In the case of supplies or equipment, the exact description of the goods, the quantity required, the price of each article, the conditions of delivery and the terms of payment;

ii.) In the case of services other than staff services, the nature of the services, the period covered, the conditions of fulfilment, the amount and terms of payment.

*(c)* The USG/AM or such other officials authorized under rule 110.16, in agreement with the USG/AM, may waive the requirements of any part of this financial rule in certain cases, such as supplies for the maintenance of buildings, where one "blanket" purchase order might be issued covering a variety of items. In the event of such a waiver, a written record shall be established to ensure that:

i.) The vendor and purchaser are in agreement as to what is being purchased;

ii.) An itemized record of sale and receipt is prepared at the time of delivery;

iii.) Payment is based on the itemized record of sale and receipt referred to in (ii) above.

*Rule 110.23*
Advance payments

Except where normal commercial practice or the interest of the United Nations so requires, no contract or purchase order shall be made on behalf of the United Nations which requires a payment or payments on account in advance of the delivery of goods or performance of contractual services. Whenever an advance payment is agreed to, the reasons therefor shall be recorded. (See also rules 108.6 and 108.9 (d) with respect to other cash advances and progress payments, respectively.)

*Rule 110.24*
Written findings

Each determination or decision required of an authorized purchasing officer by the provisions of these Rules shall be supported by the written findings of such officer. These written findings shall be placed in the appropriate case file maintained by the responsible department or office. In cases involving $2,500 or more, they shall also accompany the related obligating documents submitted to the Controller,

**Receipt, management and disposal of supplies, equipment and other property**

*Rule 110.25*
Property records

*(a)* Complete and accurate records shall be maintained of supplies, equipment and other property purchased, received, issued, sold or otherwise disposed of, and remaining on hand. Such records shall be maintained both for Head-

# ANNEX III

## FINANCIAL REGULATIONS AND RULES OF THE UNITED NATIONS

Secretary-General's Bulletin
ST/SGB/2003/7 (9 May 2003)

*EXCERPTS*

ST/SGB/2003/7
9 May 2003

United Nations

# Financial Regulations and Rules of the United Nations

Secretary-General's bulletin

# Article I

## General provisions

### Applicability and authority

**Regulation 1.1. These Regulations shall govern the financial administration of the United Nations, including the International Court of Justice.**

**Rule 101.1**

The Financial Rules are promulgated by the Secretary-General in accordance with the provisions of the Financial Regulations approved by the General Assembly. They shall govern all the financial management activities of the United Nations except as may otherwise explicitly be provided by the Assembly or unless specifically exempted therefrom by the Secretary-General. The Secretary-General hereby delegates authority and responsibility for the implementation of the Financial Regulations and Rules to the Under-Secretary-General for Management. The UnderSecretary-General for Management may in turn delegate by administrative instruction authority for specified aspects of the Financial Regulations and Rules. These administrative instructions will state whether the delegated official may assign aspects of this authority to other officials. In the application of the Financial Regulations and Rules, officials shall be guided by the principles of effective and efficient financial management and the exercise of economy.

### Responsibility and accountability

**Rule 101.2**

All United Nations staff are obligated to comply with the Financial Regulations and Rules and with administrative instructions issued in connection with those Regulations and Rules. Any staff member who contravenes the Financial Regulations and Rules or corresponding administrative instructions may be held personally accountable and financially liable for his or her actions.

**Definitions**

**Rule 101.3**

For the purpose of these Rules:
(a) "Advisory Committee" shall mean the Advisory Committee on Administrative and Budgetary Questions;
(b) "Department" shall mean any department, office or other distinct organizational entity;
(c) "Head of department" shall mean the Under-Secretary-General, Assistant Secretary-General, Director or other officer in charge of a department, as defined in subparagraph (b) above.

**Use of the Tax Equalization Fund**

**Regulation 4.11. Tax Equalization Fund revenue shall be used to refund staff members for income taxes levied by Member States in respect of their United Nations remuneration. Obligations shall be established against the Tax Equalization Fund to cover the estimated liabilities in respect of the refunds made to staff members of those income taxes. If a Member State's credit in the Tax Equalization Fund is insufficient for this purpose, the shortfall shall be added to and recovered from assessed contributions due from that Member State in the subsequent financial period. Where income tax is levied on staff financed from sources of funds that do not contribute to the Tax Equalization Fund, the additional costs for tax reimbursement shall be borne by those sources of funds.**

**Regulation 4.12. In accordance with regulation 3.2, any balance on a Member State's tax equalization account after the obligations referred to in regulation 4.11 have been satisfied shall be credited against the assessed contributions due from that Member State the following year.**

**Trust funds and reserve and special accounts**

**Regulation 4.13. Trust funds and reserve and special accounts may be established by the Secretary-General and shall be reported to the Advisory Committee.**

**Regulation 4.14. The purpose and limits of each trust fund and reserve and special account shall be clearly defined by the appropriate authority. Unless**

**otherwise provided by the General Assembly, such funds and accounts shall be administered in accordance with the present Regulations.**

**Rule 104.3**

Trust funds and reserve and special accounts may be established by the General Assembly or the Secretary-General in respect of specific activities entrusted to the Organization. The establishment, purpose and limits of trust funds and reserve and special accounts established under the authority of the Secretary-General require the approval of the Under-Secretary-General for Management.

## B. Banking

### Bank accounts, authority and policy

**Regulation 4.15. The Secretary-General shall designate the bank or banks in which the funds of the Organization shall be kept.**

**Rule 104.4**

The Under-Secretary-General for Management shall designate the banks in which the funds of the United Nations shall be kept, shall establish all official bank accounts required for the transaction of United Nations business and shall designate those officials to whom signatory authority is delegated for the operation of those accounts. The Under-Secretary-General for Management shall also authorize all bank account closures. United Nations bank accounts are to be opened and operated in accordance with the following guidelines:

(a) Bank accounts shall be designated "official accounts of the United Nations" and the relevant authority shall be notified that those accounts are exempt from all taxation;
(b) Banks shall be required to provide prompt monthly statements;
(c) Two signatures, or their electronic equivalent, shall be required on all cheques and other withdrawal instructions, including electronic modes of payment;
(d) All banks shall be required to recognize that the Under-Secretary-General for Management is authorized to receive, upon request or as promptly as is practicable, all information pertaining to official bank accounts of the United Nations.

### Bank signatories

**Rule 104.5**

Bank signatory authority and responsibility is assigned on a personal basis and cannot be delegated. Bank signatories cannot exercise the approving functions assigned in accordance with rule 105.6. Designated bank signatories must:

(a) Ensure that there are sufficient funds in the bank account when cheques and other payment instructions are presented for payment;

(b) Verify that all cheques and other payment instructions are pre-encumbered, dated and drawn to the order of the named payee approved by an approving officer (designated in accordance with rule 105.6), as indicated in the accompanying disbursement voucher, payment instructions and original invoice;

(c) Ensure that cheques and other banking instruments are properly safeguarded and that when they are obsolete they are destroyed in accordance with rule 106.11.

### Exchange of currencies

**Rule 104.6**

Officials responsible for the operation of United Nations bank accounts or for holding United Nations cash or negotiable instruments are not authorized to exchange one currency for another, except to the minimum extent necessary for the transaction of official business.

### Remittances to offices away from Headquarters

**Rule 104.7**

Offices away from Headquarters shall obtain their funds through remittances from Headquarters. In the absence of a special authorization from the Under authorizing signatures, in either conventional or electronic form. All commitments, obligations and expenditures must first be signed ("certified") by a duly designated certifying officer (rule 105.5). Following certification, duly designated approving officers (rule 105.6) must then sign to "approve" the establishment of obligations and the recording of expenditures in the accounts and the processing of payments. Expenditures recorded against an established, certified obligation do not require additional certification, provided that they do not exceed the amount obligated by more than 10 per cent or $2,500 (or its equivalent in other currencies), whichever is lower (rule 105.7). Expenditures under $2,500 (or its equivalent in other currencies) for which the recording of an obligation is unnecessary require both certification and approval.

## Certifying officers

### Rule 105.5

(a) One or more officials shall be designated by the Under-Secretary-General for Management as the certifying officer(s) for the account(s) pertaining to a section or subsection of an approved budget. Certifying authority and responsibility is assigned on a personal basis and cannot be delegated. A certifying officer cannot exercise the approving functions assigned in accordance with rule 105.6.

(b) Certifying officers are responsible for managing the utilization of resources, including posts, in accordance with the purposes for which those resources were approved, the principles of efficiency and effectiveness and the Financial Regulations and Rules of the United Nations. Certifying officers must maintain detailed records of all obligations and expenditures against the accounts for which they have been delegated responsibility. They must be prepared to submit any supporting documents, explanations and justifications requested by the Under-Secretary-General for Management.

## Approving officers

### Rule 105.6

(a) Approving officers are designated by the Under-Secretary-General for Management to approve the entry into the accounts of obligations and expenditures relating to contracts, agreements, purchase orders and other forms of undertaking after verifying that they are in order and have been certified by a duly designated certifying officer. Approving officers are also responsible for approving the making of payments once they have ensured that they are properly due, confirming that the necessary services, supplies or equipment have been received in accordance with the contract, agreement, purchase order or other form of undertaking by which they were ordered and, if the cost exceeds $2,500 (or its equivalent in other currencies), in accordance with the purpose for which the relevant financial obligation was established. Approving officers must maintain detailed records and must be prepared to submit any supporting documents, explanations and justifications requested by the Under-Secretary-General for Management.

(b) Approving authority and responsibility is assigned on a personal basis and cannot be delegated. An approving officer cannot exercise the certifying functions assigned in accordance with rule 105.5 or the bank signatory functions assigned in accordance with rule 104.5.

**Establishment and revision of obligations**

**Rule 105.7**

(a) Apart from the employment of staff against an authorized staffing table and consequential commitments under the Staff Regulations and Rules and allocations made to executing agencies, no undertaking, including by contract, agreement or purchase order, for an amount exceeding $2,500 (or its equivalent in other currencies) shall be entered into until the appropriate credit(s) has (have) been reserved in the accounts. This shall be done through the recording of obligations against which relevant payments or disbursements, made only on fulfilment of contractual and other obligations, shall be recorded as expenditure. An obligation shall be recorded in the accounts as unliquidated during the period set forth in regulation 5.3 and until such point as it is reobligated, liquidated or cancelled in accordance with regulations 5.4 and 5.5, as appropriate.

(b) If, in the time that elapses between the establishment of an obligation and the processing of final payment, the cost of the relevant goods or services has, for whatever reason, increased by less than $2,500 (or its equivalent in other currencies) or 10 per cent of the obligation, whichever is lower, no change need be made to the amount of the original obligation. If, however, the increase in costs exceeds $2,500 (or its equivalent in other currencies), the original obligation must be revised to reflect this increase in requirements and further certification is required. All increases in obligations, including those resulting from currency fluctuations, shall be subject to the same procedures as apply to the incurring of original obligations.

**Review, reobligation and cancellation of obligations**

**Rule 105.8**

(a) Outstanding obligations must be reviewed periodically by the responsible certifying officer(s). If an obligation is determined to be valid but cannot be liquidated during the period set forth in regulation 5.3, the provisions of regulations 5.4 and 5.5 shall, as appropriate, be applied. Obligations that are no longer valid shall be cancelled from the accounts forthwith and the resulting credit surrendered.

(b) When any obligation previously recorded in the accounts is, for any reason, reduced (other than by payment) or cancelled, the certifying officer shall accordingly ensure that appropriate adjustments are recorded in the accounts.

### Obligating documents

#### Rule 105.9

An obligation must be based on a formal contract, agreement, purchase order or other form of undertaking, or on a liability recognized by the United Nations. All obligations must be supported by an appropriate obligating document.

## C. Procurement

### General principles

**Regulation 5.12. Procurement functions include all actions necessary for the acquisition, by purchase or lease, of property, including products and real property, and of services, including works. The following general principles shall be given due consideration when exercising the procurement functions of the United Nations:**

**(a.) Best value for money;**
**(b.) Fairness, integrity and transparency;**
**(c.) Effective international competition;**
**(d.) The interest of the United Nations.**

**Regulation 5.13. Tenders for equipment, supplies and other requirements shall be invited by advertisement, except where the Secretary-General deems that, in the interests of the Organization, a departure from this regulation is desirable.**

### Authority and responsibility

#### Rule 105.13

(a) The Under-Secretary-General for Management is responsible for the procurement functions of the United Nations, shall establish all United Nations procurement systems and shall designate the officials responsible for performing procurement functions.

(b) The Under-Secretary-General for Management shall establish review committees, at Headquarters and other locations, to render written advice to the Under-Secretary-General for Management on procurement actions leading to the award or amendment of procurement contracts, which, for purposes of these Regulations and Rules, includes agreements or other written instruments such as purchase orders and contracts that involve income to the United Nations. The Under-Secretary-General for Management shall establish the composition and the terms of reference of such committees, which shall include the types and monetary values of proposed procurement actions subject to review.
(c) Where the advice of a review committee is required, no final action leading to the award or amendment of a procurement contract may be taken before such advice is received. In cases where the Under-Secretary-General for Management decides not to accept the advice of such a review committee, he or she shall record in writing the reasons for that decision.

**Competition**

**Rule 105.14**

Consistent with the principles set out in regulation 5.12 and except as otherwise provided in rule 105.16, procurement contracts shall be awarded on the basis of effective competition, and to this end the competitive process shall, as necessary, include:

(a.) Acquisition planning for developing an overall procurement strategy and procurement methodologies;
(b.) Market research for identifying potential suppliers;
(c.) Consideration of prudent commercial practices;
(d.) Formal methods of solicitation, utilizing invitations to bid or requests for proposals on the basis of advertisement or direct solicitation of invited suppliers, or informal methods of solicitation such as requests for quotations. The UnderSecretary-General for Management shall issue administrative instructions concerning the types of procurement activities and monetary values for which such methods of solicitation are to be used;
(e.) Public bid openings.

## Formal methods of solicitation

### Rule 105.15

(a) When a formal invitation to bid has been issued, the procurement contract shall be awarded to the qualified bidder whose bid substantially conforms to the requirements set forth in the solicitation documents and is evaluated to be the one with the lowest cost to the United Nations.
(b) When a formal request for proposals has been issued, the procurement contract shall be awarded to the qualified proposer whose proposal, all factors considered, is the most responsive to the requirements set forth in the solicitation documents.
(c) The Under-Secretary-General for Management may, in the interest of the United Nations, reject bids or proposals for a particular procurement action, recording the reasons for rejection in writing. The Under-Secretary-General for Management shall then determine whether to undertake a new solicitation, to directly negotiate a procurement contract pursuant to rule 105.16 or to terminate or suspend the procurement action.

## Exceptions to the use of formal methods of solicitation

### Rule 105.16

(a) The Under-Secretary-General for Management may determine for a particular procurement action that using formal methods of solicitation is not in the best interest of the United Nations:

- (i.) When there is no competitive marketplace for the requirement, such as where a monopoly exists, where prices are fixed by legislation or government regulation or where the requirement involves a proprietary product or service;
- (ii.) When there has been a previous determination or there is a need to standardize the requirement;
- (iii.) When the proposed procurement contract is the result of cooperation with other organizations of the United Nations system, pursuant to rule 105.17;
- (iv.) When offers for identical products and services have been obtained competitively within a reasonable period and the prices and conditions offered remain competitive;
- (v.) When, within a reasonable prior period, a formal solicitation has not produced satisfactory results;

(vi.) When the proposed procurement contract is for the purchase or lease of real property and market conditions do not allow for effective competition;

(vii.) When there is an exigency for the requirement;

(viii.) When the proposed procurement contract relates to obtaining services that cannot be evaluated objectively;

(ix.) When the Under-Secretary-General for Management otherwise determines that a formal solicitation will not give satisfactory results;

(x.) When the value of the procurement is below the monetary threshold established for formal methods of solicitation.

(b) When a determination is made pursuant to subparagraph (a) above, the Under-Secretary-General for Management shall record the reasons in writing and may then award a procurement contract, either on the basis of an informal method of solicitation or on the basis of a directly negotiated contract, to a qualified vendor whose offer substantially conforms to the requirement at an acceptable price.

**Cooperation**

**Rule 105.17**

(a) The Under-Secretary-General for Management may cooperate with other organizations of the United Nations system to meet the procurement requirements of the United Nations, provided that the regulations and rules of those organizations are consistent with those of the United Nations. The Under-Secretary-General for Management may, as appropriate, enter into agreements for such purposes. Such cooperation may include carrying out common procurement actions together or the United Nations entering into a contract relying on a procurement decision of another United Nations organization or requesting another United Nations organization to carry out procurement activities on behalf of the United Nations.

(b) The Under-Secretary-General for Management may, to the extent authorized by the General Assembly, cooperate with a Government, non-governmental organization or other public international organization in respect of procurement activities and, as appropriate, enter into agreements for such purposes.

**Written contracts**

**Rule 105.18**

(a) Written procurement contracts shall be used to formalize every procurement action with a monetary value exceeding specific thresholds established by the Under-Secretary-General for Management. Such arrangements shall, as appropriate, specify in detail:

(i.) The nature of the products or services being procured;
(ii.) The quantity being procured;
(iii.) The contract or unit price;
(iv.) The period covered;
(v.) Conditions to be fulfilled, including the United Nations general conditions of contract and implications for non-delivery;
(vi.) Terms of delivery and payment;
(vii.) Name and address of supplier.

(b) The requirement for written procurement contracts shall not be interpreted to restrict the use of any electronic means of data interchange. Before any electronic means of data interchange is used, the Under-Secretary-General for Management shall ensure that the electronic data interchange system is capable of ensuring authentication and confidentiality of the information.

**Advance and progress payments**

**Rule 105.19**

(a) Except where normal commercial practice or the interests of the United Nations so require, no contract or other form of undertaking shall be made on behalf of the United Nations which requires a payment or payments on account in advance of the delivery of products or the performance of contractual services. Whenever an advance payment is agreed to, the reasons therefor shall be recorded.

(b) In addition to subparagraph (a) above and notwithstanding rule 105.2, the Under-Secretary-General for Management may, where necessary, authorize progress payments.

## D. Property management Authority and responsibility

**Rule 105.20**

(a) The Under-Secretary-General for Management is responsible for the management of the property of the United Nations, including all systems governing its receipt, recording, utilization, safekeeping, maintenance and disposal, including by sale, and shall designate the officials responsible for performing property management functions.

(b) A summary statement of non-expendable United Nations property shall be provided to the Board of Auditors not later than three months following the end of the financial period.

# BIBLIOGRAPHY

## Monographs and Articles


ARROWSMITH, S., "Towards an Multilateral Agreement on Transparency in Government Procurement", 47 *International and Comparative Law Quarterly* 793-816 (1998).

ARROWSMITH, S., *Government Procurement in the WTO* (2004).

ARSANJANI, H. M., "Claims Against International Organizations – Quis Custodiet Ipsos Custodes?", 7 *Yale Journal of World Public Order* 131-176 (1980).

BLANK, A. and MARCEAU, G., "The History of the Government Procurement Negotiations Since 1945", 5 *Public Procurement Law Review* 77-147 (1996).

RAJESH-BABU, R., "Review of the WTO Dispute Settlement Understanding: Progress and Prospects", 2 *Asian-African Legal Consultative Organization Quarterly Bulletin* 50-74 (2005).

CANTOR, J. R., "Bid Protests and Procurement Reform: The Case for Leaving Well Enough Alone", 27 *Public Contract Law Journal* 155-178 (1997-1998).

DENDAUW, I., "New WTO Agreement on Government Procurement: an Analysis of the Framework for Bid Challenge Procedures and the Question of Direct Effect", 18 *Journal of Energy & Natural Resources Law* 254-266 (2000).

ECHÉGUT-VIGROUX, M., "The International Government Procurement Agreement and the EC Legal Order", in KRONENBERGER, V. (ed.), *The EU and the International Legal Order: Discord or Harmony?* 221-238 (2001).

GORDON, D. I., "Constructing a Bid Protest Process: Choices Every Procurement Challenge System Must Make.", 35 *Public Contract Law Journal* 1-18 (2006), available at http://papers.ssrn.com/sol3/papers.cfm?abstract_id =892781 (last visited 15 February 2008).

GOURLEY, W. H. A., HEILMAN GRIER, J. and SHAHEEN, F., "International Procurement", 35 *The International Lawyer* 395-405 (2001).

DE GRAAF, G. and KING, M., "Towards a More Global Government Procurement Market: The Expansion of the GATT Government Procurement Agreement in The Context of the Uruguay Round", 29 *The International Lawyer* 435-452 (1995).

HARPIGNIES, R. H., "Settlement of Disputes of a Private Law Character to which the United Nations is a Party – a Case in Point; the Arbitral Award of 24.9.1969, In Re Starways Ltd. v. the United Nations", 7 *Revue belge de droit international* 451-468 (1971).

HAUCK, D., HEID, S. and PRESLMAYR, K., *Handbuch des Vergaberechts* (2002).

HILAIRE, M., *United Nations Law and the Security Council* (2005).

KINSEY, M. A., "Transparency in Government Procurement: An International Consensus?", 34 *Public Contract Law Journal* 155-173 (2004-2005).

KLABBERS, J., *An Introduction to International Institutional Law* (2002).

LOCKHARDT, J. and VOON, T., "Reviewing Appellate Review in the WTO Dispute Settlement System", 6 *Melbourne Journal of International Law* 474-484 (2005).

LEVY D. A., "BOT and Public Procurement: A Conceptual Framework", 109 *Indiana International and Comparative Law Journal* 95-110 (1996-1997).

McGRATH, M., CLOSSER, A. V. and NORRETT, L. M., "International Procurement", 33 *The International Lawyer.* 315-320 (1999).

NEUHOLD, H., HUMMER, W. and SCHREUER, C., Österreichisches Handbuch des Völkerrechts. (2004).

NEUMANN P., "The Relationship between GATT and the United Nations", 3 *Cornell International Law Journal* 63-78 (1970).

NEUMANN, P., "Build, Operate, Transfer Project Financing in Emerging Countries", in, SCOTT, F. and MARTENS, C.- P. (eds.), *International Project Finance* (2001).

ORTINO, F. and PETERSMANN, E.- U., *The WTO Dispute Settlement System 1995- 2003* (2004).

POMERANTZ, M., "Toward a New International Order in Government Procurement", 12 *Public Contract Law Journal* 129-161 (1981-82).

REICH, A., "The New GATT Agreement on Government Procurement – The Pitfalls of Plurilateralism and Strict Reciprocity", 31 *Journal of World Trade* 125 (1997).

REICH, A., *International Public Procurement Law – The Evolution of International Regimes on Public Purchasing* (1999).

REINISCH, A., "Waite and Kennedy v. Germany; Beer and Regan v. Germany", 93 *American Journal of International Law* 933-938 (1999).

REINISCH, A., *International Organizations Before National Courts* (2000).

REINISCH, A., "Können Verletzungen von WTO-Recht durch einzelne Betroffene geltend gemacht werden?", 11 *Ecolex* 912-917 (2000).

REINISCH, A., "Das WTO Streitbeilegungssystem", 11 *Ecolex* 836-840 (2000).

REINISCH, A., "Securing the Accountability of International Organizations", 7 *Global Governance* 131 (2001).

ROSENNE, S., "Codification of International Law", in, BERNHARDT, R. (ed.), *Encyclopedia of Public International Law*, Vol. I (1995).

SANDS, P. and KLEIN, P., *Bowett's Law of International Institutions* (2001).

SIMMA, B., *The Charter of the United Nations – A Commentary.* Vol. I and II. (2002).

SLOAN, B., "The binding force of a 'recommendation' of the General Assembly of the United Nations." *British Yearbook of International Law* 397-424 (1948).

SPENNEMANN, C., "The WTO Agreement on Government Procurement – A Means of Furtherance of Human Rights", 1 *Zeitschrift für europarechtliche Studien* 45-95 (2001).

SØRENSEN, M., *Grundtræk af international organisation* (1952).

SZASZ, P. C., "International Organisations, Privileges and Immunities", in, BERNHARDT, R. (ed.), *Encyclopedia of Public International Law* 1325-1333, Vol. I (1995).

UNITED NATIONS, *The Work of the International Law Commission* (1996).

UNITED NATIONS, *United Nations Juridical Yearbook.* Issued annually from 1962. United Nations document ST/LEG/8.

UNDP/IAPSO, United Nations System General Business Guide for Potential Suppliers of Goods and Services with Common Guidelines for Procurement by Organizations in the UN System. UNDP (United Nations Development Programme).

VOON, S. T. and YANOVICH, A., "The Facts Aside: The Limitation of WTO Appeals to Issues of Law", 40 *Journal of World Trade* 239-258 (2006).

WEISS, F., "The WTO Dispute Settlement System", in, VAN DIJCK, P. and FABER, G. (eds.), *Challenges to the New World Trade Organization* (1996).

WELLENS, K., *Remedies against International Organizations* (2002).

WESTRING, G., International Procurement – a training manual. United Nations Institute for Training and Research (UN doc. UNITAR/MAN/3). UNITAR, New York (1977).

WILDER, M. and AHRENS, M., "Australia's Implementation of the OECD Convention on Combating Bribery of Foreign Public Officials in International Business Transactions", 2 *Melbourne Journal of International Law* 568-586 (2001).

WTO Secretariat publication, *A Handbook on the WTO Dispute Settlement System* (2004).

YUKINS, R. C., *et al.*, "International Procurement", 40 *The International Lawyer* 337–346 (2006), available at http://papers.ssrn.com/sol3/papers.cfm?abstract_id=903423 (last visited 15 February 2008).

## Documents of the Independent Inquiry Committee into the United Nations Oil-for-Food Programme

(First) Interim Report, 3 February 2005, available at http://www.iic-offp.org/documents/InterimReportFeb2005.pdf (last visited 15 February 2008).

Second Interim Report, 29 March 2005, available at http://www.iic-offp.org/documents/InterimReportMar2005.pdf (last visited 15 February 2008).

Third Interim Report, 8 August 2005, available at http://www.iic-offp.org/documents/Third%20Interim%20Report.pdf (last visited 15 February 2008).

Report of 7 September 2005 on the Impact of the Oil-for-Food Programme on the Iraqi People.

Report of 7 September 2005 on the Management of the Oil-for-Food Programme.

Report of 27 October 2005 on the Manipulation of the Oil-for-Food Programme by the Iraqi Regime.

Procedures for Law Enforcement Requests for Access to IIC Documents and Information. (November 2005).

**Völkerrecht, Europarecht und Internationales Wirtschaftsrecht**

Herausgegeben von Peter Hilpold und August Reinisch

Band 1 Florian Razesberger: The International Criminal Court. The Principle of Complementarity. 2006.

Band 2 Christian Wimpissinger: Steuerliche Verlustverrechnung nach EG-Recht. 2006.

Band 3 Christina Knahr: Participation of Non-State Actors in the Dispute Settlement System of the WTO: Benefit or Burden? 2007.

Band 4 Daniela Kröll: Toward Multilateral Competition Law? After Cancún: Reevaluating the Case for Additional International Competition Rules Under Special Consideration of the WTO Agreement. 2007.

Band 5 Georg Nolte / Peter Hilpold (Hrsg.): Auslandsinvestitionen – Entwicklung großer Kodifikationen – Fragmentierung des Völkerrechts – Status des Kosovo. Beiträge zum 31. Österreichischen Völkerrechtstag 2006 in München. 2008.

Band 6 Irmgard Marboe: Die Berechnung von Entschädigung und Schadenersatz in der internationalen Rechtsprechung. 2008.

Band 7 Peter Neumann: United Nations Procurement Regime. Description and Evaluation of the Legal Framework in the Light of International Standards and of Findings of an Inquiry into Procurement for the Iraq Oil-for-Food Programme. 2008.

www.peterlang.de

Daniela Kröll

# Toward Multilateral Competition Law?

## After Cancún: Reevaluating the Case for Additional International Competition Rules Under Special Consideration of the WTO Agreement

Frankfurt am Main, Berlin, Bern, Bruxelles, New York, Oxford, Wien, 2007.
217 pp.
Völkerrecht, Europarecht und internationales Wirtschaftsrecht.
Herausgegeben von Peter Hilpold und August Reinisch. Vol. 4
ISBN 978-3-631-56120-1 · pb. € 41.10*

In 2001, the Doha WTO Ministerial Declaration recognized a "case for a multilateral framework to enhance the contribution of competition policy to international trade and development". Yet, the negotiations on additional multilateral competition rules within the WTO were formally suspended in 2004. This book aims at providing a comprehensive overview of the current status of the discussion and is intended to suit both the advanced reader and any reader with a general interest in international economic law. The author critically reevaluates and reconfirms the case for additional international competition rules from both a competition and trade policy perspective. Taking into account the political developments around the failed Cancún Ministerial Conference and the relationship of competition policy and economic development, the author also illustrates a possible solution to break the deadlock concerning additional international competition rules within the ambit of the WTO.

*Contents*: International Competition Law · Competition Policy · Trade Policy · WTO · Economic Development · International Trade

FSC
www.fsc.org
MIX
Papier | Fördert
gute Waldnutzung
FSC® C083411

Kolibri 360 GmbH
Ferdinand-Jühlke-Straße 7
99095 Erfurt, Deutschland
produktsicherheit@kolibri360.de

Druck:
CPI Druckdienstleistungen GmbH
im Auftrag der
Kolibri 360 GmbH
Ferdinand-Jühlke-Str. 7
99095 Erfurt